Black Conservative Intellectuals in Modern America

Black Conservative Intellectuals in Modern America

Michael L. Ondaatje

UNIVERSITY OF PENNSYLVANIA PRESS

PHILADELPHIA

Published by
University of Pennsylvania Press
Philadelphia, Pennsylvania 19104-4112

Printed in the United States of America on acid-free paper
10   9   8   7   6   5   4   3   2   1

Library of Congress Cataloging-in-Publication Data

Ondaatje, Michael L.
  Black conservative intellectuals in modern America / Michael L. Ondaatje.
      p. cm.
  Includes bibliographical references and index.
  ISBN 978-0-8122-4206-5 (alk. paper)
  1. African American intellectuals—Political activity. 2. Conservatives—United States. 3. Conservatism—United States—Philosophy. 4. Affirmative action—United States. 5. African Americans—Social conditions. 6. African Americans—Economic conditions. 7. United States—Politics and government. I. Title.
  E185.89.I56O53 2010
  320.52092—dc22
                                        2009024358

Contents

Introduction

> Being a black conservative is perhaps not considered as bizarre as being a transvestite, but it is certainly considered more strange than being a vegetarian or a bird watcher.

So, in 1980, wrote Thomas Sowell, free-market economist and unofficial godfather of the "black right," delivering a stinging rebuke to the liberal critics of modern black conservatism. Although amusing, Sowell's penchant for sarcasm in this instance masks an interesting point. When one considers the extent to which American conservatism has historically been conditioned by racist notions of black inferiority, the existence of powerful conservative black spokespeople is indeed quite astonishing. Putting to one side Sowell's playful allusions to transvestites, vegetarians, and bird watchers, the obvious question becomes: "What does it mean to be both black and conservative in America?" The inevitable corollary to that question is another: "What do black conservatives actually want to conserve?"

These questions were most famously posed by the Russian anarchist Pyotr Kropotkin on his visit to the United States nearly a century ago.[1] While Kropotkin accepted that there was such a thing as an American black conservative—Booker T. Washington was widely acknowledged as the preeminent black leader of the day—he mocked the idea that their commitment to conservatism could in any way be genuine. A conservative, Kropotkin explained at the time, is someone who is satisfied with existing conditions and advocates their continuance. In the early twentieth century, no thoughtful African American could be satisfied with segregation and no thoughtful African American would advocate the continuation of second-class citizenship and the social, economic, and cultural humiliation that invariably accompanied it.[2] By Kropotkin's definition, then, a black conservative was a contradiction in terms, a freak of nature; those who claimed the mantra for themselves were opportunists, and complicit in the oppression of their own people.

Fast forward one hundred years and the question of whether it is possible for American blacks to be genuinely conservative seems old hat, even irrelevant. Black conservatism is now firmly planted on the nation's cultural landscape, its proponents having shaped policy discussion and debates over some of the most pressing matters that confront the modern black community. Most interpreters of the African American experience now acknowledge black conservatism as a phenomenon or movement of some strength, even as their judgments about its underlying significance continue to vary. Put simply, observers no longer have the luxury of pondering whether black conservatives should exist. The reality is that they do. Who, then, are these black conservatives? What do they stand for? And when and why did they emerge?

Today's black conservatives are ideologically at home on the right wing of the Republican Party, offering radically different assessments of American institutions and race relations from those of modern civil rights leaders. Although Condoleezza Rice is arguably the best known black conservative in the United States, the black conservative *phenomenon* has typically been associated with a cluster of intellectuals and public figures who, beginning in the early 1980s, carved out its ideological parameters and established its political trajectory. Thomas Sowell of the Hoover Institution and Supreme Court Justice Clarence Thomas may have been the most prominent of these personalities during the past quarter century.[3] But significant contributions to racial discourse were also made in this time by economists Walter Williams and Glenn Loury; cultural theorists Shelby Steele, Anne Wortham, and John McWhorter; and social activists Robert Woodson and Jay Parker. While these black conservatives' existence has continued to stir emotions and provoke polemical debate, no serious scholarly studies have hitherto assessed their social and political thought in the context of mainstream scholarship and the wider American political culture.

Nobody can dispute the fact that the black conservatives have had a significant impact on this culture. Indeed, for much of the 1980s and 1990s, these intellectuals were ensconced at the heart of the national dialogue on race, tapping into the enduring American philosophies of individualism and free enterprise, seeking to overturn the corrective political initiatives secured by the great civil rights movement. Insisting that their differences were not with the goals of freedom, justice, and equality, but with the methods employed to achieve them, black conservatives argued that the liberal policies associated with the Great Society of the late 1960s had failed, and that government, far from providing the solutions, was in fact exacerbating the problems faced by African American people. Paying special attention to the controversies surrounding affirmative action, welfare, and public education, they turned the language of the left on itself, charging liberal leaders—black and white—with re-enslaving black people on new plantations of government dependency. With the civil rights struggle "won," poor and even middle-class African Americans were exhorted to leave these plantations and to reestablish their independence by embracing self-help and the "gospel of business success."[4]

How exactly is one to understand these negative black perceptions of government's attempts to help black people? A cursory glance at the contemporary origins of black conservatism provides some clues. It is now widely acknowledged that as the American conservative movement gathered momentum in the 1970s, "a swarm of new, self-proclaimed black conservative . . . took flight," subsequently emerging as a visible intellectual bloc in the wake of Ronald Reagan's landslide election victory of 1980.[5] On December 12–13 of that year, as the president-elect prepared to take up residence in the White House, a delegation of mostly conservative black professionals gathered in San Francisco, at the Fairmont Hotel, to discuss ideas and policies for the incoming administration to consider in its dealings with the African American community. Sponsored by the Institute for Contemporary Studies, a prominent right-wing research organization, the two-day workshop was soon dubbed the "Black Alternatives' Conference" and its proceedings edited and later published as *The Fairmont Papers.*

Significantly, one of the editors of *The Fairmont Papers*—and one of the major organizers of the conference—was Edwin Meese, the already designated (white) legal counsel to the newly elected president. Meese was joined in San Francisco by other New Right luminaries, including Milton Friedman and Michael J. Boskin, and other recently appointed Reagan officials, to encourage the formation of (what they hoped would be) a new conservative black leadership with which the president could work. These white delegates, however, would take a back seat as the conference's star attraction, black conservative economist Thomas Sowell, rose to deliver the keynote address and establish the need to reshape the political policy debate on race. "This is a historic opportunity," Sowell declared:

The economic and social advancement of blacks in this country is still a great unfinished task. The methods and approaches currently used for dealing with this task have become familiar over the past few years and they demand reexamination for at least two reasons. First, the effectiveness of these approaches has been ever more seriously questioned in recent years. There is growing factual evidence of counterproductive results from noble intentions. . . . In addition, numerous political trends in recent years indicate declining voter and taxpayer support for these approaches, to which some of the older and more conventional black spokesmen remain committed.[6]

Over the next two days, the conference's participants laid out a philo-sophical vision and offered practical initiatives for black advancement that were vastly different from those emanating from the "older and more conventional black spokesmen." This vision and these initiatives, which centered on self-help and the free market, would challenge what the participants considered to be the hegemony enjoyed by civil rights groups in discussions relating to black America. There was hope and anticipation that they now too would be engaged in such discussions—engaged by the media as well as by the highest councils of governance. In his final remarks before the delegation at San Francisco, Meese prom-ised as much:

This conference is more than just another event. It is a significant starting point. . . . The fact that people are talking about pluralism is directly at odds with what I saw the other day when I attended a meeting, along with the then president-elect, with some of the people who purport to represent the leadership of the black community. [Reagan had recently met with leaders of the major civil rights organizations.] I am not in any way disagreeing or putting them down, but I think the difference between that meeting and this conference is significant. They were talking about the last ten years. You are talking about the ideas of the next ten years and beyond.[7]

Immediately after the Black Alternatives' Conference, the Reagan administration appointed several of the delegates to high-profile gov-ernment positions. Samuel Pierce (secretary for Housing and Urban Development), Clarence Pendleton (chairman of the Civil Rights Com-mission), and Clarence Thomas (chairman of the Equal Employment Opportunity Commission) headed the list, but several others were placed in sub-Cabinet roles or fast-tracked into the federal judiciary. As if to complement this new "African American strategy" in government, organizations such as the Heritage Foundation, the American Enterprise Institute, and the Hoover Institution began to award fellowships and pro-vide extensive monetary funding to a group of researchers who would emerge from obscurity to become leading lights in conservatism's black intellectual constellation.[8] Writing in the *New Republic* in 1985, political journalist Fred Barnes labeled the conservative movement's support for this new black leadership group an attempt to "invent a Negro Inc."[9]

The rise of conservatism during the 1980s certainly emboldened African Americans who advanced ideas consistent with the logic of the New Right. Understanding the political environment in which this logic emerged and flourished is therefore essential to a more nuanced understanding of black conservatism itself. More than anything else, Reagan's election victory in 1980 symbolized a rejection of the excesses that conservatives believed had dominated national life since the 1960s, the push for racial justice being arguably the most visible. It also signaled a renewed determination on their part to restore the values they associated with an older, better America. There would be a renewed commitment to individual liberty, market freedom, law and order, family values, and classical nationalism, and a corresponding de-emphasis on civil rights enforcement and the ethical obligations of the state to assist the poor and marginalized in society.[10] It was clear, in other words, that the president and his supporters sought a dramatic transformation in the nature and scope of political discourse in the United States. The egalitarianism that had defined the postwar era, and had provided the political space for the passage of antidiscrimination laws and the programs of the Great Society, was under attack from counterrevolutionary forces hostile to liberal social change. It was into this political milieu that the black conservatives first stepped.

As the pendulum swung to the right and Reagan's "Great Rediscovery" began, the boundaries of what was considered intellectually acceptable were radically redefined. New ways of thinking about serious social problems took hold in the public consciousness. And, not surprisingly, race was the critical symbol in the formation of the new antiliberal social consensus. It soon became clear, however, that the racist language that had traditionally defined American conservatism had been cast out by the administration in favor of a new de-radicalized discourse that emphasized equality of opportunity for all individuals.[11] The days when employers—with the approval of state and federal authorities—posted signs, "no negras need apply," might have passed, but negative stereotypes of the lazy, irresponsible "nigger" were perpetuated in terminology such as "the underclass," "matriarchy," "welfare brats," "hoodlums," and "dysfunctional."[12] Opposition to political reforms tailored specifically to the needs of the black collective was increasingly couched in terms of their violation of the newly enshrined standard of race-neutrality in American life.

In this new environment, racism was described increasingly in the media as merely an unfortunate blemish on an otherwise perfect past; it was certainly not a present-day problem of glaring inequality with grim consequences for the oppressed. This new color-blind discourse, however, could not mask the fact that for most African Americans the central political feature of the period was the sustained conservative assault on the black freedom movement and its rich traditions of resistance and sacrifice. Indeed, it seemed clear that the conservative establishment's broad denunciation of liberalism during the 1980s had a distinctly racial flavor.[13] First, it set out to discredit the African American struggle for social and economic parity through a strident campaign against affirmative action, the welfare state, and public education. Second, the race debate was to be reconstructed—the problems of the black urban poor were to be depicted as nothing more than a combination of bad behavior, over-reliance on government, and a failure to take personal responsibility.[14]

Throughout the 1980s, the black conservative network grew in size, strength, and stature, empowered, it seemed, at every turn, by the Reagan administration's determination to counteract allegations that its policies and visions for America were racist. Distancing themselves from ideas, policies, and institutions that couched the issues confronting black America in collectivist terms, members of this "new black vanguard" became associated with a style of conservatism that located social mobility and empowerment in the agency of the potentially all-conquering individual. They rejected the portrayal of black life and culture as a by-product of racial persecution, viewing traditional liberal academic engagement with racial injustice as increasingly irrelevant in the post–civil rights period. Echoing the analyses offered a decade earlier by neoconservative theorists such as Nathan Glazer, Irving Kristol, and Norman Podhoretz, black conservatives maintained that the dilemmas of race and poverty could not be addressed through the deliberate intervention of the state. Rather, explanations and solutions were to be found in the cultural sphere, among the blacks themselves—with the "criminally minded youth," the "deadbeat daddies," and the "welfare-dependent mamas" whose lives had been so utterly wrecked by flawed liberal social policies.

To be sure, some middle-class African Americans thrived in this new environment, but the great majority of black people found themselves worse off. It was they who bore the brunt of the economic recession in the early 1980s and, ironically, it was they who were hit hardest by the market policies that Reagan and his black conservative supporters championed as their salvation. "The impact of Reaganism," one scholar later wrote, "was felt across the black community as a series of devastating shocks."[15] Significantly, in 1980, 85 percent of the black electorate had voted for Jimmy Carter over Reagan.[16] And in 1984 the Democratic candidate Walter Mondale secured more than 90 percent of the black vote but still went down to the popular incumbent in a landslide defeat.[17] Devastating shocks and black voting behavior together made the black conservatives' enthusiasm for Reagan seem all the more remarkable. As pundits rushed to announce the birth of a distinctively new black intellectual species, more perceptive analysts might have asked: Had the American polity witnessed patterns of conservatism within the black community before this?

Just as the emergence of these "new black intellectuals" cannot be properly understood without reference to the political dynamics of the Reagan era, their emergence also needs to be placed in the context of the long but still largely trivialized history of black conservatism in the United States. There were, after all, notable individual black conservative figures before 1980. The contributions of such diverse thinkers as Booker T. Washington, William Hannibal Thomas, George Schuyler, Zora Neale Hurston, and Edward Brooke attest to the phenomenon's enduring presence within African American intellectual discourse. While these conservative intellectuals, writers, and political figures never presented an entirely homogeneous philosophy, many of their ideas did intersect at key junctures. Historically, the generic black conservative argument stipulated a theoretical and programmatic commitment to capitalism as a systemic vehicle for racial uplift. In this formulation, African Americans were to depoliticize their struggle, submit to white cultural power and racism, and display greater thrift, patience, hard work, and moral rectitude to overcome their circumstances.[18]

In some respects, then, the black conservatives of the early 1980s were inheritors of a tradition of black conservatism that stretched far back into the black past. Indeed, at every epoch in the nation's history in which there was a significant transformation in the status of African Americans, individual black conservative spokespersons had emerged, counseling racial caution, submission, and even retreat. At the heart of this tradition stood Booker T. Washington, whose emphasis in the late 1890s on the need for African Americans to accommodate to a capitalist system increasingly dominated by white supremacy would be hailed, a century later, by modern black conservatives. Yet one fact remained: never before in the nation's history had a group of black conservatives been elevated to a position of such prominence as in Reagan's America. In this regard, their appearance appeared to herald something new: "a bid for conservative hegemony in black political and intellectual leadership in the post–civil rights era."[19]

Above all, these black conservative intellectuals of the 1980s and 1990s sought to wrest the political initiative from liberal forces within the African American community by vigorously engaging the world of ideas in support of conservative Republicanism. To be sure, there were other prominent black conservatives operating during this period—politicians, clergymen, and, most prominently, media talk-show hosts—but these people tended to disseminate rather than generate ideas and consequently lie beyond the scope of this book. Intellectuals, to borrow Richard Hofstadter's definition, are individuals who are at once reflective and critical, and who act self-consciously to transmit, modify, and create ideas and culture.[20] Operating within conventional intellectual discourse over the past three decades, the black conservatives served such a function. Analysis of their significant contributions to social and political thought clarifies modern black conservatism's distinctive features to provide a more well-rounded definition of this controversial phenomenon in the American political culture.

Naturally, as prominent public intellectuals over the past three decades, members of this black conservative coalition have carved out various and varying positions on a whole range of contemporary issues—including abortion, same-sex marriage, and the controversial "war on terror." Yet this book is expressly concerned with evaluating these intellectuals' ideas in relation to the key debates concerning *race* and *class* in American life—debates that have centered, for the most part, on the vexed issues of affirmative action, poverty, and public education on which the black conservatives cut their political teeth. The evolution of the black conservatives' thinking in each of these three discrete subject areas demands thematic rather than chronological treatment, uninterrupted by digressions into areas with their own historical trajectories. Significantly, this structure also allows for a systematic exploration of one of the other original and defining themes of this work: the subtle, largely overlooked differences that exist among these intellectuals on fundamental matters of social policy to address racial disadvantage in the United States.

In *Challenging the Civil Rights Establishment: Profiles of a New Black Vanguard*, Joseph Conti and Brad Stetson commented: "seeing as, to our knowledge, there is no study extant explaining the often subtle disagreements among these black dissidents, we can only refer the interested reader to the primary sources—the work of the dissidents themselves."[21] By acting on this recommendation and engaging the writings of the major black conservative figures (as well as the literature of their supporters and critics), I not only analyze the merits and flaws of the ideas presented by these intellectuals, but also explore the extent to which they formed a monolithic coalition. The black conservatives emerge as more than a regimented group but as individuals with their own distinctive arguments and impressions of the conservative political tradition.

The stated objectives of this book imply that the literature on this subject remains underdeveloped, problematic, or both. That contemporary black conservatives have been severely neglected by scholars of the African American experience is beyond dispute: Sowell and company may have attracted more attention than earlier black conservatives,[22] but penetrating academic assessments of their thought and praxis remain scarce. With academic studies in short supply, much of the responsibility for explaining black conservatism's historical and contemporary significance has fallen to highly partisan journalists, whose endeavors, on the whole, have served more to inhibit than to advance understanding of the phenomenon. Indeed, a survey of articles in newspapers, magazines, and journals since the Fairmont Conference reveals a bitterly divided body of polemical commentary in which there has been virtually no middle ground; black conservatives have tended to be portrayed either as "color-blind visionaries" or "counterfeit heroes."[23]

The ideological rigidity that has undermined analyses of contemporary black conservatism demonstrates the need for more sophisticated approaches to understanding this important current in African American thought. The stakes of the debate are so high because, unlike their forebears, contemporary black conservatives—through their media visibility and financial and ideological ties with right-wing think tanks, institutions, and foundations—have had the opportunity to seriously "influence the course of the black struggle for equality" in post–civil rights America.[24] Although the 1991 nomination and confirmation of Clarence Thomas to the Supreme Court is generally credited with sparking the nation's interest in black conservatives, in reality interpretations of the group and their philosophical orientation had been emerging since the early 1980s. Still to be fully explored, this literature must be seen against the broader debates of the past three decades concerning the continuing burden of race in American society. Such an analysis yields fascinating insights not only into black conservatism, but also into the larger political currents that symbolize, in Manning Marable's judgment, "the contemporary crisis within the African American political culture."[25]

Seemingly indicative of this crisis, and in many ways the intellectual forerunner to the conflict-ridden debate over modern black conservatism, was the controversy generated in 1978 by William Julius Wilson's provocatively entitled book *The Declining Significance of Race.*[26] Then a little-known sociologist at the University of Chicago, Wilson sought to use the ghettos of Chicago as a laboratory to explore the evolution of race and class in American history, and to identify the factors behind more recent economic problems within the urban black community. Although the civil rights revolution and the rapid expansion of white-collar jobs in business and government had seen record numbers of African Americans enter the mainstream, the condition of the black poor actually deteriorated in the 1970s, with unemployment, family breakdown, and welfare dependency spiraling out of control. Wilson was both fascinated and alarmed at these trends. The rise of the black middle class, he argued, made it increasingly implausible to explain the etiology of the black underclass in terms of present-day racism alone. The situation appeared far more complex than this. Wilson maintained that while the historical consequences of racial oppression persisted and remained pertinent to any study of modern African American disadvantage, growing material divisions within the black community indicated that class had indeed supplanted race as the determining factor in poverty. Now more than ever, the problems of the black urban poor were tied to the broader issues of economic organization that had resulted from the shift from an urban manufacturing-dominated economy to a suburban service-dominated one. The political implications of Wilson's thesis were clear. To reduce racial inequality, further government action was required to attack inequality on a broad class front, to get at the heart of underlying economic dynamics.

Appearing on the stage of history at a time of conservative resurgence, *The Declining Significance of Race* was deliberately misinterpreted by right-wing ideologues to mean that "race didn't matter anymore." But if the conservative response to Wilson's research was calculating and self-serving, the heated criticism he drew on the left was often unwarranted and immature. Incensed that a fellow African American would empha-size factors other than racism to explain ghetto poverty, many black scholars "treated him as badly as Islamic fundamentalists treated Salman Rushdie, pretty much calling him a traitor and a heretic and reading him out of the race."[27] Somehow overlooking that Wilson was a committed left-liberal who favored European-style social policies and central plan-ning, critics denounced him as a black conservative and charged him with providing ammunition for those determined to destroy the African American poor.[28]

That the liberal Wilson, with his subtle analysis of race and class, could trigger an intellectual storm of such magnitude reveals a great deal about the political environment in which the black conservatives emerged and in which they would be assessed. Throughout the 1980s, the spitefulness that characterized the debate over *The Declining Signifi-cance of Race* appeared to spill over into the discourse on black conserva-tism, with name-calling substituting for scholarly scrutiny as the order of the day. Serious examination of Sowell and company was largely absent in the years "B.C.T. (Before Clarence Thomas),"[29] but numerous opin-ion pieces were nonetheless written about the new black conservative phenomenon. Indeed, by the late 1980s, a small body of literature on the subject, albeit partisan, could be discerned.

In these early years, favorable treatment of the "new black conser-vatives" was most likely to be found in periodicals sponsored by white conservative organizations, with *National Journal, Reason, National Review, Commentary,* and *Policy Review* among the most prominent.[30] Typically, in these forums, Sowell and company were depicted as authentic African American spokespeople seriously confronting black cultural deficiencies and offering new ways forward. These were the reformers, a voice in the wilderness since the 1960s, now calling for racial uplift through self-examination, self-criticism, self-motivation, and ultimately self-help. In the 1980s, "With a Friend in the White House," the black conservatives were finally "Speaking Out." Voicing bold criticism of the civil rights establishment and its commitment to government as the solution to black problems, these intellectuals had been relentlessly abused and vilified in the liberal media. But the emergence of this new cohort, its conservative supporters maintained, was an important development within the African American community, a veritable call to arms in the broader ideological battle for the very soul of black America. As sociologist Murray Friedman explained in a 1982 *Commentary* article, with one eye on this unfolding battle: "There is reason to believe . . . that the new black intellectuals reflect the views and interests of the black grass roots more accurately than do their critics and detractors."[31] In the context of Reagan's America, such an observation was controversial indeed.

Predictably, criticism of the new black conservative agenda was most apparent in the 1980s on the pages of progressive magazines and journals such as the *Nation, Dissent, Negro History Bulletin,* the *Washington DC Afro-American,* the *Village Voice,* and the *Trotter Review.*[32] But left-liberal protest at the growing influence of Sowell and company extended beyond these publications to some more unlikely ones. In *Business Week* in November 1981, for example, journalist Carl Rowan observed that "Sowell is giving aid and comfort to those who . . . are taking food out of the mouths of black children. Vidkun Quisling in his collaboration with the Nazis surely did not do as much damage to the Norwegians as Sowell is doing to the most helpless of black Americans."[33] And the vehemence of the rhetoric would only escalate. In 1984 the political scientist Alphonso Pinkney, in his book *The Myth of Black Progress,* argued that blacks who opposed the liberal policies favored by civil rights organizations were "not unlike government officials in (formerly) South Vietnam who supported American aggression against their own people."[34] The literary critic Houston Baker echoed this sentiment. Drawing on similar analogies, he portrayed black conservatives as "prospectors on the new frontiers of an urban dark continent. Gentrification and black genocide go hand in hand. Sowell and others are capitalism's and the state's new Livingstones in blackface."[35] Whatever the merits of these arguments, their virulence continue to stand out in contemporary political debate.

Symptomatic of the paucity of academic analyses in these years was the propagation on both sides of the political fence of misconceptions, distortions, and blatant fabrications about the nature of black conservatism. While the right-wing press's enthusiastic endorsement of Sowell and company as grassroots leaders appeared exaggerated, even dishonest, the numerous allegations levied against black conservatives by left-wing critics were themselves seldom verified or substantiated. In a sure blow to those who championed black conservatism as a legitimate broad-based movement, a couple of early quantitative studies in the field of political science uncovered little evidence of a support base for this agenda within the African American community.[36] These same studies, however, would find no evidence to suggest that comparisons between modern black conservatism and the murderous madness of Nazism were appropriate. The charge was simply absurd. Although unpalatable to many, the most basic tenet of black conservatism was a deep-seated respect for the culture and institutions of modern American society, whose emphasis on individualism, liberty, and limited government stood in stark contrast to the core elements of totalitarian dictatorship. More than a debate that had failed to mature, then, this was one that had failed to even get off the ground.

Most early analysts in the field appeared far too concerned with the rather trivial matter of whether black conservatism was legitimate or even possible. The serious implications of the phenomenon for the American polity were hardly touched upon and the right questions almost never asked. By shifting the onus of responsibility onto African Americans for their plight, for instance, how effective had black conservatives been in nullifying civil rights groups and restructuring the public discourse on race? Did these intellectuals' arguments hold up in the face of scholarly scrutiny? What, moreover, would scholarly scrutiny reveal about the group's emergence and increasing indispensability to the conservative movement? These questions required thoughtful analysis, not ideological posturing or the clichés and caricatures that had hitherto sufficed. The great majority of Americans, for their part, were oblivious to the fight that had been unfolding on the pages of relatively obscure intellectual publications, and most remained wholly unaware of the existence of one black conservative, let alone an entire cadre of them. But all this would change in 1991.

Whereas the appointment to the Supreme Court of that great champion of civil rights, Thurgood Marshall, was widely hailed as a defining moment in the black freedom movement in 1967, twenty-four years later the confirmation hearings of his successor, Clarence Thomas, were received altogether differently. As if to signal a changing of the guard, the hearings introduced to the general public a consortium of black supporters of the Reagan/Bush consensus in national politics, whose goal was to tear down the liberal principles Marshall had fought to establish. Now, for the first time, this new cohort appeared center stage, testifying on Thomas's behalf to discredit law professor Anita Hill's explosive allegations that he had sexually harassed her in the 1980s when both worked at the Equal Employment Opportunity Commission (EEOC).[37] Many of those African Americans who stood by Thomas then and would stand behind him into the future, were, like him, loyal Republicans and committed conservative ideologues. With the confirmation of only the second African American to the Supreme Court in serious jeopardy, and black sexuality in the spotlight, millions of people watched mesmerized as the direct, complex, and often graphic testimony of Hill and Thomas, and their respective supporters, played itself out on television. As the hearings entered their second week, and the nation took sides, two broader questions came to the fore: What was the significance of people such as Clarence Thomas to modern black politics, and what did it mean to be a black conservative anyway?

As more black conservatives emerged, journalists again offered their answers to these questions. Some sought controversially to situate Thomas within a long tradition of black conservatism in the United States, labeling as conservative such heroic figures from the African American past as Frederick Douglass, Malcolm X, and Martin Luther King.[38] Emphasizing the quintessential American-ness of his personal struggle up from poverty, but somehow overlooking his modest judicial record, these supporters dependably trumpeted the line that, in Thomas, President Bush had found the best-qualified candidate for the Court. Others—usually less partisan—downplayed the nominee's lack of professional experience and his social and political views in the hope that his disadvantaged background might "lead him to greater identification with those in America who today are victimized by poverty and discrimination."[39] Highly regarded liberal newspapers such as the *New York Times* and *Washington Post* even adopted this position, heralding Thomas's rise "From Poverty to the U.S. Bench" and proclaiming him a "Self-Made Conservative," soon after his confirmation.[40]

Many black publications, however, were incensed at these early attempts to legitimize Thomas specifically and black conservatism more generally. Within weeks of the confirmation, for example, *Emerge* ran a cover of the newly confirmed Justice with a handkerchief tied around his head.[41] The implication here was that Thomas was a "handkerchief head negro," an African American unsympathetic, even hostile, to the struggles of his own people and committed to protecting the interests of their enemies. Carl Rowan, who in the early 1980s had likened Sowell to a Nazi collaborator, now insisted that "if you give Thomas a little flour on his face, you'd think you had David Duke."[42] Author June Jordan condemned the Justice as a "virulent Oreo phenomenon," a "punk ass," and an "Uncle Tom calamity."[43] But it was the black feminist Julianne Malveaux who reserved the most vicious attack for Thomas: "I hope his wife feeds him lots of eggs and butter and he dies early, as many blacks do, of heart disease."[44] The battle lines had been drawn. A furious debate now erupted—in periodicals ranging from the *Journal of Feminist Studies in Religion* to *Playboy*[45]—between those seeking to promote the cause of

Clarence Thomas and those intent on destroying him. Thomas, to paraphrase one analyst, was being scrutinized more closely than any junior justice in American history.[46] Black conservatism was finally in full public view.

By the mid-1990s there had been no fewer than ten books written on "The Clarence Thomas Fiasco."[47] Although the bulk of these were penned for academic audiences in the fields of political science and law, two rival journalistic accounts—conservative David Brock's *The Real Anita Hill* and liberal journalists Jane Mayer and Jill Abramson's *Strange Justice*—become national bestsellers. Perhaps not surprisingly, these books' conflicting depictions of the new Justice mirrored the polarized assessments of black conservatism that had taken hold in the previous decade. Whereas Brock's account portrayed Hill as an unbalanced sexual deviant with a motive to defame the virtuous Thomas, Mayer and Abramson—relying on witnesses not heard at the confirmation hearings—sought to expose Thomas as the real liar and sexual predator.[48] Their Clarence Thomas was a career-obsessed networker who had curried favor with the conservative movement simply to secure a seat on the Supreme Court.

Although Sowell and other conservatives initially praised *The Real Anita Hill* as a carefully researched book that vindicated the black Justice,[49] revelations years later by Brock himself ultimately confirmed the veracity of the Mayer-Abramson thesis.[50] Brock's confession in 2002 that he had been at the center of a "right-wing dirty tricks operation" when he pilloried Hill—and that he had fabricated evidence as part of that operation—finally laid to rest the debates over sexual harassment and perjury. This was good news for those interested in a more nuanced interpretation of black conservatism. While Thomas's ascent to the Court had undoubtedly lifted the new black conservatives' profile, the allegations of sexual impropriety leveled against him had dominated the social commentary. In this highly charged atmosphere, it was disappointing but hardly surprising that balanced assessments of the phenomenon itself continued to be sidelined.

It was the brilliant African American philosopher Cornel West who long before Brock's admission had called into question the "crude discourse about race and gender" that emerged out of Thomas's confirmation hearings.[51] Although a significant number of black intellectuals had opposed the appointment, West was shocked generally at the "low level of discussion in black America" and dismayed particularly at the "failure of nerve of black leadership."[52] "The very fact," West wrote, "that no black leader could utter publicly that a black appointee for the Supreme Court was *unqualified* shows how captive they are to white stereotypes about black intellectual talent."[53] That Thomas, the black Republican and so-called "Uncle Tom," had secured the support of militant black nationalists such as Louis Farrakhan was even more mystifying.[54] "How," West asked, "did much of black leadership get in this bind?" Why did so many of them capitulate to Bush's cynical strategy of appointing to the Court an unqualified African American with a history of faithful service to Republican politics?[55] And what, ultimately, did this "failure of nerve," this capitulation, reveal about the decade-long debate over contemporary black conservatism? West's probing, in time, would prove critical to the development of a more mature discourse centered on the new black conservatives.

Most African American leaders had responded so inadequately to the Thomas nomination, West insisted, because they were caught in a "vulgar form of racial reasoning." This form of reasoning privileged claims to black authenticity and black patriarchy "in the interests of the black community in a hostile white racist country." It had led to the application of a simplistic line of questioning in relation to Thomas, the individual, while simultaneously stifling rational debate about the wider black conservative impulse he had come to represent. "Was Thomas really black?" "Was he black enough to be defended?" Or "was he just black on the outside?" That these were the questions being "asked, debated and answered throughout black America"—by leaders of the major political organizations and by ordinary people in "barbershops, beauty salons, living rooms, churches, mosques, and schoolrooms"—pointed, in West's view, to a deeper crisis within the African American community. So long as this essentialist framework continued to regulate black thought and action, he warned, people such as Clarence Thomas would "continue to haunt black America—as Bush and other conservatives sit back, watch, and prosper." Thus, racial reasoning needed to be replaced with prophetic moral reasoning in the best tradition of the black freedom movement.[56] Since, according to West, this was the only genuinely illuminating analytical framework, it had the potential to elevate the discussion of black conservatism to a new level.

If the debate over Thomas's personal legitimacy, both racial and sexual, initially failed to generate better work on the broader black conservative phenomenon, by the mid-1990s the intellectual landscape had changed: those working in the area could now point to a more sophisticated body of literature "demystifying the new black conservatism."[57] Although exaggeration and distortion continued to feature prominently in many assessments of the new black intellectuals, a small number of serious analysts—following West's lead—had belatedly emerged. By eschewing the stale polemics of the 1980s and the crude racial essentialism of the early 1990s, West had offered in a chapter of *Race Matters* one of the first—and arguably one of the most impressive—interpretive studies of contemporary black conservatism to date. Unlike previous commentators who insisted that black conservatives had only emerged because white conservatives wanted them to emerge, or those who saw in these intellectuals' prominence confirmation of a broader rightward shift within the black community, West sought to *explain* the rise of these alternative thinkers in the context of three major currents in American society since the late 1960s—the collapse of American liberalism, the structural transformation of the national economy, and the moral breakdown of communities across the country. Rather than ridicule or endorse the black conservatives' ideas, West sought to *engage* with these ideas and to offer a reasoned assessment of their political significance. Although his analysis was only brief, and further inquiry would be necessary, West had offered a constructive intellectual model for future scholarship in the field.[58]

Historians, philosophers, economists, anthropologists, literary theorists, and political scientists now joined journalists in focusing on modern black conservatism, but seemingly with a commitment to move beyond the exaggerations and distortions of the past. Some of these new scholars explored the black conservatives' alliance with the New Right and Republican Party and evaluated their role in the nation's rightward cultural shift.[59] Others took a different approach, investigating these intellectuals' relationship to the black community and attempting to explain their emergence and prominence in the context of sociopolitical currents within that community.[60] Increasingly those scholars in the second category wrote of a contemporary "crisis of black leadership" as the critical factor in the rise of these alternative black thinkers, even as their assessments of the thinkers themselves continued to vary.[61] How exactly was this crisis to be understood? And how, specifically, did it relate to black conservatism?

In *Race Matters* Cornel West explained the modern political dilemma confronting black America as follows: "There has not been a time in the history of black people in this country when the quantity of politicians and intellectuals was so great, yet the quality of both groups has been so low."[62] In this sense, he continued, "the crisis of black leadership contributes to political cynicism among black people; it encourages the idea that we cannot really make a difference in changing our society."[63] Indeed, as the 1990s wore on and racial inequality persisted, the political cynicism to which West referred only intensified. Some commentators argued that the controversial removal of Benjamin Chavis as executive director of the NAACP, alongside the demise of Jesse Jackson and the perceived middle-class bias of civil rights groups, had heightened black people's disillusionment with traditional black liberalism.[64] At the same time, the racial controversies generated by Nation of Islam leaders' Khalid Muhammad and Louis Farrakhan raised serious doubts about the political credibility of black nationalism.[65] With the Republican landslide victory in the 1994 mid-term elections virtually destroying the influence of the solidly Democratic Congressional Black Caucus, and House Leader Newt Gingrich touting a new Contract with America to deliver smaller government,[66] the crisis of black political culture seemed complete. According to some commentators, black conservatives were now well positioned to make their bid for political and intellectual hegemony within the African American community.[67]

To be sure, this bid had been foreshadowed one year earlier in what remains the only comprehensive book-length study favorable to contemporary black conservatism. Published in 1993, Joseph Conti and Brad Stetson's *Challenging the Civil Rights Establishment: Profiles of a New Black Vanguard*[68] offered an abridged version of black conservative thought and a neat summary of the social and political philosophies of arguably the four best-known black conservative intellectuals in modern America—Thomas Sowell, Shelby Steele, Glenn Loury, and Robert Woodson. These four African Americans were hailed as the architects of an unparalleled political phenomenon symbolizing not just evolution but complete innovation in black thought.[69] By advancing an alternative political creed of self-empowerment for black people, they were said to have "broken the liberal mold of black thought" to the benefit of all Americans.[70] What is more, Sowell and company had exposed civil rights leaders as corrupt and self-serving, and utterly disconnected from the hopes and aspirations of the "black silent majority."[71] This silent majority would seemingly soon be theirs. As the twentieth century drew to a close, Conti and Stetson predicted that black conservatism—so long confined to the political margins—would become one of the most culturally significant trends in American public life.[72]

"Dedicated, in admiration and gratitude, to the New Black Vanguard," *Challenging the Civil Rights Establishment* was—as this quotation suggests—a contribution to the debate over black conservatism best viewed as political. The book simply presented and endorsed the theories of the black conservatives while dismissing as "a kind of black political correctness" alternative views promoted by the "civil rights establishment" and its supporters.[73] This unbridled enthusiasm for these intellectuals' arguments predictably delighted right-wing reviewers, who praised Conti and Stetson's "thoughtful" and "fascinating" work. But it enraged liberals and radicals, who saw the failure to engage with the counterarguments of critics as emblematic of the methodological deficiencies and intellectual bias that underpinned the entire project. Indeed, in time, Stetson's position as director of the David Institute—a Californian think tank openly supportive of black conservative politics—was noted by progressives as yet further evidence that Sowell and company were "a new breed of

Uncle Tom" in "opportunistic service,"[74] "akin to client or satellite states who do the ideological bidding of the WASP establishment."[75]

In one sense, Conti and Stetson's hagiography was a "profound hoax," amounting, in the words of Hanes Walton, to little more than a series of "hoorays, hurrahs, praises, joyous songs, flips, firecrackers, and loud toots and hoots" for the black conservatives themselves.[76] Some two years after Clarence Thomas's appointment to the Supreme Court, the book certainly confirmed the high esteem in which these intellectuals were held by the American right. But why, one might ask, this book in 1993? The voices of the black conservatives were hardly new in 1993; they had already occupied the spotlight for the twelve years of the Reagan and Bush administrations. Nor were they any longer, in the truest sense, "a social force in ascendance," since their corrective reform proposals for the African American community had been emphatically rejected by the incoming Clinton administration. The black conservatives, however, remained useful in 1993 because of the symbolism attached to their rejection of the structural analyses of disadvantage that were resurfacing in the aftermath of the Los Angeles riots.[77] By reinforcing in the media the behavioral interpretation of the black underclass, these intellectuals arguably conferred upon it some semblance of authentic legitimacy. Conti and Stetson's lot, therefore, was to confer upon the black conservatives this same legitimacy.

Although literature on black conservatism continued to appear into the late 1990s, there would be no left-wing equivalent of the Conti-Stetson study. For the pundits, new racial obsessions had emerged. The writings of black conservative intellectuals would take a back seat during this period as the controversies generated by two new book titles—Charles Murray and Richard Herrnstein's *The Bell Curve*[78] and Dinesh D'Souza's *The End of Racism*[79]—captured a disproportionate amount of media attention, provoking fierce debate. While the first of these books, *The Bell Curve*, argued that blacks' innate intellectual inferiority lay at the root of American racial inequality, the second, *The End of Racism*, explained the problem as a function of primitive and pathological black culture. Despite this critical difference, implicit in both texts was the assumption that state intervention was powerless to redress what were (according to these authors) irrefutably African American deficiencies. Published in the mid-1990s with the endorsement of the American Enterprise Institute—a strong supporter of black conservatives—both *The Bell Curve* and *The End of Racism* were also reviewed favorably in the wider right-wing press. Yet the conservative movement continued to deny racist intentions.

With such explosive new, and yet familiarly old, arguments to wrestle with, it was hardly surprising that black conservatives were no longer the headline act. Even so, their activities were never far from the public eye. When Sowell hailed *The Bell Curve* as "one of the most sober, responsible, thorough and thoughtful books to be published in years,"[80] and Walter Williams followed with praise for *The End of Racism*,[81] the legitimacy of black conservatism was again called into question. When a new cluster of black conservative media personalities emerged in the shadow of Rush Limbaugh, bashing civil rights leaders for the amusement of white audiences, this was said to illustrate, once and for all, "The Descent of Black Conservatism."[82] And when University of California regent and African American businessman Ward Connerly launched his very public campaign to end race-based affirmative action at that institution, his credentials as a black conservative were scrutinized almost as much as the campaign itself.[83] Observing these developments in the mid- to late 1990s, Khalid Muhammad would offer what remains arguably the most extreme assessment of black conservatives to date—"boot-licking, butt-licking, bamboozled, half-baked, half-fried, sissified, punkified, pasteurized, homogenized Nigger[s]" who had "sold out" to "the man" and no longer spoke in an "authentically black voice."[84] These "homogenized Niggers" may not have made the political inroads that some commentators had earlier predicted, but they certainly continued to stir emotions.

Refusing to be drawn into the unproductive realm of personal denigration, the moderate African American journalist Clarence Page stood out in the media as an important voice of reason in this highly charged racial climate, expressing some sympathy for black conservatives in the late 1990s. Although at times these intellectuals' "proselytizing sounded like sloganeering," their "boldness and brashness," he insisted, had sometimes been refreshing.[85] It was difficult, moreover, to argue with their core contentions that liberalism had failed the black poor and that these people now needed to assume more responsibility for alleviating their condition. Since, in Page's view, there appeared little alternative in the modern American polity, the black conservatives' emphasis on self-help—a longstanding black tradition—positioned them as legitimate spokespeople in debates over the black future.[86]

Perhaps. And yet Page also wrote powerfully about some of the problems associated with such a view. The most obvious problem was the fact that contemporary black conservatives continued to lack an institutional base within the African American community. Attacking traditional civil rights leaders may have raised these intellectuals' public profile, but this combative strategy had simultaneously repelled most African Americans. The idea—promoted by black conservatives and their supporters—that black people were more conservative than the modern media stereotype, thus needed to be examined and put in perspective. Page, to this end, noted that there had always been a powerful conservative streak in black

America, and that on moral questions in particular, black core culture had historically displayed views that were more traditional than liberal. But it was not sufficient, he continued, for the black conservatives simply to present the moral conservatism of African Americans as evidence of political conservatism's legitimacy with the black masses. Research had shown, after all, that poverty, education, and civil rights remained "the three principal public policy concerns of black people"—the very areas in which the views of black conservatives deviated most dramatically from those of most black Americans.[87] Since elements drawn from political and economic liberalism appeared firmly embedded in the African American community, Page offered this explication of black conservatism: "I distinguish between black conservatives and conservative blacks. The former is a relatively small, if high profile movement of avowed conservatives who happen to be black. The latter best describes the black masses who harbor many conservative attitudes, but part company with traditional conservative party lines, especially the line that says black people make too much of racism."[88]

Page's compelling distinction represented yet another decisive blow against those who continued to claim that black conservatives enjoyed significant black grassroots support. But this Chicago journalist's contribution to the debate over black conservatism went beyond this. Having lowered the rhetorical temperature and paused to reflect on the phenomenon with an open mind, Page, like West before him, had implicitly rejected the old ideological boundaries of interpretation and posited an alternative way of thinking about the subject, disengaged from the old invective of personal denunciation so characteristic of the past. What was now required was a detailed examination of contemporary black conservatism to build upon this methodological progress.

Notwithstanding some significant advances in the way black conservatism was analyzed in the mid- to late 1990s, the fact remained that at the turn of the century a comprehensive academic study of this important phenomenon had yet to be written. Then, in 2001, Angela Dillard's *Guess Who's Coming to Dinner Now? Multicultural Conservatism in America* appeared.[89] Some eight years after the publication of the Conti-Stetson polemic, Dillard claimed to have produced the first in-depth analysis of modern black conservatism. But *Guess Who's Coming to Dinner Now?* did not focus on black conservatives alone. Rather, it was a study of a more diverse ideological movement the author called "multicultural" or "minority" conservatism, encompassing Latino, women, and homosexual conservatives as well. Even so, as the most prominent of the species, black conservative intellectuals attracted the most attention. Dillard's primary concern was their rhetorical positioning, especially the relation-

ship between their autobiographies and the social policies they championed. How, she asked, had these new conservatives conceptualized and
presented their public political selves?[90]

Modern black conservatives, Dillard argued, had essentially appealed
to two separate historical traditions to legitimate their presence in
American politics. On the one hand, they had sought to crawl inside the
"American Jeremiad," invoking God and the sentiments expressed in the
Constitution and the Declaration of Independence as evidence of their
faith in the political project that is America. On the other hand, they
had sought to create an authentic intellectual tradition inside the black
community, poaching several heroic figures from the African American
past—such as Frederick Douglass and Booker T. Washington—and setting them up as their intellectual forebears.[91] In highlighting the dual
heritage on which black conservatives had drawn in seeking to package
themselves for public consumption, Dillard made a point that seems self-
evident in 2009. It must nonetheless be recognized that Dillard's analysis
at the time of its publication represented a highly original contribution
to contemporary scholarship.

Guess Who's Coming to Dinner Now? also looked closely at the political implications of modern black conservatism and the significance of its white
conservative patronage. Uncomfortable with the old stereotype of black
conservatives as intellectual slaves of New Right masters, Dillard started
from a different premise—that their prominence reflected a change in
racial attitudes in the post–civil rights era. Ad hominem attacks were off
the menu. By following West's and Page's example and repudiating the
polemics of the past, *Guess Who's Coming to Dinner Now?* unearthed some
provocative questions about the relationship between identity and politics, and claims to authenticity in modern America. Moreover, Dillard's
conclusion that Sowell and company were a nascent political force that
had already transformed the complexion and character of American
conservatism appeared to suggest that a study devoted specifically to the
black conservatives' ideas was long overdue.

With their 2002 edited collection *Dimensions of Black Conservatism in the
United States: Made in America*,[92] political scientists Gayle T. Tate and Lewis
A. Randolph sought to fill this gaping hole in the historiography, producing the first comprehensive liberal/radical work evaluating the core
tenets of modern black conservative thought. Featuring twelve individual essays by black scholars, the book attempted not only to explore the
historical and political function of black conservatives, but also to dissect
and assess the validity of these intellectuals' interpretations of black life.
The contributors examined, among other things, Sowell and company's
critiques of liberalism and the federal government; the significance of
their institutional ties, particularly to the Republican Party; their fraught

relationship with the media; and their standing within the African American community. But while engaging some of the most complex issues of race, class, gender, and identity in American life, *Dimensions* fell into the trap of so many edited volumes in failing to present a clear thesis in a systematic fashion. There was general agreement among the authors that black conservatives "do not have a concrete program to operationalize politically and economically the values they espouse,"[93] but beyond this, few thematic connections existed between the various chapters. Problematic, too, was the collection's failure to address adequately two of the most controversial issues on which contemporary black conservatives have focused—public education and affirmative action.[94] Considering that the black conservatives had forged their public identities largely through their reflections on these issues, Tate and Randolph's decision to afford them limited analysis was puzzling.

Dimensions may have fallen short of its scholarly objectives, but it remained a far superior work to Godfrey Mwakikagile's 2004 polemic, *Black Conservatives: Are They Right or Wrong?*[95] Seemingly unable to grasp that black conservatism was an enormously complex ideological nexus in the contemporary American political culture, this Tanzanian journalist set out—as the title suggests—to answer the extraordinarily unsophisticated question of whether the black conservatives' views were right or wrong. Without so much as an attempt to assess their arguments with reference to the work of academic experts in the relevant fields, Sowell and company were pronounced wrong. This was not, therefore, historical writing in the usual mold. It did not state a problem to be solved or a set of questions to be answered through the interrogation of evidence or indeed a body of literature. Rather, Mwakikagile's intention was to expose the black conservatives as frauds pushing unconvincing arguments that served only to harm the larger African American community. Indeed, the author's argumentation attempted to lay a trap for these intellectuals. If they espoused Friedmanite views on economics they were, by definition, race traitors, because Friedmanite policies would maintain racial inequality. Since it was assumed—but not proven—from the outset that white conservatives controlled black conservatives as ventriloquists controlled their dummies, Mwakikagile's thesis as an argument went nowhere. A decade on, then, this was the left's stylistically inferior equivalent of the Conti-Stetson study.

If the publication of Thomas Sowell's *Race and Economics* in 1975 marked "the rise of . . . a visible and aggressive black intellectual conservative assault on traditional black liberal ideas,"[96] aided and abetted by the conservative movement, more than three decades later it was equally true that this novel phenomenon had itself been the target of a visible and aggressive counterassault by the very forces it had set out to topple. Although the positions adopted by liberals, black nationalists, and radical egalitarians on this subject sometimes varied, there was a general consensus among these groups that contemporary black conservatism was not only undesirable but unacceptable. Those African Americans who championed the New Right agenda were cunning political opportunists, the argument went, opportunists who had gravitated toward Republican power and privilege solely to further their professional ambitions.

Where liberals had emphasized individual debility in framing this thesis, black nationalists and radical egalitarians typically relied on more deterministic approaches. Black nationalists, on the whole, had very little intelligent to say about the modern black conservative phenomenon. Blinded by an overwhelming loyalty to race, they appeared in a perpetual state of confusion, unsure whether to denounce the black conservatives as race traitors or to support them solely on account of their race. Considering the preeminence in these circles of fanatics such as Louis Farrakhan and Khalid Muhummad, this lack of analytical sophistication was fairly predictable. The same judgment, however, could not be applied to black conservatism's radical egalitarian critics. These critics tended to combine liberal and nationalist analyses, deploying the individual debility thesis alongside essentialist criticism of the black conservatives. Manning Marable's condemnation of Sowell and company as race traitors, as late as 2002, epitomized the seeming eternalness of this fruitless approach to the subject.[97]

With the notable exceptions of Cornel West and Angela Dillard, then, radical egalitarians failed for the most part to critique contemporary black conservatism effectively. By favoring character assassination over idea assassination, these and other critics often remained closed to the possibility that alternative explanations of the phenomenon might have some validity. Black conservatives might actually be correct in their individualist and cultureless diagnosis of the black condition. Their positions, while flawed, might reflect the overwhelming hegemonic force of American capitalism over individual debility. Sowell and company's refusal to see black disadvantage as solely a function of race and racism may indeed be hard to refute. But such a concession does not mean that the explanations of black disadvantage offered by black conservatives have themselves been irrefutable.

Despite some modest improvements in the level of inquiry into black conservatism from the mid-1990s—extending into this century with the publication of two useful scholarly books—fixed notions and preconceived prejudices about these intellectuals, among pundits both left and right, have continued to impede the field. With luminaries of the conservative movement determined to promote them and liberal and radical commentators resolved (overwhelmingly) to condemn them, the black conservatives' contributions to racial discourse have continued to be exaggerated and misrepresented in the press. This observation serves merely to reinforce the need for more scholarship focused on modern black conservatism—scholarship not only to document these intellectuals' involvement in the racial policy debates of the past three decades, but also to assess the significance of this involvement through a systematic analysis of the ideas they put forward for public consumption.

Before engaging the relevant debates over affirmative action, welfare, and public education, any such analysis must take seriously three preliminary, but nevertheless fundamental, historical questions. Who were these intellectuals? What had they thought and written? And why? Forming part of an introduction to the dramatis personae of the subject, these questions have the potential to yield productive insights not only into the lives of the most prominent individual black conservatives, but into the complex nature of their intellectual philosophies.

Pursuit of these previously underdeveloped considerations is essential to a more nuanced assessment of black conservative thought.

Chapter 1
Profiles of an Intellectual Vanguard

During the 1980s and 1990s, a relatively small group of right-wing African American intellectuals—supported by the networks and institutions of the New Right—defined the parameters of contemporary black conservative thought. Derided by progressive critics for lacking racial and cultural authenticity, these intellectuals frequently hit back by writing in personal and political terms about their dual heritage as *African Americans.* On the one hand, the black conservatives emphasized humble origins—the fact that many of them had grown up poor in black communities before "making it"—to establish their authority to speak to the myriad problems confronting African Americans. But they also drew on the rhetorical traditions of black America, reconfiguring them with the U.S. constitutional tradition and neoclassical economics, to construct something resembling their own distinctive canon. Examination of the personal histories and the nature and content of the thought of the most influential of these intellectuals is essential in the quest for broader conclusions about the phenomenon they represent.

The words "canon" and "phenomenon" imply something monolithic, when, in reality, contemporary black conservatism was more complex and multifaceted than either supporters or critics recognized. Just as there were ideas and opinions that united the cohort, so there were variations and crosscurrents that divided them. Some black conservatives were serious intellectuals; others were media pundits. Some deployed empirical evidence to advance arguments; others relied almost entirely on individual experience. Some were libertarians beholden to complex free-market theory and philosophically opposed to government; others emphasized morality and, in some instances, the need for government to enforce it. Some believed in politics and the importance of engaging the black community; others eschewed politics and spoke of, but never with or to, that community. Some yearned for the death of race and the dawn of a color-blind America; others expressed antipathy toward integration and assimilation, celebrating a golden age of black achievement before civil rights.

Clearly, these intellectuals did not simply offer "a sickeningly familiar neo-conservatism in blackface,"[1] as some charged. That being the case, the question of what each intellectual did offer—and why—becomes central to a more comprehensive and sophisticated appreciation of black conservatism itself. If the black conservatives were not products of the same school or students of the same teacher, but pointed to a variety of influences that helped shape their views, what were these influences and how diverse were the views they subsequently embraced? By drawing together threads of information about the various intellectuals and giving a coherence to personal narratives that have only been presented in snippet form in the past, the medium of biography allows for a new and more complex addition to scholarship on this powerful current in American society.

Any discussion of the major black conservative thinkers of the past three decades must take as its starting point Clarence Thomas, for he, more than any other individual, personified the rise of black conservatism during this period. Described by one commentator as "perhaps the only Supreme Court Justice who might be recognized in the check-out line at the Giant,"[2] Thomas became, upon appointment to the bench in 1991, one of the most divisive figures in national life.[3] Of course, this black conservative might not be considered an "intellectual" in the traditional academic sense; however, many of his pre–Supreme Court writings on race and class displayed an intellectual flavor and, in the 1980s, were critical in popularizing contemporary black conservative thought. But while Thomas the "public figure" has been the focus of a torrent of analysis and opinion, sophisticated treatments of the political philosophy of Thomas the "conservative legal intellectual" have remained scarce.

Perhaps part of the reason for this reluctance to engage Thomas's philosophy was that it was so fraught with internal inconsistencies, making it difficult to pin down and explain. On the one hand, for example, Thomas condemned affirmative action for placing the interests of groups before individuals.[4] He also charged that the policy stamped minorities with a badge of inferiority that "may cause them to develop dependencies or to adopt an attitude that they are entitled to preferences."[5] Yet Thomas claimed to identify with Malcolm X, a leader whose popularity with blacks stemmed largely from his emphasis on the power of the collective.[6] Moreover, racial preferences did not appear to have harmed Thomas himself. In yet another paradoxical display, he once conceded that, if not "for affirmative action programs, God only knows where I would be today. These laws and their proper application are all that stand between the first 17 years of my life and the second 17 years."[7]

Consistency appeared to elude the Justice in other areas too. As a member of the administrations of Reagan and Bush, Thomas firmly insisted "the Constitution be interpreted in a colorblind fashion," since apparently "it was futile to talk of a colorblind society unless this constitutional principle is first established."[8] But there was another Clarence Thomas who openly questioned the value of pursuing such a society, seeing colorblindness as impossible in a country where "blacks will never be seen as equal to whites."[9] Too often, a commitment to color-blindness, he believed, sent a message to African Americans that black institutions—and thereby black people—were inferior. For this reason, Thomas attacked the 1954 *Brown v. Board of Education* decision—which abolished segregation in public schools—as being based on "dubious social science evidence." "Black children," he argued, "gain nothing from simply sitting next to whites and can do quite well in their own schools."[10]

Thomas's ideas were often credited to Booker T. Washington.[11] This was not surprising, since—like Washington—Thomas had declared that the issue "is economics—not who likes you," imploring blacks to eschew government and do for themselves.[12] But unlike Washington, who preached a *collectivist* message of economic empowerment for the black community, the Justice's idea of racial salvation was predicated, almost entirely, on an appeal for more *individual* effort in the service of self and family. An admirer of Ayn Rand's libertarian tracts *The Fountainhead* and *Atlas Shrugged*, Thomas warned his son that he would "personally hunt you down and kick your behind from one end of America to the other" if he ever heard any "whining about how you can't make it because you are black."[13] While perceiving "a mean callous world out there . . . still very much filled with discrimination,"[14] this black conservative went on, contradictorily, to reject the view that racism continued to inhibit black social mobility, offering his own life experiences as evidence for his claim.

Thomas's past—his life and work—offers the key to understanding what can only be described as an enigmatic worldview. Born into the segregated world of rural Georgia in 1948, Thomas wrote frequently of a childhood marred by racial poverty and hardship. Raised by his sharecropper grandfather in a house without indoor plumbing, he claimed to have worked the land, struggling to "survive under the totalitarianism of segregation, not only without the active assistance of government but with its active opposition."[15] It was in these early years, Thomas later recalled, that his hostility to state intervention developed: since government was the problem, not the solution, for Southern blacks, economic self-reliance seemed the best—indeed, the only—way forward.[16]

Schooled by nuns at a small segregated Catholic school in Savannah, Thomas briefly contemplated life as a priest before being accepted to study liberal arts at Holy Cross, a Jesuit college in Massachusetts.[17] If his Catholicism had already consigned him to outsider status in the

Southern black community, Thomas's voyage into higher education in the North would set him even further apart. Admitted to Holy Cross as part of a special scholarship program set up for African Americans in the wake of Martin Luther King's assassination, he flirted with political radicalism for a time, donning the beret of the Black Panther Party and declaring himself a disciple of Malcolm X.[18] Yet, as one commentator noted, "in an era when Malcolm X's autobiography was on the school's freshman reading list and torn fatigues and berets were the fashion, it was easy to confuse style with substance."[19] In Thomas's case, style appeared to trump substance. According to one former classmate, the future Supreme Court Justice's penchant for iconoclasm and controversy was already well known: he was always "seeking out isolated, idiosyncratic positions where, characteristically, he could be alone."[20]

Despite modest academic results at Holy Cross, Thomas was accepted to Yale Law School as part of an aggressive affirmative action program to increase black student representation.[21] But stung by a succession of personal failures early on in his tenure,[22] he began to feel "stigmatized rather than helped by race-conscious aid" and to suspect resentment on the part of white faculty at his presence in the classroom.[23] The personal uncertainty that plagued Thomas during these years led him to reject affirmative action and was arguably the catalyst for his subsequent conversion to conservative politics.[24] Abandoning his commitment to "radical social justice" in only his second year at Yale, the new Clarence Thomas declared his intention to work in private practice to earn "a lot of money."[25] This about-face turned out to be his making.

Thomas was employed in a number of high-profile government and legal positions upon graduation in 1974.[26] Yet visibility in the conservative movement eluded him until the Fairmont Conference in 1980. Having wandered for so long "in the desert of political and ideological alienation," he arrived at the conference "bubbling, bursting with excitement," relieved finally to have "found a home" among like-minded African Americans.[27] Dazzling the luminaries of the New Right with his uncompromisingly conservative approach to black issues, Thomas was soon profiled in the *Washington Post* in an article that served as a virtual "advertisement for employment in the new administration" of Ronald Reagan.[28] This article would be the first of many about Clarence Thomas and mark the beginning of his rapid ascent into the highest echelons of American society.

Appointed in 1981 to the high-ranking position of Assistant Secretary for Civil Rights in the Department of Education, Thomas was soon promoted to chair the Equal Employment Opportunity Commission (EEOC), supervising until 1990 the entire federal effort to curb prejudice in the workplace. He dramatically transformed the culture of the

EEOC, shifting the burden of proof from employers to employees in discrimination suits and rejecting group remedies to workplace inequity. He also abandoned the use of timetables and numeric goals, which allowed companies greater flexibility in the hiring of minorities, even though he himself had been a beneficiary of these mandates.[29] Indeed, by the mid-1980s, Thomas had become linked with the broader onslaught against civil rights occurring under Reagan and developed into a fully fledged ideologue of the New Right.[30] Courting a close political relationship with George Bush in the election year of 1988, he poured all his energy into the Republican campaign, assuming special responsibility for promoting the presidential hopeful's credentials with African Americans.[31] Thomas's efforts were duly rewarded. After a brief stint at the U.S. Court of Appeals (for the District of Columbia) to gain "some experience," President Bush appointed him to the Supreme Court, insisting he was "the best qualified man for the job on the merits."[32]

How was Thomas's climb from rural poverty to the heart of American judicial power to be explained? The new Justice offered his own interpretation. "Only in America," Thomas exclaimed, on the day Bush nominated him to the Supreme Court, could a person from such humble origins have risen to a position of such eminence. He continued: "As a child, I could not dare dream that I would ever see the Supreme Court—not to mention to be nominated to it. Indeed, my most vivid childhood memory of a Supreme Court was the 'impeach Earl Warren' signs that lined Highway 17 near Savannah. I didn't quite understand who this Earl Warren fellow was, but I knew he was in some kind of trouble. I thank all those who have helped me along the way and who helped me to this point and this moment in my life, especially my grandparents, my mother, and the nuns—all of whom were adamant that I grow up to make something of myself."[33]

Here and elsewhere Thomas would invoke his humble black origins to explain his professional achievements and conservative political philosophy. He spoke of a grandfather who had put "a premium on self-help"; of nuns who had taught him discipline; and of his own unflinching drive to be somebody, consistent with the values of dignity and pride he had learned as a child. This was a story, then, that—on the face of it—was both authentically black and quintessentially American. But the Justice's account of his noble past was problematic to say the least. Not only did he typically neglect to mention that he owed much of his professional success to affirmative action policies—policies he subsequently went to great lengths to excoriate—but he failed to recognize the significance of his "noteworthy service as a partisan ideologue for conservative Republicanism."[34] Even Thomas's famous claims to childhood deprivation were exposed as exaggerated. Although far from privileged, his grandfather's

small business had been sufficient to provide him with childhood com-
forts that most of his Southern black contemporaries did not enjoy.[35] As
these and other facts came to light, the philosophical content of Thomas's black conservatism appeared increasingly dubious, more a function
of self-serving justification than of intellectual rigor.

This same charge could not be leveled at the man Thomas identified as
his intellectual mentor, the indefatigable Thomas Sowell.[36] Perched at
the forefront of the new black vanguard and certainly its unofficial intellectual messiah since the mid-1970s, Sowell was the most prolific black
conservative writer of the era. Sometimes referred to as the "black Milton Friedman,"[37] he was the author of numerous academic books challenging liberal social policies on topics ranging from affirmative action
and welfare to immigration and education.[38] But not one to be confined
to the ivory tower, he also cut a distinctive figure in the media. A syndicated newspaper columnist and regular contributor to the nation's most
influential conservative magazines,[39] in the 1980s Sowell also appeared
as a regular guest on television and radio as an expert on race relations.
   As was perhaps appropriate for a conservative economist in Reagan's
America, Sowell collected evidence and marshaled statistics to refute the
"myth" that racism continued to determine black life chances and to
criticize those who saw government intervention as a solution to black
problems.[40] Trained for life by the great capitalist theorist Milton Friedman, Sowell maintained that black America's long-term future depended
on the ability of black people to obtain—in the short-term—low-paid
private-sector jobs in a stable free-market economy.[41] Drawing concepts
from microeconomic theory and functionalist sociology, Sowell's writings were also heavily directed toward an assessment of the progress of
different ethnic cultures in American life. "What determines how rapidly
a group moves ahead is not discrimination," he argued, "but the fit between elements of its culture and the requirements of the economy." "To
get ahead," Sowell continued, "you have to have some ability to work,
some ability at entrepreneurship or something else that the society values."[42] Clearly, black Americans lacked these basic ingredients. Clearly,
Sowell's conservatism displayed a more scholarly flavor than Thomas's.
   By taking his empirical axe to "liberal mythology" and offering the market as the cure for all of society's ills, Sowell emerged in the early 1980s
as "the Administration's favored black spokesman."[43] Few were aware,
though, that he had hesitated before writing about African Americans.
But in the preface to *Ethnic America*, Sowell explained that he initially intended to write a book about Marxism but was persuaded by colleagues
to write about race and ethnicity instead.[44] Doubtless his colleagues and
supporters understood that a book critical of liberalism and civil rights

by a black person who had moved from Harlem to Harvard would carry considerable symbolic weight. And they were right. The 1981 *Ethnic America* became "one of the best-selling books on American ethnicity to have appeared in recent years."[45] Before long, Sowell was being hailed as "one of the towering intellectuals of conservative thought."[46]

This assessment of Sowell's intellectual status was almost certainly an exaggeration. But there was no doubt that the controversial black economist was an impressive figure in several respects. Born into segregated North Carolina in 1930 to parents who were "low-skilled workers," Sowell moved to Harlem at the age of nine. Dropping out of school at the age of sixteen, he worked in a number of menial jobs before being drafted during the Korean War and spending two years in the Marine Corps.[47] Returning to civilian life at the war's end, the reformed Sowell completed high school with sufficient competence to earn entry to Howard University, before going on to Harvard. Although "a bitterly eloquent critic of racism in his writings," Sowell's mentor at Howard, Sterling Brown, offered his young student the following advice before he departed for the Ivy League: "Don't come back here and tell me you didn't make it 'cause white folks were mean . . . Harvard has ruined more niggers than bad liquor."[48] These words would stay with Sowell throughout his life and arguably form the basis of his renowned contempt for the politics of victimhood.

Whether it was the discipline he had learned in the Marine Corps or the stirring words of Sterling Brown that motivated him, Sowell's newfound resolve brought him great success in the Ivy League. Writing up his senior honors thesis at Harvard on Karl Marx, he graduated from that institution *magna cum laude* before earning a doctorate in economics at the University of Chicago under the supervision of Milton Friedman.[49] In search of an academic career, Sowell received strong support from his mentor Friedman, who wrote years later of the job opportunities the young man initially considered: "He talked to several of us about which to accept, expressing a strong preference for one of the least attractive offers—at Howard University in Washington—on the purely emotional grounds that it would enable him to make the greatest contribution to members of his race. I tried to dissuade him—as did many of my colleagues."[50] But Sowell ignored the advice and went to Howard, only to leave after a year in frustration at what he considered to be loose academic standards and the institution's capitulation to black student militancy. Although the Howard experiment was swiftly aborted, a promising career had been born. From the late 1960s until the late 1970s, Sowell held positions at Cornell, Rutgers, Amherst, Brandeis, and UCLA, and wrote several books—including *Say's Law, Black Education: Myths and Tragedies, Race and Economics*, and *Knowledge and Decisions*—that established his credentials with the conservative movement.[51] Yet as late as 1979, when the final draft of *Knowledge and Decisions* was completed, Sowell remained on the margins of mainstream political debate.

Of course, "the cause of Sowell's rise to prominence," one scholar noted, was not to "be found in his books," but in Reagan's election victory and the conservative movement's ensuing search for blacks who would support the new administration's urban reform agenda.[52] Having accepted a senior fellowship at the Hoover Institution in September 1980, Sowell—freed from the burden of teaching—produced a succession of books strongly supportive of this agenda. These books reiterated his fundamental thesis that the preeminent structural element of political-economic life relevant to the plight of the black poor was the negative role of the state and the positive role of the market. New Right luminaries liked what they read. Although he continued to deny a political relationship with Reagan, Sowell was soon appointed to the president's Economic Policy Advisory Committee and widely touted as a candidate for one of three high-profile political posts: Secretary of Housing and Development, Secretary of Education, and Secretary of Labor.[53] This one-time ghetto resident had become a valued expert at White House domestic policy discussions and a living testament to the enduring power of the American Dream.

Following *Ethnic America, Markets and Minorities,* and *The Economics and Politics of Race,* Sowell's star continued to rise with the publication in 1984 of *Civil Rights: Rhetoric or Reality,* an all-out academic assault on an undeniably complacent and hardly visionary civil rights establishment. While books such as these relied on detailed, statistical analysis to dent the credibility of racial liberalism, his newspaper columns were polemics—abrasive and egoistic, employing the art of sarcasm to put down political adversaries. Some years earlier, for example, in the *Washington Post,* Sowell had launched the most extraordinary attack on black leaders since the days of George Schuyler. Failing to exercise the intellectual civility he so often demanded of others, he accused civil rights activists Andrew Young and Patricia Roberts Harris of exploiting race for personal gain—of seeking to be "Blacker Than Thou"—even though as "light-skinned Negroes they historically had more in common with whites than with the darker members of their ethnic group."[54] Having grown up middle class, these liberals could never be truly representative spokespeople for the black masses. That role, apparently, was reserved for Sowell himself.

Indeed, a recurring theme in Sowell's work was his determination to portray himself as an authentic spokesman for African American interests in response to those who would question his blackness. His autobiography, *A Personal Odyssey,* revealed a man steeped in racial pride as he battled to make it from Harlem to Harvard and beyond. By invoking his tortuous personal path to becoming a respected international economist, Sowell sought to legitimize his attacks on liberalism on the one hand and to establish a connection with the black poor on the other. As a rising black conservative economist in the 1980s, it was absolutely essential for him to earn the trust of African Americans while working on behalf of New Right interests.

To this end, Sowell wrote frequently of how he had not lived in a home with running water, electricity, or heating before moving to Harlem, and how, once in Harlem, he had lived "amid rats and with un-soled shoes" until he was a teenager.[55] He explained how his rejection of black student militancy in the late 1960s—far from being motivated by conservatism—had been compelled by a determination to hold black students to high academic standards—for the sake of their families and for the good of the race.[56] He also expressed admiration for the Washington model of uplift and praised the journalistic writings of George Schuyler.[57] Yet he wrote little favorable about the civil rights movement. In fact, he criticized the movement's emphasis on integration, drawing on an authentic sense of blackness and idealizing the 1940s Harlem of his childhood—a separated community structured by the reality of de facto segregation. There was much in this world worth preserving, Sowell insisted. Not one to get carried away with the lofty rhetoric of color-blindness, he steadfastly maintained that the entire rationale behind the political effort to gain admittance to formerly white educational institutions had been deeply flawed. But these arguments Sowell rarely made within the black community: there he was persona non grata, someone known to talk *about*, rather than with, African Americans.[58]

Although he continued to write prolifically and be praised in right-wing circles as "a unique figure in American scholarship"[59] into the 1990s and beyond, Sowell's political utility had virtually expired by the late 1980s. The Republican Party's brain trust appeared to recognize that, if their goal was to make political inroads into the African American community, summoning to the front line a man so unpopular with black people was hardly an effective strategy. Sowell's tendency to flaunt his ego—to "match ridicule with ridicule, sanctimony with sanctimony, truculence with truculence"[60]—had come to be seen as a liability. His persistent characterization of the homeless as "sanctifying bums who refuse to work,"[61] for example, was extreme even by the administration's standards. The underlying message might have been legitimate, conservatives surmised, but the abrasive style of delivery was politically counterproductive. Indeed, outside the conservative labyrinth, Sowell had come to be seen as "an ultra-right crank of the H.L. Hunt or Jesse Helms variety."[62] The political space was now clear for a new—more restrained—black conservative voice.

*   *   *

In Reagan's second term, Sowell was displaced as the "Administration's favored black spokesperson" by the young Harvard economist Glenn Loury. Although less combative than his predecessor, Loury's life appeared to resemble Sowell's in several ways. Born and raised on the south side of Chicago, "where the color line was an inescapable fact of life,"[63] this son of working-class parents also reported overcoming prejudice, poverty, and profligacy in youth. By the age of nineteen, Loury had already fathered two children out of wedlock, dropped out of college, and was employed in a menial capacity at a printing plant. But displaying the initiative he would later call for in other blacks, Loury's fortunes soon improved: he began taking courses at Southeast Junior College and won a scholarship to Northwestern University, before going on to graduate work in economics at MIT under the supervision of the Nobel laureate Robert Solow.[64]

Loury's 1976 doctoral dissertation was widely credited with pioneering the study of social capital—those informal features of social organization that, as much as money or brains, facilitate mobility in the labor market.[65] As the condition of the nation's inner cities deteriorated in the 1970s under the weight of an outbreak of violence, drugs, and family breakdown, this former liberal came to insist that the greatest barrier to racial equality was no longer the "enemy without"—white racism—but the "enemy within": social problems within the black community itself. These problems, he continued, would need to be tackled directly in the 1980s if blacks were to achieve anything approaching social and economic parity in national life. Old strategies would have to be discarded and new ones pursued in what loomed as a critical decade for the future of black America.[66] Loury, however, could not have foreseen how important his own work would come to be in the context of this changing racial climate.

If disillusionment with the simplistic antiracism of some civil rights leaders drove this young black economist into the arms of the conservative establishment, his views on social capital—on what blacks needed to do for themselves—soon made him a conservative intellectual sensation. In 1982, aged only thirty-three, Loury became Harvard's first tenured black professor of economics.[67] By the mid-1980s, his work was featuring prominently on the pages of *Commentary*, *The Public Interest*, and the *Wall Street Journal*, and he had become a virtual celebrity on the right-wing lecture circuit.[68] Whether writing or speaking, Loury's message to blacks was blunt: since revolution was unlikely in America, pragmatism dictated the need for greater self-reflection and open-mindedness toward the president's social policy agenda. Citing the failure of government to improve the lives of the black poor, he exhorted civil rights leaders to rise above their self-serving commitment to affirmative action and to explore alternative approaches to assist those blacks who were truly disadvantaged.[69] Like Sowell, Loury was an enthusiastic "supply-sider" who believed that the American free market conduced to social mobility. But unlike Sowell he never argued for the abolition of the welfare state.[70] Indeed, his exposition of market economics was often punctuated by a profound realism about the *enduring* legacy of discrimination against black Americans under capitalism.[71]

Government, then, in Loury's view, could be employed legitimately to address the symptoms of racism's enduring legacy—serious criminality, drug abuse, inadequate educational preparation, and the like. But such intervention, he argued, should be minimal and geared only to enable individuals to become self-supporting moral agents.[72] Moral considerations were often the priority in Loury's work. Since, in the post–civil rights era, "a large and growing body of data and evidence" suggested that "the behavior and values of persons in the underclass . . . play an important part in perpetuating their poverty,"[73] it was absolutely essential, he argued, that black people rediscover the ethics and values that had underpinned the black community before civil rights.[74] Only self-reliance and the mediating structures of the family, church, schools, social clubs, and neighborhoods could deliver the spiritual regeneration and moral leadership required to uplift—and save—this community in the "age of crack."[75] In putting this argument, Loury was effectively calling on black people to reclaim their past in order to secure their future: "The great challenge facing black America today is the task of taking control of its own future by exerting the necessary leadership, making the required sacrifices, and building the needed institutions so that black social and economic development becomes a reality. No matter how windy the debates become among white liberals and conservatives as to what should be done, meeting this self-creating challenge ultimately depends on black action."[76]

Central to Loury's call for black action was his explanation of the importance of black responsibility. While acknowledging that African Americans had been hampered by a history of racism in the United States that partially explained the depth of their contemporary disadvantage, he also suggested that fault and responsibility were separable. "It is absolutely vital," Loury wrote, in a manner reminiscent of Washington, "that blacks distinguish the fault which may be attributable to racism, and the responsibility for relieving that condition."[77] But liberal leaders, black and white, had steadfastly rejected this premise, preferring to adhere to a victim-status conception of blackness that suggested it was sufficient to construct an identity based upon the guilt and the pity of one's former oppressor.[78] Not only had this "loyalty trap" blinded these leaders to the genuinely harmful aspects of black behavior, in Loury's view it had also led them to rebuke other blacks who were willing to breach cultural sensibilities and talk openly about the internal problems of the black community.[79]

It was the breaching of these cultural sensibilities, however, that made Loury popular with the Reagan administration—so popular that, by the mid-1980s, he was a regular guest at the White House and privy to most federal policy discussions concerning African Americans. With his humble origins giving him the cloak of racial authenticity—a connection, one might say, to the streets—it was little surprise when the boy from Chicago's South Side was selected by the then Secretary of Education William Bennett to serve as his deputy.[80] Of this spectacular rise to prominence, the journalist Robert Boynton wrote: "With two years left in Reagan's second term, Bennett would be giving Loury a bully pulpit from which to push a conservative agenda. . . . Because his writings promoted self-help and family values, Loury seemed the ideal spokesman to inform black America that, despite rumors to the contrary, it had a friend in the Republican Party."[81]

Loury certainly appeared to be an effective political operator. Socially more agreeable than Sowell, he was also distinguished by a genuine commitment to engage the African American community.[82] Like other black conservatives, he drew heavily on the ideas of Washington, advocating a program of pragmatism, morality, and economic development in the present, while recalling a black epoch in which "a great people striving under terrible odds" had pursued such a program. But unlike some of his black conservative counterparts, Loury also sought to situate his thought within the context of civil rights, drawing on the legacy of Martin Luther King.[83] Claiming to believe, like King, in American potential and the need for "compromise and cooperation with whites of good will," Loury attacked the pessimism of contemporary black leaders who expressed "a profound antagonism toward the American state."[84] Yet he was not averse to criticizing the approach to race adopted by other black conservatives, believing they had a responsibility to establish a dialogue with liberals and to improve their image within the black community. "A black critic speaking with the backing of the political and intellectual right," Loury wrote, "bears a difficult burden of showing that he is not a tool of forces hostile to his own people."[85] Never entirely comfortable with the black conservative label, this black scholar situated himself between those who argued that behavioral problems were the sole impediment to black progress and those who argued that structural factors were the only reason for the lack of progress.[86]

As it turned out, Loury's political career was extinguished before it ignited: within three months of his nomination as deputy to the Secretary of Education, news emerged that he had withdrawn from the confirmation process, citing personal reasons. Not only had assault charges been laid against Loury by his twenty-three-year-old mistress, but he was soon in court again charged with possession of marijuana and cocaine, drugs for which he had developed an addiction.[87] Buoyant critics noted that the good Harvard professor had come to epitomize the very kind of black man he often criticized in his work: "a violent, irresponsible, drug-using womanizer who put his own pleasure above the needs of his career and the needs of his family."[88] Disgraced and humiliated, Loury retreated into intellectual exile to rethink the meaning of his life. Re-emerging in the early 1990s was an altogether different man—politically moderate, religiously devout, and with an eye increasingly to scholarship.[89] Referring years later to his bitter personal history, Loury wrote: "I thought if I hung out in the community and engaged in certain kinds of social activity, in a way I was being black."[90] Time and again, thereafter, he would invoke this troubled past to claim a special status to speak to the problems of black America.

Having spent so long deriding blacks for claiming victim status, the notoriously prickly Walter Williams would have been troubled by the intellectualization of such irresponsibility.[91] A professor of economics at George Mason University since 1980, as well as a nationally syndicated newspaper columnist and media pundit,[92] Williams may have been politically less visible than Sowell and Loury, but his role in the development of contemporary black conservatism was nevertheless significant. Indeed, so significant was Williams's contribution in the early 1980s that he and Sowell reportedly made a pact never to fly together on the same plane: an accident, they joked, would spell the end of black conservatism in the United States.[93]

As with Sowell, Williams looked to portray himself as a harsh truth teller who was motivated by a deep concern for the people he criticized— namely, black people. The author of six books on economic and racial themes, he was undoubtedly the most controversial member of the cohort, adopting what often seemed like an unending number of needlessly provocative positions. Not only did Williams denounce welfare as "twentieth century slavery" and applaud the South for its stand during the Civil War, but he supported the right of state legislatures to publicly display the Confederate flag.[94] With these and other peculiarities, this black conservative did not always appear to meet the requisites of a serious academic. But there was another—indeed more scholarly—Walter Williams who was a formidable intellectual mind in his own right.

In addition to courting controversy with his divisive columns and public relations stunts, Williams acquired a reputation in academic and political circles as a fierce exponent of unfettered market capitalism, it being in his view the most rational and egalitarian system of human organization yet devised.[95] In fact, poverty and racial inequality only existed in America, he argued, because politically imposed distortions in the market such as minimum wage legislation and occupational licensing schemes priced new competitors out of certain sectors and entrenched the positions of groups already established.[96] Praising the founding fathers and the system of limited government they had set down in the Constitution,[97] Williams insisted that the removal of these distortions—together with other forms of "big government" such as affirmative action and welfare—would inevitably pave the way for greater black economic advancement.[98] "Any way we cut it," he concluded, "the free market is a friend to discriminated-against people."[99] Any way *we* cut it, Williams's worldview fitted neatly within the parameters that had traditionally defined the libertarian wing of American conservatism.

This black economist, then, was perhaps best seen as a libertarian conservative.[100] Whereas Loury's skepticism toward government was based on a practical historical assessment of welfare's failure to uplift the black poor, Williams saw state intervention, in principle, as a violation of individual rights in a free-market economy. People have an inalienable right, he maintained, "to engage in *any* voluntary exchange without interference, control, or coercion by third parties," and to own the product of their labor. Any attempt to interfere with this process, by confiscating or transferring a part of that product, was immoral, unjust, even criminal.[101] This was natural law.[102] By focusing on race and endorsing the redistributive measures of the Great Society, not only had modern civil rights leaders violated this law, they had fundamentally misunderstood the real problem confronting black Americans—the regulated market—and thereby blocked innumerable opportunities for black mobility. Of course, "racial discrimination *was*," Williams conceded, "an ugly part of U.S. history." It used to be "a *reasonably satisfactory* explanation" for the socioeconomic disadvantage of African Americans. But that had changed. The civil rights struggle was "over" and "won."[103] Now, rather than a racial problem, Williams argued, what modern blacks confronted was an economic problem. Its resolution would require not only a principled commitment to limited government but also a "recapturing" of the "can-do-spirit" that had defined so much of black history.[104]

Just as Williams's relegation of race to the theoretical margins could be interpreted as a strategy to win influence in Reagan's America, his emphasis on the individual might also be understood as a product of his remarkable personal history. Like Thomas and Sowell, Williams consistently offered his own life as an example of what could be achieved in America with discipline and hard work. "From exceedingly humble beginnings," Williams wrote, "I am now in the top 1 percent of income-earners." Raised by his domestic servant mother in the slums of Philadelphia after his father abandoned the family, Williams recalled shining shoes and shoveling snow as a teenager to help pay the bills. Graduating from high school in the mid-1950s, he married and worked as a taxi driver for several years before being drafted—like Sowell—into military service toward the end of that decade. It was while stationed in Korea in 1960, at the age of twenty-four, that Williams purportedly made the decision that changed his life. "My wife and I agreed that when my Army tour was over and we had saved $700, we'd move to California and I'd go to college." Shortly after his discharge, Williams enrolled to study economics at California State University, taking an all-night job in a juvenile detention facility "to help pay his way." For over a decade, he remembered, he would "study on the job and sleep in the afternoon after attending morning classes."[105] Awarded his Ph.D. in 1971, this former projects resident found a whole new world replete with opportunities.

If Williams's Horatio Alger–style account of his life journey appeared to mirror Sowell's, so did his unwavering commitment to neoclassical economics. Although he too had flirted briefly with political radicalism in the late 1960s—expressing, among other things, support for the efficacy of government[106]—Williams's subsequent metamorphosis presented little in the way of mystery. Milton Friedman, it turned out, had influenced him too.[107] A relatively obscure figure at Temple University in the 1970s, Williams nevertheless sprang to prominence at the Fairmont Conference, joining the Republican side of politics on a number of highly partisan policy debates.

With his opposition to affirmative action and welfare well established, and his commitment to school choice unconditional, Williams's views were perfectly attuned to the times. As well as becoming a valued member of Reagan's inflation and welfare task forces and an important voice on the transition team for Health and Human Services, this black economist appeared regularly before congressional hearings as an expert supportive of Reagan's controversial new urban agenda.[108] Perhaps nowhere was Williams's work more valuable to the administration than in his call for government to "get off people's backs" so that business could grow the economy to the benefit of all citizens. But certainly nowhere was his work more controversial than when it defended racist employment practices under the cover of protecting business choice and capitalist rationality. Williams argued passionately that prejudice was "simply a process of prejudging, making a judgment based upon pre-existing knowledge." Hence if employers refused to hire young black males in Reagan's America, it was not due to prejudice but to their "pre-existing knowledge" about young black males' low levels of education and "poor work habits."

Discrimination, then, was informed preference, similar to being discriminating in one's taste.[109] With these views, it was little wonder that Williams felt little affinity for the ongoing struggle for racial equality.

Capitalist advocacy was never a major theme in Shelby Steele's work. Indeed, in contrast to the statistics and explanations of market forces offered by Sowell, Williams, and (to a lesser extent) Loury, this former English professor employed the essay format and personal experience to discuss racial inequality in American life. Emerging in the late 1980s with a series of articles addressing this problem,[110] Steele ultimately captured national attention in 1990 with the publication of his first book, *The Content of Our Character*.[111]

Although presented as a collection of nine essays, *The Content of Our Character* was perhaps best seen as nine versions of the same essay. Each recounted an occasion in Steele's life—suburban cocktail party conversations, childhood conflicts, encounters with strangers in shopping centers—to make essentially the same point: black people's continuing obsession with their own oppression had become the greatest barrier to their full equality. These same autobiographical anecdotes were deployed, moreover, to censure liberals for foisting an ideology of self-defeating victimization onto African Americans and to condemn affirmative action—"the great swindle of black Americans"[112]—for stigmatizing its recipients and fostering self-doubt. "I believe we are freer than we think and that the white man is nowhere as omnipotent as he used to be," Steele wrote confidently.[113] That being the case, the time had come to return to the integrationist agenda championed by Martin Luther King—to reinvest in the ideology of individualism and to start "thinking beyond race."[114]

By conceptualizing modern racial politics as a psychological issue, Steele was implicitly suggesting that, in order to fully understand black disadvantage, one did not require expertise in economics or politics, simply a solid grasp of how individuals think and act. Consistent with his thesis, Steele called for leadership to tackle the psychological consequences of oppression—"victimology," "racial inversion," "race fatigue," "race-holding," "race bargaining," "integration shock," "white guilt," and the "anti-self."[115] Together, these "consequences of oppression" had culminated in a black fear of opportunity, which now lay beyond the scope of government remedy. Yet Steele did not oppose state intervention per se. Like Loury, he urged a role for government, but one that supplemented, rather than supplanted, individual effort and the meeting of social responsibilities.[116] In the meantime, though, the counterproductive liberal programs of the past four decades—which had "bred the black underclass"—needed urgently to be rescinded.

Given the general tenor of his thesis, it was hardly surprising that Steele was embraced as a conservative by the same forces that had earlier propelled the careers of Thomas, Sowell, Loury, and Williams. Like them, after all, he had attributed manifest racial inequality principally to defects among black people and maintained that it was somehow problematic for these people to view government action and public policy as vehicles for egalitarian redress. Although there were to be no invitations to the White House, Steele soon found a comfortable home at the Hoover Institution and was being compared favorably to the likes of James Baldwin, Richard Wright, and Frederick Douglass.[117] Although his first-person narrative structure too often blurred the distinction between singular and plural—leaping from passing discussions with strangers to mass racial psychoanalysis—he had become, according to one conservative admirer, an expert in the study of race relations, multiculturalism, and affirmative action, the "perfect voice of reason in a sea of hate."[118]

Indeed, by the mid-1990s, Steele was writing extensively on these subjects for major national publications.[119] He had produced and narrated an award-winning PBS documentary on racial politics—*Seven Days in Bensonhurst*—and also appeared on popular current affairs programs as an expert in this field.[120] In 1996 he founded, with Glenn Loury, the Center for New Black Leadership to "revive and encourage traditional solutions to social and economic problems in the African American community."[121] But while this flirtation with practical action turned out to be fleeting, by 1999 Steele was in the headlines again with the publication of his second book, *A Dream Deferred: The Second Betrayal of Black Freedom in America.*[122] In this essentially updated version of *The Content of Our Character,* Steele argued that, if the first betrayal of black freedom in America was slavery and segregation, the second had come at the hands of a redemptive liberal politics that had mired blacks in victimization even as it went about the main business of assuaging white guilt.[123] Such had been the legacy of Great Society liberalism.

Despite his rising fortunes within the conservative movement, Steele remained a somewhat unlikely figure to have forged a career as an antiliberal essayist. Born in Chicago in 1946 to a black truck driver father and white social worker mother who were both active members of the Congress of Racial Equality (CORE), Steele was what might be called a "civil rights baby."[124] Educated at a segregated school in a black working-class district of Phoenix, he went on to university at Coe College, where—as one of only a handful of black students in his class—he became active in a youth organization affiliated with King's Southern Christian Leadership Conference. Graduating from Coe in 1968, Steele earned a master's degree in sociology from Southern Illinois University before completing a Ph.D. in English literature at the University of Utah in 1974 and securing a position on the faculty at San Jose State. Beginning his academic career as an occasional fiction writer for *Black World* and a teacher of African American literature and creative writing,[125] Steele claimed years later that he had been moved to write about racial politics because of his loathing of white guilt—"the standard media formula" by which the white elite accepts responsibility for the inability of black America to fulfill its socioeconomic potential.[126] Yet in his own work, Steele was not averse to exploiting this standard media formula. Not only was his parents' civil rights activism invoked to establish his credentials as an authentic black spokesman, references to childhood hardship were also commonplace, serving to counter liberal charges of racial detachment. "I am a black nigger from the South Side of Chicago," Steele snapped in a tense 1991 interview with Julianne Malveaux. "I grew up in a tough world and had every kind of racism. . . . I know what it's about. . . . I believe profoundly in civil rights."[127] But sadly, he continued, "the dialogue in the black community is full of too many lies because we're not after the truth—we're just playing this game of racial politics with white people, we're trying to chalk up points against them."[128] Beholden only to their victimhood in an "Age of White Guilt," black people had lost sight of the individualism that propelled the civil rights movement and, in the process, ceased to be individuals themselves.[129]

If Steele's determination to portray himself as racially authentic was surprising in view of his spirited individualism, so perhaps was his willingness to participate in (what were often fiery) debates within the African American community. But Steele was a complex figure. Recognizing the paternalism of the liberal left, which criticized him,[130] and the indifference of the conservative right, which lauded him,[131] this black intellectual sought—at least symbolically—to occupy a middle ground, imploring black success rather than dwelling on the myriad structural obstacles that, arguably, accounted for the disproportionately high level of black failure. While rarely backing away from controversial positions, Steele seemed determined to combat charges of "blaming the victim," presenting himself as an inspiring and unifying figure in African American life rather than a disparaging and divisive critic of black people. Nowhere was this determination more apparent than in his harkening back to the moral power and relentless passion of the civil rights movement. Seeking to lay claim to the legacy of the movement's most celebrated leaders and intellectuals, the title of Steele's first book—*The Content of Our Character*—was appropriated from Martin Luther King's "I Have a Dream" speech, while the title of his second book—*A Dream Deferred*—had its genesis in a 1951 poem by the writer Langston Hughes.[132] Whatever one's political criticisms of this black conservative, his media savvy lay beyond doubt.

Steele, then, was an existential neoconservative rather than an anti-statist economic conservative, a former liberal who—to invoke Irving Kristol's words—had been "mugged by reality" and come to believe that the urgency of the times mandated fresh ideas and approaches. But while Steele presented fresh ideas in the form of psycho-racial analysis, he offered little by way of practical solution to improve the black condition.

This same criticism could not be leveled so easily at the scholar-activist Robert Woodson, for his approach to the African American community differed markedly. A civil rights advocate in the 1960s and 1970s, Woodson's frustration at the failure of liberalism to address black poverty eventually led him to renounce the movement and explore alternative methods to deliver economic equality.[133] Falling under the influence of the conservative sociologist Peter Berger, who had popularized the theoretical framework of "mediating structures" in the late 1970s, this former liberal came to view market-based initiatives—together with voluntary associations and moral leadership—as the most effective weapon in the fight against contemporary racial disadvantage.[134] In 1981, following this epiphany, Woodson established the National Center for Neighborhood Enterprise (NCNE) to provide technical assistance to local businesses and associations in poor communities as an "empowering alternative" to the government "largesse" favored by black liberal leaders.[135] Subsequently recognized by the conservative movement as "by far the most successful pro-free enterprise grassroots organization dedicated to solving black and urban problems,"[136] the NCNE initiative served to distinguish Woodson from other black conservatives seemingly more concerned with intellectual matters.

Although resisting political categorization, Woodson's platform made him one of the few African Americans Presidents Reagan and Bush consulted over urban policy.[137] What is more, like the preceding intellectuals, Woodson's personal history appeared to befit his new role as a black conservative. He too reported being born into poverty—to a single mother who worked long hours to support her family in the slums of Philadelphia. He too had been wayward in youth, dropping out of school as a teenager, before signing up for the Air Force. And he too had straightened out during national service, learning to turn "some of his energy and anger into achievement."[138] With the philosophy of self-reliance drummed into him during his military sojourn, Woodson resolved to practice this philosophy in civilian life, completing high school before enrolling in college and earning a master's degree in social work at the University of Pennsylvania.[139]

If Woodson had both the personal background and professional credentials to be a legitimate advocate for the poor in his own right, his ferocious attacks upon modern civil rights leaders—whom he accused of "hustling" poor blacks to obtain perks and privileges for themselves— only enhanced his reputation with the Reagan administration.[140] Determined to see an economic world through civil rights glasses, these leaders, he charged, continued to support a system that had "proven tragically ineffective . . . to the economic improvement of poor black Americans," a system that "should never have been regarded as an omnicompetent source of service delivery in the first place."[141] That system was social welfare. Although welfare agencies provided a source of nominal cash to the poor in the short term, in Woodson's view they hindered the development of the self-sufficiency and personal resourcefulness so crucial to poverty alleviation in the long term. This "Poverty Pentagon" had already turned millions of underprivileged people into "passive clients" and trapped them in a kind of "poverty limbo."[142] It needed to be dismantled and the money and power given directly to the poor who could use the resources to take control of their own lives. Woodson fiercely maintained that these people had the capacity to think and act for themselves.[143]

The NCNE president claimed to offer these observations—and economic agenda—to honor the memory of Martin Luther King. By condemning the welfare state and establishing his grassroots organization, he had hoped, he said, to put the ideas of self-determination and social pragmatism back on the black political map and to carry on where King had left off—fighting economic injustice.[144] Inspired by Berger and Richard Neuhaus's 1977 study *To Empower People*,[145] and drawing on his experiences growing up in a segregated neighborhood, Woodson placed greatest emphasis on the mediating structures of family, church, and neighborhood associations in the belief that these local structures could best facilitate the economic development, educational improvement, and crime prevention so essential to community stability and strength in the long term.[146] An important component of Woodson's strategy for black social mobility from the outset, then, was its emphasis on neighborhood solidarity and racial pride.[147]

By calling for a diminished role for government and greater individual responsibility, the NCNE was able to secure considerable financial support from the conservative movement's traditional donors and to deliver some tangible results to the truly disadvantaged.[148] The organization's micro-enterprise approach to black poverty appeared most effective in inner-city areas where mega-governmental structures had clearly failed, building businesses, encouraging home ownership, improving schools, and instilling in residents a sense of community where previously there had been only dysfunction. Indeed, so impressed was the moderate black journalist Clarence Page that he was moved to write: "Woodson's grass-roots revolution of local block clubs, public housing residents, independent schools and black churches may show the best hope for picking up where the civil rights revolution left off."[149]

Offered the position of Undersecretary of the Department of Housing and Urban Development (HUD) in the late 1980s, Woodson turned it down, citing as his reason President Bush's alleged "pandering" to civil rights leaders.[150] Even so, his star continued to rise in the 1990s with his ongoing efforts on behalf of the black poor and the publication of a stream of articles and books on contemporary racial inequality.[151] Terminating very publicly—in 1996—his long-standing association with that bastion of American conservatism, the American Enterprise Institute, over its decision to publish and endorse Dinesh D'Souza's controversial tract, *The End of Racism*, Woodson's stand revealed divisions not only between himself and the conservative movement, but among black conservatives as well.

Woodson was an unusual figure among modern black conservatives. Of course, much connected the NCNE president to this cohort—his contention that racism was no longer the principal enemy of African Americans; his support for the free market as a remedy for racial inequality; and his contempt for the black liberal leadership. But unlike the others, Woodson was, first and foremost, a community activist committed to making his ideas "socially real." Although a critic of black liberalism, he did not appear to have "sold out"; rather, his past suggested that he had paid his dues to the movement and changed his views on the racial question over time. What is more, Woodson spoke *knowingly* of the black poor, not as statistics or as pitiable residents who were psychologically and culturally damaged, but as decent people with the intelligence and the will to transform their lives.[152] Although he criticized government programs, he did not seek to eliminate them: in contrast to some black conservatives, he only wanted to remove the bureaucratic middleman who soaked up resources that he believed were better off in the hands of poor people themselves.

Indeed, as the 1990s wore on, Woodson would take many of his fellow black conservatives to task for being "reflexive, me-too conservatives" who simply parroted the prevailing orthodoxies of the New Right. For their own credibility, he continued, these intellectuals needed to move beyond the ivory tower and to forge connections with the low-income people they claimed to represent. "It's not enough to challenge ideas," Woodson argued. It was incumbent upon black conservatives to offer "positive alternatives," to be "originators of ideas and policies" that "go beyond the current hi-polar debates of the left and the right," if they sought to contribute meaningfully to the lives of the black poor. Only then, he predicted, would Sowell and company garner the respect they had long coveted with the "black silent majority."[153]

One black conservative who wrote frequently of the black silent majority but who appeared himself to lack any grassroots connection to this constituency was John McWhorter.[154] For different reasons from Woodson, McWhorter appeared to be somewhat of an anomaly among contemporary black conservatives when he burst onto the American intellectual scene in the late 1990s, leading the fight against the use of Ebonics as a teaching aid for black students.[155] Born in Philadelphia in 1965, he was by far the youngest of the cohort, a mere teenager when the others began to cut their political teeth in Reagan's America. Moreover, in contrast to his older counterparts, McWhorter's formative years were spent in a middle-class setting replete with stable family and private schooling.[156] Neither an academic economist nor a social policy analyst, his chosen field was initially linguistics, but in time this would change.[157] Lauded by the conservative establishment for his anti-Ebonics stance, McWhorter soon moved outside his area of expertise and began writing broader social commentaries on race. A professor of linguistics at the University of California, Berkeley, and a senior fellow at the Manhattan Institute, he managed to redefine himself as a black conservative critic specializing in self-sabotaging black culture.

Between 2001 and 2006, McWhorter wrote three books and numerous articles on African American themes and became a huge name in the media. While the 2001 *Losing the Race* was a *New York Times* bestseller, his more recent works—*Authentically Black* and *Winning the Race*—were also popularly received.[158] Conservative claims about McWhorter's enduring originality notwithstanding, these books shared a common methodology and thesis, and did not appear, at first glance, to represent a significant addition to the preceding black conservative analyses. Proclaiming black culture and big government the causes of, and the free market the solution to, black people's problems, McWhorter nevertheless added to this standard right-wing argument a unique psychological dimension. This psychological dimension—which combined empirical data with his own life experiences—arguably set his work apart from other black conservatives.

McWhorter's core thesis could be neatly summarized, revolving as it did around an "interlocking set of three mentalities."[159] Black America's contemporary problems, he argued in a manner similar to Steele, stemmed primarily from a misperception that racism remained a serious obstacle to advancement. Although the civil rights revolution had marked a high point in American history, in McWhorter's view it also had some tragic and long-lasting side effects, this misperception being the most devastating. As racism's potency receded over the years, he contended, more and more black people were led into a self-destructive ideological detour where their victimhood was exaggerated in order to extract political concessions. This detour had nurtured a "cult of victimology," a crippling mindset of "therapeutic alienation" that encouraged blacks to blame all their problems on racism.[160] Growing out of this victimhood was a "cult of separatism," the "sense that being black is a thing apart from being a human being in the United States . . . the sense that black people are subject to different rules."[161] Still more damaging, though, according to McWhorter, was the "cult of anti-intellectualism that had come to pervade the black community as a result of victimology and separatism." The final component of a self-sabotaging culture, this "disconnect from the school endeavor" had fostered an atmosphere in the African American community where intelligence and good grades were equated with "selling out" and "acting white."[162] This atmosphere needed to change, he insisted, if the black condition was to change.

If these arguments made McWhorter popular with the conservative movement, his dramatic position on affirmative action further enhanced this reputation. The young black conservative compared the policy to chemotherapy: it was necessary in the 1960s, but the "toxic effects" had come gradually to outweigh the benefits.[163] By assuming that blacks had been "so profoundly broken by their history" as to require ongoing treatment as "emotional cripples," affirmative action left them with "the most systematically diluted responsibility for their fate of any group in America."[164] What is more, it reinforced the very "defeatist thought patterns"— the victimology, the separatism, and the anti-intellectualism—that were black Americans' major stumbling blocks in the first place.[165] Focused on this psychological aspect of McWhorter's thesis, most commentators overlooked the fact that the Berkeley linguist had acknowledged, albeit pithily, that government could be—and, in the case of affirmative action, initially had been—employed legitimately as an instrument for the social betterment of African Americans. McWhorter's worldview was somewhat different, then, from the one embraced by Thomas, Sowell, and Williams.

Unable to lay claim to a racially disadvantaged past like the other black conservative intellectuals, McWhorter emphasized instead the black students he mentored, the black academic support programs he designed, as well as his black pride, to establish his racial legitimacy and lend weight to his criticisms of modern black life.[166] This strategy of self-authentication was similar to those pursued by other black conservatives. What made McWhorter different, however, was his attempt to combine history and statistics with his own life experiences as part of what remained, nevertheless, a psychological interpretation of racial inequality. By wrestling with empirical data and events, he sought to avoid the criticisms of "simple-minded, one-dimensional psychological reductionism" that had been leveled at Shelby Steele's work in the early 1990s. While clearly much united McWhorter's and Steele's analyses, another critical difference was McWhorter's rejection of Steele's emphasis on the calculating uses of "victim power." The younger black conservative insisted that widespread black abstentions from professional pursuits were not deliberate tactics or poses, but symptoms of "a subconscious psychological gangrene" that had outgrown the white racism that had generated it.[167]

Despite obvious methodological differences, two members of the black conservative old guard—Thomas Sowell and Walter Williams—responded favorably to McWhorter's contentious psychological thesis.[168] But two other black conservative veterans—the lesser known Jay Parker and Anne Wortham—remained silent. This was not altogether surprising, since both had been increasingly disconnected from public debate after the battle-laden days of the 1980s. Although frequently overlooked in the literature on contemporary black conservatism, these intellectuals' contributions in the Reagan era remain important to any study of this controversial strand of African American thought. Their ideas, while extreme, were nonetheless significant, sometimes even serving as a yardstick for their fellow black conservatives. Of the two, however, Parker stands out for analysis first, his long-standing involvement with the conservative movement arguably critical to the emergence of black conservatism itself.

In 1987 that symbol of black conservatism, Clarence Thomas, had praised Parker for "refusing to give in to the cult mentality and childish obedience that hypnotize black Americans into a mindless political trance."[169] Thomas went on to say that he admired the older black conservative's courage and strength and aspired to similar qualities in himself.[170] Parker was certainly a fascinating figure. The first of the cohort to attach his name to something distinctive called black conservatism, in 1978 he had founded the Lincoln Institute for Research and Education—a black conservative think tank in Washington, D.C.—and established under its auspices a quarterly policy journal called the *Lincoln Review*. Socially conservative and economically libertarian, the *Lincoln Review*'s main purpose was to reevaluate the liberal "theories and programs of the last decades" and to highlight their failure in relation to the black community. Downplaying the significance of racism in American life while emphasizing low-paid employment opportunities for black mobility, the Institute and the *Review* sought "to bind America's black minority to its white majority," to stress that this was "one nation with one national destiny."[171]

Although racial and economic divisions across the nation appeared to tell a different story, the Lincoln Institute's black conservative vision was perhaps best understood in terms of Parker's life story. Born into poverty in the slums of South Philadelphia, Parker was raised by a single mother who worked as a domestic servant to support her seven children. "I'm a conservative because I was poor," he later claimed. "I learned early that there is no free lunch, no Santa Claus, no Easter Bunny. . . . When you're poor, you just have to get up early and stay late."[172] By the age of nine, Parker claimed to be practicing the self-help philosophy he would later champion politically—"hustling and scuffling, delivering orders for people, putting trash out for them," shoveling snow and working as a step scrubber.[173] Graduating from the Philadelphia public school system in 1954, he signed up with the Delaware County Young Republicans the following year, on his way to becoming a "long-time movement conservative."[174]

In the 1960s Parker denounced as "lawless" the great mass democratic movement to challenge racism in America: civil rights.[175] Roused by the writings of George Schuyler and influenced by arguably the three most popular conservative treatises of the day—*The Conservative Mind, Up from Liberalism,* and *The Conscience of a Conservative*—he spoke regularly on college campuses as a representative of Young Americans for Freedom, gathering support for the anti–civil rights presidential candidate Barry Goldwater. "I had no intention of joining the civil rights movement," Parker insisted years later. "I was interested in a color-blind society, not something exclusively ethnic-oriented."[176] This detachment from the African American community would only become more marked as time passed. Significantly, in the late 1960s, as more and more disillusioned black people turned to a more ethnic-oriented politics, embracing variants of black nationalism, Parker again found himself out of step with black sentiment. His deliberately provocative but little-known 1973 biography of the black communist Angela Davis confirmed this growing pariah status.[177] Not content with dealing in caricatures of Davis, the book presented conservatism as the ideology of "Negro Americans," seemingly ignorant of Nixon's unpopularity with the black masses.

Exaggeratedly described by one admirer as "one of the founders of the modern conservative movement,"[178] Parker's political philosophy appeared to have been forged in direct opposition to the collectivist fires that fuelled the black insurgency. "Problems in America," he argued like Goldwater, "can only be truly fixed by individuals convincing individuals, one at a time, how to behave properly—just as in business the only way to achieve success is through good, old-fashioned hard work."[179] This was Reagan's view too. In the early 1980s Parker became one of the president's few trusted black leaders, heading the transition team at the

EEOC and declining a government position only because he believed he could be "more effective as an independent critic."[180] But Parker was never really an independent critic. Proclaiming Reagan the "best President for American blacks" because he had cut the tax rate and stimulated economic growth, this black conservative's only criticism of the administration was that its black reform agenda had not gone far enough.[181] The president had failed, for example, to eliminate the social safety net in order to encourage greater black self-reliance.[182] What is more, he had occasionally flouted the color-blind principle by letting "race creep into many decisions," most notably with political appointments.[183] To "return to the goal of a color-blind society," Parker implored Reagan to rescind Executive Order 11246, which had been introduced in the mid-1960s to reduce discrimination in the workplace.[184]

Not surprisingly with these views, Parker was an unpopular figure in the black community, an unpopularity that was only exacerbated by his work as a paid consultant for the apartheid regime in South Africa.[185] Dismissing depictions of that country as a brutal racist police state, he insisted that it was best viewed as "a society in the midst of peaceful evolution" toward freedom.[186] The "vocal campaign" to isolate it economically by withdrawing U.S. investment was misguided, Parker maintained, and almost certainly destined to hurt poor black South Africans the most.[187] Although he remained president of the Lincoln Institute and editor of the *Lincoln Review*, Parker's public profile plummeted in the second half of the 1980s as support for South Africa became increasingly politically untenable. With his reputation in tatters, little more would be written by or about him.

Little had ever been written about Anne Wortham. Although by far the least prominent black conservative intellectual to have an impact on racial discourse in the 1980s and 1990s—and the only woman—the sociologist Wortham was arguably the group's most independent thinker. This product of black Southern working-class parents, who taught at Harvard in the early 1980s before moving to Illinois State University, acquired a reputation early in her career as a quixotic nonconformist.[188] Drawing heavily on the works of Ayn Rand and Nathaniel Branden, Wortham deployed their conceptions of natural rights and human nature to offer a philosophical treatise on race in American life, dismissing blacks who would subordinate their individuality to "ethno-race consciousness." In 1981 her exposition of the relationship between individual and collective identity in *The Other Side of Racism* provided a distinctive theoretical framework for conservatives to frame their opposition to modern racial identity politics.[189]

Wortham may have emphasized the "sovereign individual" and challenged the efficacy of "ethno-racial consciousness," but she did not offer conservative economic policies as the solution to problems in the black community. She believed, simply, that socioeconomic and political policies ignored the individual personality.[190] This obsession with individualism served to distinguish her thought from other black conservatives who merely thought "the individual" important. While these other intellectuals argued against collectivist strategies as the key to black advancement and against collectivist solutions to the problem of race relations, they still dependably detailed group cultural characteristics of African Americans as being at the root of both problems. What is more, these intellectuals appeared determined to deal with their alienation from the black community by emphasizing the cultural ties that bound them to that community. Wortham, by contrast, discussed the causes of racism and the cure for strained race relations solely in terms of the individual.[191] She also made no attempt to identify with or appeal to African Americans, remarking in the preface to *The Other Side of Racism* that she was neither against "Negroes" nor for "Negroes."[192]

Wortham was, however, explicitly against the civil rights movement. Unlike many black conservatives who sought to cast themselves in the image of the movement (or, otherwise, to ignore it), she looked to undermine the movement's credibility by criticizing not only its goals and achievements but also the character of its greatest icon: Martin Luther King Jr.[193] Recasting civil rights as a struggle to escape individual responsibility and to enshrine arbitrary privileges rather than constitutional rights, Wortham argued that the antiracism laws enacted in the 1960s, in the name of freedom, were actually an assault on freedom. She offered the 1964 Civil Rights Act as a case in point. By making it illegal for merchants to withhold services from people on account of their race, color, religion, or national origin, Wortham believed the act trampled a fundamental individual economic right, since "a businessman who cannot serve whom he pleases is not a businessman but a slave."[194] If the movement's greatest contradiction had been "its effort to achieve justice for all at the expense of the rights of some," King's greatest contradiction had been to lay claim to the mantle of nonviolent individualist while supporting the coercive force of government and the implied threat of violence to achieve his goals. Far from being a peacemaker, Wortham asserted, violence was an inherent part of the civil rights leader's philosophy that he was "in no way blind to."[195]

Yet Wortham's rejection of black identity went beyond these attacks on the movement and its most prominent symbol. Her scholarship sought not only to eliminate King but *all* sources of black intellectual and political thought as potential leaders of the black community—the "conventional integrationists," "power-seeking nationalists," "spiritual separatists," and "independent militants."[196] If Wortham's unflinching commitment to "rational individualism" placed her squarely at odds with those who would espouse a collectivist vision of racial consciousness (be they radical, liberal, or conservative), it also explained her resistance to being categorized politically as a black conservative. But while refusing to be boxed into any group, Wortham's writings critical of affirmative action, welfare, and public education in the 1980s and 1990s necessitated her inclusion in this book, albeit with some qualification, as a black libertarian conservative. Arguably more than any other intellectual profiled here, her work was a reminder of the diversity and complexity that characterized so much of contemporary black conservative thought.

Since "diversity" and "complexity" were obviously words congruent with black conservatism, one might reasonably have expected the black conservatives to elicit in commentators a more diverse and complex response. Firstly, characterizations of these intellectuals as "middle-class people who don't understand what it is like to live in the ghetto" appeared not only simple-minded but almost certainly wrong.[197] Since the black conservatives, overwhelmingly, had lived in the ghetto, their liberal and radical adversaries confronted a dilemma. On the one hand, these critics' focus on identity had led them to rebuke Sowell and company on the grounds that, as conservative blacks who were privileged, they lacked the necessary pedigree to understand the black experience. Yet with their ghetto origins revealing that they too had done it tough, the black conservatives appeared to satisfy at least one of their critics' prerequisites for what constituted black authenticity in modern America: hardship. Citing their poverty as a source of insight not available to those analysts who came from more privileged settings, these intellectuals steadfastly maintained that their proposals might help the black community, and that surely the liberal social programs from the 1960s had hurt African Americans.

In response to the question, "what have blacks to conserve in the United States?" the black conservatives identified several long-standing traditions within African American social and political reasoning, and pointed to a number of conservative figures in black history. Yet even as they set out to muster a usable black past to further demonstrate their racial legitimacy, these intellectuals' emphases tended to vary. Some invoked the self-help doctrine of Booker T. Washington. Others paid to tribute to the iconoclasm of George Schuyler. Some applauded the economic nationalism of Malcolm X. Others acknowledged a debt to Martin Luther King, Jr., and civil rights. Some even recognized the contributions of white mentors from inside the conservative movement. Considering these widely divergent influences, it was hardly remarkable that the black conservatives should present a less than monolithic worldview.

Clearly, the most conspicuous aspect of these intellectuals' work and biographies is the diversity within black conservative ranks. Just as the ideas and approaches of Sowell and Williams differed markedly from those of Steele and McWhorter, the individualism embraced by Parker and Wortham contrasted sharply with the collectivist visions of Loury and Woodson. Clarence Thomas's conservatism was different again, more the product, one senses, of political machination than of sustained intellectual reflection. Rather than a bloc of black conservative opinion, then, what had in fact emerged was a spectrum of black conservative opinion, one that drew elements from neoconservative, populist, libertarian, and even liberal thought and reflected the different interests and experiences of what can only be described as an eclectic array of thinkers.

Yet it would be foolish to dispute that this eclectic array of thinkers had coalesced around a set of key principles, since the black conservatives were in broad agreement that the free market, limited government, and personal responsibility represented the best way forward for African Americans. Indeed, it was precisely because of this agreement that these intellectuals had been labeled black conservatives in the first place. Less well documented, however, had been their attempts to establish their racial credibility to speak to matters concerning the African American community. In seeking to legitimize their ideas and challenge the crude Uncle Tom stereotype, not only had the black conservatives constructed a humble origins thesis and written about their experiences in black communities, they had poached several prominent figures from the black past and set them up as intellectual forebears. With the exceptions of Wortham and possibly Parker, then, these intellectuals appeared to share a common strategy for political and cultural engagement. While rejecting identity politics in principle, most black conservatives inadvertently embraced a version of it in practice.

The unwillingness of these intellectuals to reject a group-based racial identity led some, such as Elizabeth Wright, to suggest that they were "the real nationalists."[198] But this interpretation was problematic to say the least. Although the philosophical tenets of black conservatism and black nationalism sometimes converged, it was clear that, at the most basic level, black conservative intellectuals presented no claim to nationhood. In essence, Sowell and company looked to have endorsed Richard Nixon's reinterpretation of black nationalism as black capitalism; here, race was important but only as it was useful for organizing self-help initiatives in the African American community.[199] In this deliberate, if dubious, synthesis of black nationalism and Americanism, the category of race was effectively stripped of its political content and deemed significant only within the private realm of black life. Significantly, moreover, modern black conservatives rejected any hint of racial essentialism, lest that essentialism imperiled the possibility of transcending race in the future.

Although drawing elements from Richard Nixon's racial conservatism, the resulting critiques of integration presented by some of these intellectuals put them somewhat out of step with a modern conservative movement now symbolically committed to color-blindness. Criticism of the black conservatives for simply "parroting the issues and rhetoric of contemporary conservatism" consequently appeared misguided.[200] Sowell and company may have endorsed many of the ideas and policies of the New Right. But it was also clear that these intellectuals had their own priorities and areas of emphasis. Most of the black conservatives had reconfigured elements of American conservatism and tied them to notions of racial solidarity deeply rooted in the black experience. Yet, even as they did, divisions among these intellectuals were apparent, not only in terms of what they thought but also in the methods they employed to reach their positions. While their ideas and approaches were controversial, they were also often serious. These ideas and approaches certainly warranted sincere intellectual scrutiny, perhaps nowhere more so than in the bitterly contested area of affirmative action.

Chapter 2
Affirmative Action Dilemmas

Freedom is not enough. You do not wipe away the scars of centuries by saying: Now you are free to go where you want, do as you desire, choose the leaders you please. You do not take a person who, for centuries, has been hobbled by chains and liberate him, bring him to the starting line of a race and then say "you are free to compete with all the others," and still justly believe that you have been completely fair. It is not enough just to open the gates of opportunity. All our citizens must have the ability to walk through those gates. . . . We seek not just legal equity but human ability, not just equality as a right and a theory but equality as a fact and equality as a result.

—*President Lyndon Johnson*

Affirmative action is dividing us in ways its creators could never have intended because most Americans who do support equal opportunity and are not biased don't think it's fair to discriminate against some Americans to make up for historic discrimination against other Americans.

—*Joseph Lieberman*

Affirmative action, the policy of giving preferences for jobs, university admissions, or government contracts to members of historically oppressed racial groups, has long been a source of division in American political life. Forged out of the cauldron of black insurgency at the height of the civil rights movement, affirmative action was intended to be a corrective to generations of entrenched racial discrimination in educational institutions and the workplace; a challenge to social structures that, for centuries, had denied blacks' equality and preserved the racist status quo. That a practice seemingly so at odds with one of the most celebrated American values—to judge individuals on merit alone—became a part of the nation's policy fabric was quite remarkable. Less remarkable was the fierce and often violent resistance it provoked. In the 1960s and 1970s affirmative action incensed millions of white Americans—rich and poor, intellectual and anti-intellectual—who believed that the demands of the civil rights movement had simply gone too far.

In the 1980s and 1990s black conservative intellectuals began to express similar concerns about the trajectory of civil rights and the legitimacy of affirmative action. Explicit double standards in the workplace and large disparities in the test scores of blacks and whites admitted to universities were unwise practices, in their view deservedly under attack. Not only did racial preferences flout principles of fairness and individualism, they were also counterproductive, exacerbating rather than addressing the worst aspects of the black condition. Affirmative action, then, needed to be dismantled *for the sake of African Americans*, so they might one day grasp the individualistic imperative at the heart of national life. But while unanimous in their opposition to preference, Sowell and company's critiques of the policy sometimes displayed subtle variations that demand a more nuanced assessment than scholarly literature has provided of black conservative attitudes to this contentious social policy.

An evaluation of the challenges posed by black conservatives to affirmative action in modern America requires as its starting point a detailed analysis of the concept of affirmative action itself—its definition, history, and political evolution. It was John Kennedy who first used the term "affirmative action" in a 1961 executive order urging federal contractors to pursue nondiscrimination in the recruitment, hiring, and promotion of workers.[1] From this point on, all Americans, in theory, were to be treated equally, to compete and be judged on merit alone. But implementation of the Kennedy order proved near-impossible and in 1962 the overall rate of black unemployment remained twice that of whites.[2] It was only in the second half of the decade, during the presidency of Lyndon Johnson, that something resembling a concrete set of affirmative action policies emerged. Johnson established numerical "goals and timetables" in the fight to desegregate the labor force, thereby taking affirmative action beyond a passive instruction not to discriminate. It now meant special assistance—compensatory justice—for black people through a series of outreach programs, training courses, and most controversially, preferential policies in the workplace and at universities.[3] Results had become the order of the day.

The evolution of affirmative action reflected the growing realization in liberal policy-making circles that efforts to increase African American representation during the first phase of affirmative action had been largely unsuccessful. A more interventionist approach was required if the goal was racial equality, "not just as a right and a theory, but as a fact and a result."[4] Curiously, however, it was not Johnson but the conservative Richard Nixon who, in the late 1960s and early 1970s, laid the foundation for affirmative action as it came to be known. Nixon bolstered the programs set in motion by his liberal predecessors. He expanded the Equal Employment Opportunity Commission (EEOC) and the Office of Federal Contract Compliance (OFCC) while reviving the so-called Philadelphia Plan that required all contractors on federally funded projects to hire African Americans at a rate consistent with their representation in the local population.[5] The Nixon administration also supported provisions for minority set-asides to promote black business and placed Federal Reserve funds in black-owned banks.[6] If this was not enough, the Supreme Court, stacked with recent Nixon appointees, set a series of precedents recognizing the potential for race-neutral programs to reinforce existing racial hierarchies, and supported forced busing to achieve racial balance in the nation's schools.[7]

Affirmative action, however, was not only driven by presidents and the courts; it was also inspired by significant social pressures from below. With legal equality for African Americans secured by the mid-1960s, black leaders immediately turned their attention to material equality, expressing frustration at how "institutional racism" was retarding black economic progress after the momentous earlier civil rights victories. Joined by white liberals in government and academia, these leaders now sought to explain racial disadvantage not only as a legacy of 350 years of slavery and second-class citizenship, but also as a consequence of countless hidden practices of discrimination allegedly woven into the fabric of national life. So entrenched was white America's Old Boys Network that only hiring goals, they argued, closely monitored by the federal government, could take the majority of black people from unemployment and poverty into mainstream employment.[8] Some supporters of affirmative action even championed these hiring goals in the interest of the national good, believing a large and stable black middle class the best defense against the urban unrest of the mid- to late 1960s.[9]

From the late 1960s into the 1970s, black people experienced social mobility at a pace unparalleled in U.S. history. The occupational spheres in which African Americans made the most gains—government service, major blue-collar employment, corporate management, and the professions—were all areas where affirmative action programs were firmly in place.[10] At this time, new admissions and hiring policies were also being introduced at universities to boost black student numbers. Some universities developed "flexible admission plans," which considered the applicant's race alongside their grades, test scores, personal characteristics, and extracurricular talents in the sporting arena and in music and the arts. Others went further, establishing strict numerical targets for minority enrollments.[11] By the end of the 1970s, these measures had more than doubled black student representation at the nation's institutions of higher learning.[12] Since it was clear that Americans were witnessing for the first time in their history the emergence and growth of a genuinely upwardly mobile stratum of black people, affirmative action appeared to have done what court decisions and executive decrees had been powerless to do: position a large pool of African Americans within striking range of the American Dream.[13]

For liberals and radicals, black progress during this period suggested that affirmative action was having an important democratizing effect in American life. The shift in philosophy from color-blindness to color consciousness, from opportunity to outcome, and from individual to group rights, had been tremendously successful, they argued.[14] Yet despite the achievements credited to affirmative action, the meaning of the term itself remained elusive. Indeed, Edward C. Sylvester, the director of the OFCC, had inadvertently betrayed this confusion at the time of the policy's inception, saying: "There is no fixed and firm definition of affirmative action. I would say that in a general way, affirmative action is anything you have to do to get results."[15] What, then, had to be done to get results?

Contrary to received wisdom, affirmative action was neither a law, nor even a coherent policy formulation. Rather, as we have seen, it developed through an ad hoc series of executive orders, government programs, civil rights initiatives, and court decisions, linked only by their shared goal of uprooting bigotry and facilitating employment and college opportunities historically denied to African Americans.[16] In implementing these measures, the state was acknowledging race as a dynamic that impacted every facet of American life, creating winners and losers. Such an acknowledgment in turn required the government to intervene to influence the way in which that dynamic played itself out between Americans. The U.S. Commission on Civil Rights was clear on this point. Affirmative action went "beyond simple termination of a discriminatory practice [against a group]"; it was adopted "to correct or compensate for past or present [group] discrimination" and "to prevent [such group] discrimination from recurring in the future."[17] The decision to extend affirmative action to all minorities—including women—in the 1970s would be welcomed in some quarters as a sign of the nation's growing commitment to the disadvantaged. Mandated and legitimized by the courts and enforced by the expanding government bureaucracy, these programs were being implemented virtually everywhere.[18]

But widespread implementation and enforcement did not translate into widespread acceptance. By the mid-1970s, it was obvious to all but a few that supporters of affirmative action were losing the battle for the hearts and minds of the American people.[19] Across the nation, discontent at the new politics of compensation had been brewing for years.

Brought to a head in 1978 by the landmark *Regents of the University of California v. Bakke* Supreme Court decision, which allowed race to be considered among other factors in university admissions,[20] millions of Americans openly questioned the fairness of a system that appeared to penalize white males in order to make up for past discrimination against minorities and women. Not only did these people think such attempts to ameliorate the sins of the past excessive, they were tired, in particular, of racial analyses that continued to implicate them in the social inequalities afflicting American society.[21] Throughout the 1970s, this sense of white victimization threatened to boil over. And on occasions it did.

Predictably, expressions of white victimization varied. Some were visibly class-based, some reflected regional anxieties, while others were rooted in regressive political ideology.[22] But the most sophisticated early critiques of affirmative action came from a group of disillusioned liberals or "neoconservatives" at American universities and New Right think tanks. Through the pages of prominent journals such as *Commentary, Conservative Digest, Policy Review,* and *Public Interest,* and in their own books, the likes of Nathan Glazer, Daniel Moynihan, and Charles Murray criticized the new direction in which government was steering civil rights.[23] In their view, the original vision of civil rights required that public policy be exercised without regard to the distinctions of race, color, or creed. Thus, any policy that went beyond protecting the individual against explicit acts of discrimination, they argued, was a contravention of the 1964 Civil Rights Act. In fact, any such measure would constitute a form of "affirmative" or "reverse" discrimination against whites.[24] Supposing racism against blacks to be all but dead in the wake of civil rights legislation, these intellectuals called for a renewed commitment to the principle of individual merit that had formerly served the nation so well.

For much of the 1970s, white neoconservatives effectively consolidated their opposition to affirmative action around an absolutist interpretation of color-blind individualism. But it was not until Ronald Reagan's election in 1980 that a serious political campaign against the policy was waged at the heart of government. Rejecting the broad definitions of systemic discrimination that had underpinned affirmative action since the late 1960s, Reagan's new civil rights approach promised a society in which all individuals would be judged on merit and one in which individuals rather than groups would have constitutional rights. Getting back to color-blind hiring was the goal, Americans were told, because this remained the most effective strategy to deliver equality. According to the new president, not only had affirmative action crippled the economy, reduced efficiency, and burdened business, but it had also stifled the individualism and entrepreneurialism so vital for black progress. A dramatic u-turn in social policy was sought.[25]

One might have expected the Reagan administration, in its drive to dismantle affirmative action, to rely on the arguments of those pioneering white neoconservatives from the 1970s. But the frontal assault on the policy launched by those intellectuals throughout that decade had been too easily dismissed as "racist" by civil rights leaders and the broader liberal establishment. Reagan's presidency heralded a shift in tactics. Although white conservative critiques of affirmative action appeared throughout the 1980s and 1990s, they were arguably upstaged by the trenchant analyses offered by the new black conservatives, which carried greater symbolic value within the context of the new political culture. As former Harvard law professor Derrick Bell observed at the time: "Today, as policy makers again seek to abandon civil rights enforcement, certain experts assert that the plight of blacks is the fault of blacks or of the social programs on which the poor rely. When such claims are expounded by blacks, they obtain a deceptive authenticity."[26]

For much of the 1980s, the new black conservatives were content to repeat verbatim the white conservative objections to affirmative action that had drawn fierce criticism from liberal and radical commentators in the 1970s. Borrowing the language of social policy analysts and conservative critics, but adding to it an authentic black spin, these new intellectuals merely resubmitted the charge that affirmative action was "reverse racism," a case of blacks exploiting white guilt and creating for themselves a special status in order to hustle social benefits denied to other Americans.[27] While conceding that it had indeed been wrong to discriminate against blacks in the past, they now concluded that it was equally wrong to give blacks preferential treatment and thereby discriminate against whites. This "cheap social engineering device" was taking from innocent white individuals who had inflicted no injury, and giving to a black collective that had suffered none.[28] Black conservatives feared that race relations had deteriorated as a result and some, imagining the worst, wondered whether affirmative action policies might lead the nation down the dark path to civil war.[29]

In 1982 Jay Parker, writing in the *Lincoln Review*, had made clear his objections to affirmative action along these lines: "Current affirmative action programs represent a new racism which we should oppose as contrary to our goal of a color-blind society. . . . It violates our very basic principles of individual freedom and our hope for continuing progress."[30] Clarence Thomas and Anne Wortham would in time echo Parker's sentiments. Since American constitutionalism was predicated on the rights of individuals, not groups, in Thomas's view affirmative action was "at war with the principle of inherent equality that underlies and infuses our Constitution."[31] The policy had not only moved society further away from its ideal of individualized merit; in highlighting societal differences, it had also created resentments and exacerbated racial conflict across the nation. Wortham despaired openly of affirmative action's consequences but expressed little surprise at these consequences. The policy, she wrote, "could not and never can go right," for it was based, fundamentally, on false premises: "collectivism," "socio-cultural determinism," "the psychology of victimization," and "intergroup egalitarianism." And affirmative action was simply unjust. Expanding upon Thomas's critique, Wortham insisted that "it violates the equal protection clause of the Fourteenth Amendment of the Constitution," and, in doing so, "violates the basic right of individuals to their own lives and the products of their own labor."[32] It was depressing that blacks, who had known the worst oppression and exploitation by the state, had chosen to institutionalize the primacy of the state through their support for this policy.

It was not Wortham, however, who was the symbol of the early black backlash against affirmative action; that distinction belonged to Thomas Sowell. In scores of books and articles throughout the 1980s, Sowell argued that, in breaking with the principle of color-blindness, color-conscious policies had created new victims of racial discrimination: white victims.[33] Aggrieved that "live people were being sacrificed because of what dead people did,"[34] many had turned to white extremist groups in order to vent frustration at the new racial-spoils system. These developments, Sowell warned, were nothing short of alarming since a "multi-ethnic society like the United States can ill-afford continually to build up stores of inter-group resentments."[35] Pointing to other multiethnic societies such as Indonesia, Malaysia, and Sri Lanka, where certain groups received government-sanctioned preference, he noted that hundreds of thousands of people had lost their lives in massive racial riots and pogroms. If America went down the road of racial polarization, it too could find interracial violence at the end.[36]

Not content with demonstrating the perils associated with "quotas" in the modern world, Sowell also set out to show the disastrous impact of quotas in history,[37] as did his friend Walter Williams. Williams concurred with Sowell that government subversion of the labor market to apportion coveted positions to a particular group was not a new phenomenon. The practice apparently had a long and destructive past in South Africa. Focusing inevitably on apartheid, Williams noted that under this system citizens had been classified according to race so that governments could award jobs preferentially to whites, to effectively practice affirmative action *against* blacks.[38] The impact of the policy on the black South African population had been devastating. Even more devastating, according to Sowell, was the impact of Nazi persecution on the Jews. Sowell, in his analyses of affirmative action, would periodically raise the specter of the Holocaust, accusing bureaucrats of the modern American state of engaging in racial classification reminiscent of Hitler's Germany. Were the *numerus clausus* laws used to restrict the opportunities of Jews in pre-war Germany, he asked indirectly, not similar in principle to the current quota systems employed in the United States to restrict the opportunities of white males?[39] Williams eschewed this comparison but drew another controversial link of his own. Civil rights organizations advocating affirmative action, he maintained, differed "only in degree, but not in kind, from white supremacist organizations" like the Ku Klux Klan.[40]

Liberal-minded Americans could be forgiven for being caught off guard by this initial black conservative foray into the affirmative action debate. Caught in a "thicket of racial reasoning," there was an assumption that black faces in high places had to be credible representatives of black popular opinion.[41] However, from the outset, civil rights leaders and progressive scholars were resolute in their opposition to the reverse racism thesis so enthusiastically embraced by some members of the new black conservative cohort. Led by Jesse Jackson in the public domain and Manning Marable in academe, elements within the black left rallied strongly. It was, they argued, inaccurate—and perhaps dishonest too—for analysts, particularly black ones, to equate genuine endeavors to remedy a people's plight with the racist actions and practices that had produced it. A clear moral distinction had to be made between the ideological hostility of the oppressor and the corrective measures undertaken on behalf of the oppressed.[42] Indeed, when this line was drawn, the initial theoretical concerns of Sowell and Williams about the racist character of affirmative action appeared exaggerated. Trite invocations of South African apartheid, Nazi racialism, and Klan terror were not sufficient to sustain an argument against compensatory measures for the black victims of American injustice.

Appearing rather more credible was Sowell's and Williams's other contention that affirmative action had ignited in millions of whites a counter-chauvinism with the potential to erupt in racial violence in the future. But this was an argument that many liberal and radical scholars initially sought to avoid, seemingly unable to acknowledge that a policy to deliver racial justice might have flaws. In contrast, the broader white public dwelled on these flaws. To them, Sowell's and Williams's sentiments would have contained more than a kernel of truth; the struggle for multicultural democracy—of which affirmative action was so crucial a part—had clearly provoked the ire of millions of whites and provided ammunition for a resurgent Ku Klux Klan.[43] Yet these black conservatives' predictions in the 1980s of a looming race war in the United States had proven wrong. Although the Klan reemerged in the 1970s, bringing increasing incidence of racist violence to the nation's streets, their new presence never reached the scale of the racial unrest in Indonesia, Malaysia, and Sri Lanka. Without acknowledging fundamental differences in national histories, the attempt by Sowell and Williams to compare the United States with these countries had created the misleading impression that what happened abroad upon introduction of a policy inevitably happened at home. Such a simplistic assumption was a serious methodological flaw. Historians could have told these two black intellectuals that the human condition had always been more complex.

If these black conservatives' fears of affirmative action-fueled bloodshed in America were empirically misguided, their counter-chauvinism thesis displayed several other problems as well. Sowell, Williams, and Thomas were effectively calling on African Americans to forgo new opportunities and abandon their push for access to historically discriminatory job markets in order to placate racists. Instead of repudiating racism and the perception that blacks were to blame for shrinking employment opportunities, these intellectuals found it easier, or more expedient, to insist that blacks renounce affirmative action policies. Their position—which stipulated the importance of appeasing whites, whatever the political cost to blacks—arguably had some striking theoretical parallels in U.S. history. Was their logic not similar to the rationale of 1960s segregationists who claimed that there would be peace between "negras" and whites if only civil rights campaigners left the South? Did their arguments not resemble those who opposed federal anti-lynching legislation in the 1920s on the grounds that such legislation would endanger states' rights and only encourage further reprisals against blacks in the future? And what about slavery? Millions of whites had opposed abolitionism, warning that divisions over slavery would lead eventually to civil war. Given that war was the outcome, had the abolitionists been wrong to seek the destruction of the "peculiar institution"?

Since the early years of the republic, American conservatives—supported in many instances by "Negroes"—had gone to great lengths to persuade blacks that they would antagonize the rest of society, and thereby harm themselves, by pressing for the same life opportunities as whites.[44] Now, in the 1980s, the counter-chauvinism thesis promoted by Sowell, Williams, and Thomas appeared to bear resemblance to the strategies employed in those past campaigns. Progressive critics of the black conservatives might have focused more attention on the historical significance of this argument in their quest to neutralize its contemporary intellectual impact. On the one hand, these critics might have conceded that the problems caused by racist reactions to affirmative action were real and often serious (though, in America, unlikely to lead to war). But they might then have suggested, with a nod to history, that the proper response to racist reactions was to challenge the false assumptions that had provoked them in the first place. Since statistical data appeared to confirm that white men in contemporary America had not been the victims of reverse discrimination, there was neither a need to appease the campaign to undercut affirmative action, nor to attack in ad hominem terms the black conservatives for supporting seemingly false conjecture.[45] By pointing to the evidence and the not insignificant fact that racial hostility in the United States antedated preferential policies, a clear and decisive intellectual blow against Sowell and company would have been struck.

But, on the whole, liberal and radical scholars did not point to the evidence. And so, in the absence of a forceful response to their counter-chauvinism thesis, the black conservatives would continue to assert that affirmative action was little more than a racist policy of rigid quotas that rewarded "unqualified" blacks at the expense of "qualified" whites.[46] But as time wore on, an increasing number of these intellectuals—perhaps troubled by the simplicity of this analysis—relegated it to a suitably marginal place in their work. Gradually they turned their attention to how affirmative action had inadvertently harmed the very group that it was intended to help: black people themselves.

From the early 1990s, in addition to fueling white resentment, racial preferences were charged with fostering a psychological demoralization among African Americans and reinforcing their self-doubt. A growing number of black conservatives would argue that, since it was the "implied inferiority" of black people that justified their preferential treatment, it was foolish to think that this treatment could uplift them.[47] In fact, it was humiliating that such an exchange between black weakness and white power had become the basic paradigm for progressive race relations in America.[48] Rather than putting black people on the road to self-reliance and autonomy, affirmative action policies had wedded them to a new victim status and encouraged them to exploit this status as a source of contemporary power and privilege.[49] At the nation's institutions of higher learning, in particular, these policies were said to have implicitly endorsed lower expectations for African Americans and undermined the achievements of the most talented black students and faculty by making them look like gifts from government.[50] Eschewing a focus on symbolic "feel-good" victories in favor of pragmatic cost-benefit analysis, black conservatives insisted that the psychological costs of affirmative action far outweighed any related benefits. This generic position, however, masked subtle differences among the intellectuals.

The black conservative most associated with the position that affirmative action had a debilitating impact on the mental state of African Americans was Shelby Steele. This was hardly remarkable: the Hoover Fellow had been propounding this view with vigor since the late 1980s. When stripped of its egalitarian hyperbole, Steele argued, the basic premise of affirmative action lay exposed: since blacks simply could not measure up to the academic standards of whites, standards had to be lowered to "do for us what we could not do for ourselves."[51] But not only did the policy impute "a certain helplessness to blacks that diminishes our self-esteem," it also heightened racial consciousness, teaching blacks to internalize the message of their own inferiority.[52] By the early 1990s, so serious was this "internalization of inferiority" that it stood as the greatest impediment to black progress in the United States. Steele's message, then, was clear: since affirmative action had "shown itself to be more bad than good," good intentions did not always translate into sound social policy."[53]

In any case, the notoriously prickly Thomas Sowell cared little for intentions. He claimed, like Steele, to be far more concerned at the undermining of African American confidence by the fundamental message that affirmative action was sending every day: that blacks were "losers who will never have anything unless someone gives it to them."[54] But while Steele focused mainly on blacks' self-esteem, Sowell was preoccupied with the perception of whites. "Today," he wrote, "many Americans will refuse to visit a black physician or dentist because of their assumption that he or she was admitted both to medical school and to the position held through "special preferences," set-aside quotas, and relaxed standards. The same is true for many other professionals and for other beneficiaries of 'affirmative action.' Even if a minority professional is a qualified, rational practitioner, he or she will be shunned due to the stereotype, created by affirmative action, that he or she is a puppet of special interest wars."[55]

Black law professor Stephen Carter shared a number of Steele's and Sowell's concerns, offering a variation on both men's arguments in his 1991 book, *Reflections of an Affirmative Action Baby*.[56] Venturing (with them) into the world of amateur psychology, this self-proclaimed "victim" of preference also decried the indignities and pressures that "inevitably" befall recipients of affirmative action. Like Sowell, Carter insisted the policy created doubts not only about the abilities of its beneficiaries, but all blacks, who were tarnished by the suspicion they had moved ahead because of race rather than merit. And like Steele, he expressed concern about the psychological impact of this stigma on black people. Since affirmative action set up a dichotomy in which employers and admissions officers were forced to make an unenviable distinction between the best candidate and the "best black" candidate, Carter thought it natural that black students should wonder: "Do I really deserve to be here?" and for white students to ask: "Is this one among the best, or merely among the best blacks?"[57] Setting Carter apart from Steele and Sowell was that he drew on his personal experience as an object of preferential treatment in law school admissions to frame his argument. Although an academic at Yale University and by all objective measures a talented and successful scholar, Carter nevertheless described the racial stigmatization that had tormented him and countless other black "victims" of this policy:

For many, perhaps most, black professionals of my generation, the matter of who got where and how is left in a studied and, I think, purposeful ambiguity. Most of us, perhaps nearly all of us, have learned to bury the matter far back in our minds. . . . Those of us who have graduated professional schools over the past fifteen to twenty years, and are not white, travel career paths that are frequently bumpy with suspicions that we did not earn the right to be where we are. We bristle when others raise what might be called the qualification question—"Did you get into school or get hired because of a special program?"—and that prickly sensitivity is the best evidence, if any is needed, of one of the principal costs of racial preferences.[58]

Since affirmative action had created agonizing conflicts of status and identity for black students and faculty at American universities, these programs were not only denigrating, in Carter's view, but also counterproductive and unnecessary.[59]

If Carter's admixture of analysis and autobiographical reflection made for an important contribution to the public debate on race and social policy, so, years later, did John McWhorter's *Losing the Race*. McWhorter began by restating the by now familiar argument that affirmative action had nurtured a "cult of victimology" among blacks and simultaneously encouraged them to exploit this identity in order to extract concessions from whites.[60] But the Berkeley linguist went further, exploring what he saw as the powerful disincentive effects of these policies on black motivation and achievement.[61] Years earlier, in 1992, Glenn Loury had provided the intellectual template for this analysis by contemplating incentive patterns in the workplace after these policies were introduced. The black economist worried that affirmative action "may alter the terms on which employers and workers interact with each other so as to perpetuate, rather than eliminate, existing disparities in productivity between minority and majority populations."[62] If workers felt they would be favored by affirmative action, he argued, they would have less incentive to work hard and improve their skills. "They may invest less," Loury concluded, "because . . . it has become easier for them to get high level positions."[63] A decade later, the younger black conservative, McWhorter, was making similar arguments about black students in the tertiary sector.

Drawing upon his personal experiences as a teacher of undergraduates, McWhorter casually compared students from different racial backgrounds and suggested, rather tenuously, that an inferior commitment to academic endeavor plagued blacks disproportionately.[64] Although an "anti-intellectual strain" within black culture was partly to blame for their apparent lack of motivation, the "perverse incentive system" institutionalized by racial preferences was deemed the real force holding these students back.[65] "The maintenance of affirmative action," he wrote, "hinders the completion of the very task it was designed to accomplish, because it deprives black students of a basic incentive to reach out for that highest bar. If every black in the country knows that not even the most selective schools in the country require the very top grades or test scores of black students . . . then what incentive is there for any but the occasional highly driven black student to devote his most deeply committed effort to school?"[66]

As if to validate his theory that preference served as a deterrent to hard work, McWhorter offered as evidence his own schooling: "In secondary school, I quite deliberately refrained from working to my highest potential because I knew that I would be accepted to even top universities without doing so. Almost any black child knows from an early age that there is something called affirmative action which means that black students are admitted to schools under lower standards than whites; I was aware of this from at least the age of ten."[67]

The entire process was deeply insidious, said McWhorter, because, for all its emphasis on self-esteem, affirmative action deprived talented blacks of the satisfaction of an accomplishment legitimately earned.[68] Ironically, then, blacks' sense of self-worth was systematically undermined by the very policy that was supposed to uplift them.

Not surprisingly, the self-esteem critiques offered by black conservatives were enthusiastically taken up by white conservative ideologues. Journalist Charles Krauthammer, writing in the *Washington Post*, lauded Steele's and Carter's view on the "terrible psychic toll of affirmative action," employing their arguments to demonstrate that the policy "costs more than it is worth."[69] Not only did affirmative action dispense "unequal justice," "balkanize communities," and "distort the merit system," but it also attached "a question mark to every real black achievement."[70] In *The End of Affirmative Action: Where Do We Go From Here?* Darien McWhirter agreed. Pointing to various black analyses, McWhirter claimed that preferential policies stigmatized African Americans and were, in the end, "not a very good deal for them. They get little concrete benefit in exchange for being stigmatized."[71] Clearly there could be no emancipation here! But for those who continued to believe in affirmative action's emancipatory potential, Stephen and Abigail Thernstrom recommended McWhorter's "brilliant, sparkling, effervescent book" that "courageously confronts the problem of black underachievement."[72] Far from a solution to this underachievement, affirmative action was now a cause of it.

For white conservatives, it seemed, the psychological consequences of affirmative action were clear.[73]

Yet in academia, liberal and radical scholars moved quickly to illustrate the intellectual bankruptcy of the claim that affirmative action had infected large numbers of African Americans with a disease called low self-esteem. Harvard political scientist Martin Kilson accused the black conservatives of making far-reaching empirical claims about African American life while offering only personal accounts as evidence.[74] The black radical Adolph Reed would stake out a similar position. Focusing mainly on Steele, Reed charged that the black conservatives' psychological analyses were "unburdened with facts outside a particularly limited compass of personal experience." Devoid of "social and political complexity," they did little else than build "castles of psychobabble on platitudes and banal autobiographical anecdotes."[75] Not to be outdone, the sociologist Stephen Steinberg took aim at Carter's *Reflections of an Affirmative Action Baby*, suggesting that, while the book might be useful as a case study of "one affirmative action baby's" personal paranoia, it carried absolutely no weight as an intellectual analysis of affirmative action itself. Like McWhorter's *Losing the Race*, it offered no historical overview of the relevant policies; no recognition of their success in counteracting institutionalized racism in the workplace; indeed no awareness that affirmative action existed outside the professions at all.[76] These were major flaws.

Most black intellectuals appeared wholly unperturbed by such conceptual speculation on the part of the black conservatives and their supporters in politics and the media. For genuinely confident African Americans, it mattered little that a small network of unrepresentative black elites had questioned their success and attributed it to "unjust race preferences."[77] These scholars sought to demonstrate the considerable practical achievements of affirmative action in increasing the size of the black middle class and in creating for the first time in American history a genuinely upwardly mobile stratum of black people.[78] Many expressed great satisfaction in achievements that would have been unlikely without affirmative action, and a sense of pride that they were a part of a new and promising generation (even a talented tenth?) bringing "dignity to the race."[79] In fighting hard to defend these programs during the 1980s and 1990s, black liberals and radicals demonstrated their belief that the opportunities afforded by affirmative action far outweighed any threat of psychological damage. To the extent that there was evidence of low self-esteem and a preference-induced victim-focused identity among African Americans, it appeared to be confined almost exclusively to those within the black conservative collective.

And how was psychological damage to be measured anyway? Based as it was on speculation and little or no empirical evidence, the legitimacy of this black conservative view of preference was easily challenged. As political scientist Jennifer Hochschild noted: "Anecdotes pull in equal but opposite directions."[80] Incensed that the personal angst of a Shelby Steele or a Thomas Sowell would be taken as confirmation that affirmative action diminished black self-esteem, black liberal and radical scholars countered with their own experiences to show that the policy may in fact enhance black self-esteem.[81] Every year since the introduction of the policy, large numbers of African Americans had won prizes, appointments, and promotions that previously would have been unthinkable because of their color. How many of these new lawyers, businessmen, army officers, doctors, and academics, who were given opportunities because of affirmative action, had subsequently complained of the damage done to them? Colin Powell had not complained of being harmed by the policy. Seemingly psychologically intact, this beneficiary of military preference had enjoyed a decorated career in the armed forces and government, significantly without abandoning his commitment to the principle of affirmative action. Cornel West's defense of preference was similarly steadfast. Asked whether he had ever felt anxiety about being at Harvard, West replied:

Not at all. I knew that I would not be at Harvard in 1970 if there had not been 187 rebellions the night of April 4, 1968. There's a direct correlation between the large numbers of black folk who were upset at the murder of Martin Luther King Jr. who shook the foundations of this nation, and the opening of doors that followed. The question became, How could I use whatever talent I had, cultivate that talent, sharpen my sense of discipline, and retain a commitment to service, given my entrée to Harvard? Because I would have had that same talent, discipline, and sense of service if I'd gone to Howard. . . . It was a challenge. Of course, I had some anxiety about going to college and about going to Harvard in particular, but that would be true of anybody. But I didn't suffer the kind of anxiety you hear about from Thomas Sowell or Shelby Steele or Glenn Loury—a feeling of inferiority. I never felt like I was inferior to white folk; that wasn't part of my tradition. That was the most absurd notion. . . . I couldn't wait to compete . . . because I'm confident of my talents.[82]

The message emerging out of this discourse on the psychological impact of affirmative action on its beneficiaries was that self-esteem was an individual "thing." Some beneficiaries obviously questioned their accomplishments, others were secure in them, and many more would have suffered low self-esteem no matter their background. Since affirmative action was at best a weak indicator of self-esteem, it was unclear why some black professionals—and not others—felt diminished by its existence. Speculation was rife that the black conservatives' defense of merit as the sole criterion for selection and advancement was related more to their sense of personal diminishment by affirmative action labels than anything else.[83] This theory seemed plausible for a group whose reputation in Reagan's America had rested largely on their public persona as self-help heroes. Given the rugged individualism that defined the political period, that these intellectuals should seek to escape identification with a people who appeared to have "preferential treatment" stamped across their forehead was hardly surprising.[84] Nothing less than the political utility of black conservatism was at stake.

If the underlying motivation for the black conservatives' psychological thesis was clear to some observers, even clearer were the thesis's analytical deficiencies. The first fact ignored by these intellectuals was that racist assumptions about blacks' abilities had existed in America long before the inception of affirmative action.[85] The second fact they ignored was that their own continued speculation about blacks' low self-esteem, as a product of affirmative action, may have exacerbated the problem, to the extent that it existed. The charge that affirmative action constituted a form of reverse discrimination—where blacks were widely presumed to be unqualified beneficiaries of undeserved preference—may have been untrue. But this had not always mitigated the harmful effects the charge produced, from blacks questioning their own abilities to racist assumptions about them by others. As the philosopher Stanley Fish noted: "People who never would have questioned their achievements might begin to do so if it was raised every night on the evening news."[86]

Never in their work—or on the evening news—did the black conservatives cite academic studies to bolster their argument about affirmative action's psychological toll on recipients. The reasons for this failure to engage scholarship were arguably twofold: studies often contradicted the black conservatives' rigid position while also suggesting a complexity to social policy considerations these intellectuals had long denied. To the extent that they were an accurate indicator of social phenomena, opinion surveys uncovered little evidence of a black self-esteem sapped by affirmative action. Usually focused on universities, these surveys revealed that only one-tenth of black faculty believed that the policy perpetuated the myth of inferiority or robbed beneficiaries of a clear sense of deserved accomplishment. They also revealed that less than 15 percent of black managers believed it had lowered standards in the workplace and that four times as many considered it had enhanced their opportunities. On the whole, more than 80 percent of blacks saw affirmative action as "effective" while only 4 percent believed these programs hurt recipients.[87] Yet these research findings, released in the mid-1990s, had minimal impact in discrediting the black conservatives, who continued to offer unsubstantiated pronouncements about the "inevitable" effects of affirmative action as truth.

It was arguably William Bowen and Derek Bok's *The Shape of the*

River: Long Term Consequences of Considering Race in College and University Admission—published in 1998—that did the most to dent the credibility of the black conservatives' psychological thesis.[88] Based on a study of 45,184 students who entered twenty-eight selective colleges in 1976 or 1989, the book provided the most comprehensive examination to date of how students who had benefited from affirmative action fared during and after university. Significantly, little evidence was uncovered to suggest that psychological demoralization had afflicted a generation of blacks since the late 1960s. The book's other conclusions, however, were alarming. Bowen and Bok warned that, in the absence of affirmative action, the number of African Americans attending highly regarded universities would fall dramatically. Turning the black conservatives' reasoning on its head, they then speculated that this reduction in black numbers would surely have the most devastating impact on black morale, as white racial stereotypes about black intellectual inferiority would inevitably gain momentum.[89] Affirmative action policies, in their view, were evidently worth fighting for.

Afro-American studies professor William M. Banks arrived at much the same conclusion albeit with a different approach. Banks simply noted that self-esteem theorists such as Steele and Carter never spoke about "the other side of the coin." For centuries, white men had not competed fairly with blacks—the law had seen to that. White mobility had also received considerable affirmative assistance from public policy at many levels, as well as buddy and status networks that had always excluded blacks. Yet curiously, white Americans had never felt stigmatized, preferring to believe their mobility was a strict product of self-reliance and merit. They had certainly never felt the need to qualify their professional achievements by publishing titles such as "Reflections of a Racial Privilege Product"![90] Invoking his own career path, the historian Eric Foner agreed that a clear double standard existed: "Thirty-two years ago, I graduated from Columbia College. My class was all-male and virtually all-white. Most of us were young men of ability, yet had we been forced to compete for admission with women and racial minorities, fewer than half of us would have been at Columbia. None of us, to my knowledge, suffered debilitating self-doubt because we were the beneficiaries of affirmative action—that is, favored treatment on the basis of our race and gender."[91]

To this day, thousands of students continue to be admitted to the nation's most prestigious universities simply because their fathers or mothers went to these institutions.[92] Have these students been irreparably harmed by the spoils they received outside the "merit system"? Have they wondered—like Steele, Sowell, Carter, and McWhorter—whether they should be in the Ivy League or whether they deserved that top job that came after college? It was problematic that black conservatives never expressed concerns about the psychological diminishment that may have affected these white people. Theirs was arguably selective ideological commentary at best.

There were other reasons to resist the black conservative broadside against preferential treatment. Historian John Hope Franklin would cheekily point out that in America "quotas had existed long before affirmative action, but the figure for blacks was zero."[93] Others, including Kilson and West, supported affirmative action policies because they seriously questioned the legitimacy of the claim that antidiscrimination laws enacted in the mid-1960s had eliminated all major obstacles to African American advancement. Minimalist civil rights legislation may have contributed to the widespread belief that racial discrimination no longer existed, but there was no objective evidence to suggest that its passage had fostered a color-blind milieu in which merit figured as the only relevant criterion in selection processes.[94] In fact, to the extent that evidence did exist, it revealed racism as a force that continued to affect the employment prospects of all blacks, even those with education and skills.[95] Fears that the abandonment of affirmative action might occasion a return to the anti-black discrimination of the past were not without foundation.

The problem, progressives now suggested, lay with the very concept of merit itself. In the 1980s and 1990s, black conservatives had assured the nation that, in the absence of affirmative action, whites would judge African Americans "not by the color of their skin, but by the content of their character."[96] However, the black conservatives steadfastly refused to accept that affirmative action was a practical response to the persistent refusal of most whites to do just this.[97] Indeed, upon closer academic scrutiny the merit principle seemed to flounder, resting as it did on a slippery theoretical foundation of "fairness" to the individual, and amounting in substance to little more than an idealized paradigm. The "merit versus race" debate, to which the black conservatives were so devoted, ignored the essential fact that any selection process was ultimately "the combination of some imperfect assessment of merit (skill and talent) and purely personal filtering processes."[98] The assumption that race considerations were neutral at the personal filtering process was problematic to say the least. Unchallenged, it would only serve to "justify actual practices of discrimination against blacks" in the future.[99]

In their highly lauded works, black conservatives such as Sowell and Steele disagreed with this assessment, pointing to the tremendous gains in employment, income, and university admissions that African Americans were making prior to the onset of affirmative action. "In the period from 1954 to 1964," Sowell wrote, the "number of blacks in professional, technical, and similar high-level positions more than doubled." In other occupations, he continued, "the advance of blacks was even greater during the 1940s—when there was little or no civil rights policy—than during the 1950s when the civil rights revolution was in its heyday."[100] And similar progress was afoot within higher education. During the 1960s, after the enactment of major antidiscrimination legislation but before the advent of affirmative action, black college enrollments had increased by 83 percent to 417,000.[101] These historical trends suggested to Sowell that liberal and radical analysts were wrong to attribute the spectacular gains of the 1970s to preferential treatment. His thesis was that these gains would have occurred regardless.

Sowell's provocative observations certainly warranted further consideration. He had effectively thrown down the gauntlet to a generation of progressive intellectuals who had long assumed a direct correlation between racial development and affirmative action. Charting African American economic progress from 1940, the black economist claimed to have discovered facts showing this policy had never been the driving force behind black mobility and that its impact on black life had always been exaggerated. Steele backed this view, even suggesting that blacks would have moved ahead faster without racial preferences. "I think affirmative action takes credit for underlying changes that were already in place in American life. . . . If we had just protected them [blacks] against discrimination, my guess is that blacks would be farther ahead today than they are now via the patronization of affirmative action."[102]

The support subsequently afforded this position by Stephen and Abigail Thernstrom in their monumental analysis of black life—*America in Black and White*—would see it become a staple of anti–affirmative action discourse.[103]

These black intellectuals' challenge to a central tenet of progressive thought on affirmative action, however, initially elicited little response from liberal and radical scholars. Merit skeptics such as Kilson and West would no doubt have objected to the essence of the thesis in light of their firm views on the enduring significance of race within the opportunity structure of U.S. employment. But neither academic offered a systematic rebuttal of Sowell's and Steele's argument. That task fell to prominent New York sociologist Stephen Steinberg. A passionate advocate of African American equality, as well as an outstanding scholar, Steinberg expressed outrage at all intellectuals who had adopted this position as well as bewilderment at how quickly it had become the conventional wisdom in some academic circles. In his judgment, such a view was only possible through a "gross misuse of statistics" and a calculated failure to consider the demographic changes within the black community in the quarter century before the Civil Rights Act of 1964.[104] The critique mounted by Steinberg would be most compelling.

Far from signaling the dawn of genuine employment opportunities for African Americans, rising black incomes between 1940 and 1964 were perhaps best understood in terms of the "push" and "pull" factors that triggered Southern blacks' northern migration during the period.[105] To this end, Steinberg documented the 1.6 million black workers who had been pulled North in the 1940s to take up jobs in what was, necessarily, a racially less restrictive war-production workforce. It was a development that represented, in his view, "an unprecedented breach in the nation's system of occupational apartheid—one that set the stage for future change as well."[106] Significantly, in the 1950s, an even greater number of African Americans were pushed north—driven by the mechanization of Southern agriculture that had effectively rendered them rurally obsolete. Although these new migrants were forced to contend with severe employment discrimination in their new urban setting, even the lowest-paid jobs in the North, Steinberg explained, were a considerable improvement on the pittance they had received in the old Confederacy.[107] But it was not as if these black arrivals penetrated core industries in the 1940s and 1950s: the black middle class that E. Franklin Frazier derided in *Black Bourgeoisie* was comprised of only a handful of professionals whose lives were rooted in the ghetto.[108] Access to mainstream occupational structures for these and other blacks had come later, after the introduction of affirmative action. Numerous studies appeared to bear out Steinberg's conclusion: after all, it was companies subject to EEOC scrutiny that provided the most professional employment opportunities for African Americans. In contrast, black people continued to struggle for decent employment in those companies not subject to the same scrutiny.[109]

Sowell and Steele were obviously not historians. Devoid of critical social context, their discussions of black employment mobility appeared conveniently skewed. These intellectuals' attitude to racial preferences in higher education—that such preferences were unnecessary and even counterproductive—was similarly problematic. In a 1999 article in the *Journal of Blacks in Higher Education*, social scientists Theodore Cross and Robert B. Slater moved decisively to show just how problematic.[110] While acknowledging the leap in black university enrollments before affirmative action, Cross and Slater took aim at both black and white conservatives for failing to contextualize the figures and for overlooking important facts. The increase of 83 percent, they pointed out, had occurred in the early 1960s after the passage of antidiscrimination laws; that is to say, "during a period in which a Jim Crow starting base was very low and in many cases almost zero." Their point was significant. Arguably even more significant was the fact that, after the widespread introduction of affirmative action in 1970, that figure of 83 percent had risen to 259 percent—and this time from a much higher base.[111] Since 1970 the black middle class had quadrupled.[112] Although Sowell and Steele criticized racial preferences for being ineffective, the statistics appeared to tell a different story.

The black conservatives' economic appraisals of affirmative action were more resilient in the face of criticism; they appeared to display a scholarly traction lacking in the preceding analyses. As the 1990s dawned, most of these intellectuals would grudgingly concede that preferential policies had indeed "furthered the careers of some blacks," adding, however, that "any policy of favoritism would."[113] Their main objection now became that, while affirmative action had contributed significantly to the growth of the black middle class, government benevolence had failed miserably to improve the life prospects of the black poor.[114] The black conservatives explained that part of the moral aura surrounding affirmative action policies rested on the belief that such policies benefited the "less fortunate."[115] This "falsehood" had been entrenched through "repetition and vehemence, rather than evidence," and had "become part of the folklore of the land."[116] But what had in fact happened in America in the era of affirmative action was that the lot of middle-class black people had improved while the condition of lower-class black people had worsened.[117]

The black conservatives explained this apparent deficiency in social policy strategically. Preferential treatment, they argued, tended to be focused on prestigious markers such as university admission or white-collar job promotion and consequently was only within striking range of those already well beyond the category of the less fortunate. While these policies may have given academically oriented students a few more options for college, secured a black professor an endowed chair or enabled minority businessmen to break into the "old boys' network," they had limited value for the masses of unemployed workers dependent on welfare. Indeed, during the 1970s, when affirmative-action policies were being implemented most vigorously, Sowell and Williams noted that the most disadvantaged black families—often those headed by single women— had suffered a large decline in real income. Far from empowering poor blacks, these policies appeared to have exacerbated their economic woes. Depicting themselves as "partisans of the poor," black conservatives condemned affirmative action as a cheap tool geared toward getting those already privileged better jobs rather than bringing the underprivileged into the system. Sowell, in particular, lamented that the practical outcomes of these policies had received much less attention than the moral rationale that lay behind them.[118]

While Sowell and Williams focused on the devastating economic impact of affirmative action on the black poor, Woodson drew on their analyses but shifted focus to the policy's moral legitimacy. In a 1992 article in the *Harvard Journal of Law and Public Policy*, the NCNE president charged that preference was being used by the black middle class as part of a "bait and switch game."[119] In this game, he explained, statistics highlighting the extent of American racial inequality were documented and emphasized primarily to justify the allocation of a larger pool of positions to African Americans as if they were a monolithic group. Civil rights leaders, for instance, had stressed that black people in the aggregate were underrepresented at universities and in positions of management, even though well aware that poorer blacks would almost certainly not be candidates for positions in either sphere.[120] Thus, in a curious twist of logic, Woodson noted, the people who provided the statistical validation for affirmative action—the racially disadvantaged—received next to nothing from it.[121] It followed that the policy was best viewed as middle-class welfare. Drawing on his personal circumstances to illustrate his point, this moderate black conservative wrote: "My own children and the children of most members of the Congressional Black Caucus have better prospects for a successful future than many children, white, black, or brown, who live in impoverished communities. It should come as no surprise that when preferential treatment is offered without regard to economic circumstances, those who have the most training and resources will be best equipped to take advantage of any opportunities offered."[122]

An important distinction needs to be drawn between Sowell's and Williams's argument and the one presented by Woodson. In contrast to the two economists, Woodson did not claim that affirmative action had been directly harmful to the black poor, only that it had failed to assist those most in need. In fact, very few scholars argued that the policy had directly harmed poor blacks. How could Sowell and Williams make such an extraordinary claim?

The first explanation offered by these black conservatives for why affirmative action had wounded the most disadvantaged African Americans was rooted in theory: anything that interfered with the natural order of the marketplace, they insisted, was by definition damaging to the poor's best interests. This rationalist assumption constituted, as we have seen, the essence of both men's intellectual identities. Their second explanation went beyond theory, however, relying on what might liberally be termed an empirical approach. Critical of liberal and radical commentators for entrenching falsehoods through repetition and vehemence, Sowell and Williams routinely demanded that these supporters of affirmative action show proof that the policy delivered positive results to the African American community—clearly oblivious to a number of studies that had done precisely that.[123] Yet in their own work, these two black economists were content simply to point out that in the 1970s—in the so-called "era of affirmative action"—black progress had stagnated while the condition of the poorest blacks grew worse.[124] Curiously, for economists, there was no acknowledgment of the economic developments of the period, in particular how deindustrialization had contributed to the increasingly difficult circumstances in which millions of blacks found themselves. What is more, neither Sowell nor Williams showed how abolishing affirmative action would contribute to economic parity.

These black conservatives were not the only black intellectuals challenging the efficacy of racial preferences in this era. Some years earlier, in *The Declining Significance of Race*, William Wilson had turned his attention to this controversial issue in the context of his broader discussion of how economic restructuring—rather than white racism—was dictating black life chances in the post-industrial age.[125] Elevating class over race in his analysis of black poverty, Wilson expressed similar concern about the powerlessness of race-based affirmative action "to deal with the problem of the disproportionate concentration of blacks in the low-wage labor market," calling instead for race-neutral programs that would address the new economic realities.[126] His proposal for uplift was therefore consistent with his analysis. Since the causes of black unemployment and underemployment were not race-specific—that is, based on patterns of deliberate racial exclusion—neither could the solutions be race-specific.

Sometimes referred to as "a man of the left" because of his determination to promote government solutions to black poverty, Wilson would expand on this theme in his award-winning 1987 book, *The Truly Disadvantaged.*[127] Renewing his call for full employment policies, job skills training, public school reform, and the like in poor communities, this black sociologist was nevertheless forced to concede that such initiatives were unlikely in Reagan's America. Wilson held affirmative action partly responsible for the nation's declining commitment to the disadvantaged: more a distraction than anything else, it had triggered a formidable white backlash and destroyed what was left of the fragile New Deal coalition of working class whites and blacks.[128] With this racial wedge dividing the poor, a movement addressing itself to socioeconomic disadvantage had become nothing short of inconceivable.

Wilson's position on affirmative action must be distinguished from the views of Sowell, Williams, and Woodson. Wilson never argued that racial preferences were inherently detrimental to the poor, nor did he upbraid civil rights leaders and the broader black middle class for supporting such measures. With a cool scholarly detachment, he simply criticized these policies on the basis that they had done very little for the black poor and because he supported alternative policies—universal spending programs—that he believed would more effectively address their plight.[129] These policies, however, would not be presented as strategies to tackle the problems of poor minorities—despite the fact that they would disproportionately help these people—but as strategies to assist all disadvantaged groups, irrespective of race. By bridging the racial divide, Wilson insisted that a movement dedicated to the nation's truly disadvantaged—to which people of all races and ethnicities could positively relate—was not only possible, but likely.[130]

Clearly, a concern with racial disparity did not always entail an endorsement of racially preferential hiring and admissions, as the case of Glenn Loury further illustrated. Loury had long expressed concerns similar to those of Wilson about the inability of affirmative action to target the sources and symptoms of black hardship: he also believed the policy had delivered only minor trickle-down employment benefits to black workers.[131] How, he asked repeatedly, had such a poorly targeted method of intervention that conferred benefits almost exclusively on better-off African Americans become the symbol of progressive race relations in America?[132] Loury's skepticism when it came to affirmative action was not motivated, however, by a desire to see the emergence of a new "war on poverty," for unlike Wilson, this moderate black conservative economist had never supported big government. Rather, his reservations stemmed from two, albeit different, assumptions: the belief that the black middle class were now equipped to compete on merit and the conviction that the black poor stood to gain more from voluntarism and the market than from state intervention.[133]

Agreeing, then, with Cornel West that racial preferences were neither "a major solution to poverty nor a sufficient means to equality,"[134] Loury went on to question why so much black political energy had been expended fighting for them.[135] But in doing so, he and other critics of affirmative action failed to recognize that this was never really the driving principle behind the policy in the first place. The impetus for affirmative action was a determination to stamp out institutional prejudice—to tackle discrimination rather than disadvantage, to counteract the evils of caste rather than class. Supporters of affirmative action insisted that racism remained a historical and contemporary cultural reality with the potential to cut across socioeconomic boundaries.[136] Their policy was thus designed to confront the prejudice that all African Americans—affluent and poor—experienced collectively every day. It was also a recognition that blacks in the United States had been the victims of a system of domination that went beyond the difficulties associated with poverty and demanded a special solution.

The politically centrist Harvard sociologist Orlando Patterson was one of many black intellectuals to grasp this fundamental distinction. Although far from an unqualified supporter of affirmative action, Patterson explained that the function of these programs had always been different from antipoverty initiatives.[137] The black radical Manning Marable displayed a similar awareness of the underlying rationale for preference. Initiatives based on "narrowly defined economic criteria"—which sought to expand employment, access to education, and other social benefits for poor people, regardless of race—were "absolutely essential," he insisted, and needed to be vigorously expanded. But given the "statistical profile of racial inequality," he continued, progressives needed to resist the temptation to choose between race or class in what was almost certainly a "false debate."[138] It was unlikely that class-based programs would appease "angry white males" in the contemporary political climate. In Marable's view, racial tensions would in all likelihood persist as race-neutral policies came inevitably to be seen as race-conscious given the large overlap between "black" and "poor."[139]

Neo-enlightenment leftists such as Wilson, who were optimistic that a class-based model of preference could "restore interracial unity under the umbrella of the labor movement" while simultaneously tackling the problem of American racism, often failed to take account of the long and tortuous history of discrimination within organized labor.[140] That the white working class, through the medium of the unions, played a critical role in upholding the system of occupational apartheid in the United States is undeniable; typically excluding blacks from membership, unions rarely lived up to the slogan, "Black and White, Unite and Fight."[141] Instead, these organizations reserved jobs for whites while relegating African Americans to either the pre-industrial sector of the national economy or to a small number of menial manufacturing jobs spurned by whites.[142] When Wilson and others criticized affirmative action for being an obstacle to restoring interracial unity, it was unclear to which interracial unity these scholars were referring. Not only was this major proposition unsubstantiated, but it rested on assumptions that were implausible if not patently false in terms of history. Since class unity had never really existed in America, it was difficult to see how repealing racial preferences would magically deliver class unity.

The black conservatives, to be sure, never endorsed this component of the Wilson thesis; critical of the role of labor unions as free-market enthusiasts, they only agreed with him that race-based affirmative action unfairly privileged those blacks who were already privileged. In fact, these intellectuals challenged Wilson's thesis from the right, attacking its ahistorical assumptions about the working class as part of their larger campaign to promote the market—as opposed to unions or government—as the salvation of the black poor. The pro-market campaign of the black conservatives would, of course, itself be attacked. But their argument that affirmative action had only benefited elite blacks was one that continued to enjoy considerable support across the political spectrum. Notably, it was an argument that afforded politicians hostile to preference—such as Reagan—the opportunity to pursue the policy's destruction out of an apparently higher concern for the struggling black masses. It was only remarkable, given this significance, that the intellectual merits of Sowell and company's thesis so often escaped scholarly scrutiny.

Stephen Steinberg and Yale law professor William Taylor offered arguably the most penetrating critiques of the black conservatives' contention that affirmative action was but a form of black middle-class welfare. In the 1980s and 1990s they conducted empirical studies of affirmative action, exposing as incorrect the view that the policy had disproportionately assisted those blacks already comfortable. In making such a claim, Steinberg argued, critics of affirmative action appeared only to have in mind programs in higher education and the professions that—he too conceded—had done little to uplift African Americans at the lower end of the social spectrum.[143] But rather than constituting a compelling case against racial preferences, their position revealed, in his view, an extraordinary unfamiliarity with the history of the black freedom struggle. Those familiar with that history would have known that these programs had always extended beyond higher education and the professions, providing, among other things, unparalleled opportunities for black advancement in historically racist job markets.[144] The "focus of much of the effort," Taylor concurred, had been "not just on white collar jobs but also on law enforcement, construction work, and craft and production jobs in large companies—all areas in which the extension of new opportunities have provided upward mobility for less advantaged minority workers."[145]

Beginning in 1969 with Nixon's Philadelphia Plan—one of the first applications of race-conscious employment policy—there had always been affirmative action programs targeted specifically at blacks with little or no formal education. In Philadelphia, after the introduction of goals and timetables for federal contractors, the percentage of skilled minority construction workers rose from less than 1 percent to more than 12 percent of the total workforce. Similarly impressive developments were afoot in law enforcement, where the number of black police officers almost doubled between 1970 and 1980.[146] These were occupations not usually associated with privilege. But for the people concerned, the new opportunities afforded by affirmative action were arguably the difference, Steinberg explained, between being "relatively advantaged" and "truly disadvantaged" in contemporary America.[147]

Indeed, during the 1970s, Americans witnessed the first significant racial integration of blue-collar industries in the nation's history. By the mid-1990s, merit and effort, in conjunction with affirmative action, had ensured that close to 65 percent of all African Americans were living in either stable working-class or middle-class households.[148] Although this progress could not mask the poverty crisis in the so-called "static-strata," which comprised 30 percent of blacks, these trends remained significant.[149] Buoyed by this progress, Steinberg went so far as to suggest that affirmative action had gone a long way to reconstituting the racial division of labor that had existed since slavery. In the light of America's bitter racial history, to argue that this policy had been an ineffective weapon in the fight against economic inequality in the workplace, yielding only a modest impact on the structure of opportunity, seemed problematic to say the least. The empirical research of reputable scholars in the field had rendered yet another seemingly credible black conservative assumption dubious.

Even in higher education there was evidence that affirmative action had resulted not only in greater choice for middle-class blacks but in improving social mobility for the black poor; it turned out that a substantial number of the increased black enrollments since the late 1960s had come from low-income families.[150] The black conservatives did not seek to dispute the empirical validity of this fact. But they did seek to turn the optimism that inevitably accompanied the fact into a source of pessimism rather than hope. Concerned at the disastrous college completion rate of African Americans in the 1990s, these intellectuals now insisted that the politics of racial preference had placed black students in learning environments beyond their capabilities and thereby systematically set up them for failure. Blacks who were sufficiently qualified to attend less competitive universities were allegedly being admitted to more prestigious ones where they were ill-equipped to deal with the rigorous demands thrust upon them.[151] "Instead of becoming University of Texas graduates," Sowell charged, these "temporary tokens" usually became "Harvard dropouts."[152]

From Sowell and Williams to Steele and McWhorter, the black conservatives assumed primary responsibility for publicizing this academic "mismatch" theory beyond the walls of the ivory tower. And to many observers, it was a theory that appeared convincing. How could it not? It was widely documented, after all, that at some universities the black graduation rate hovered below 10 percent and that at most universities it failed to exceed 50 percent.[153] Williams's statistics—and his accompanying explanation—confirmed a seemingly grim situation. "Nationally," he wrote, "only 26 percent of black students graduate six years after entering college. That's about half the graduation rate of white students. At some colleges no more than 20 percent of black students admitted graduate. Many who do graduate do so with grade point averages that are lower than their white or Asian counterparts. These statistics on academic failure are not new. They've existed since colleges began racial double-standards in admission."[154]

In the mode of Sowell's "temporary tokens" jibe, this black economist then offered his own typically dramatic illustration of the problem. "You say to me, teach me to box and the first match I get for you is with Lennox Lewis. You are going to get your brains beaten out."[155] Graduating from "a less prestigious university" was "better than flunking out of a prestigious one," Williams reasoned. "It's better for both the student and blacks as a group."[156] Steele agreed with Williams's assessment. Insisting, like him, that 75 percent of black students admitted to American universities drop out, he argued that the time had come to scale back affirmative action in higher education.[157] Scaling back would ultimately benefit blacks, since, according to McWhorter, these students would find themselves better able to compete in academic environments for which they were more adequately prepared.[158]

Despite its popularity, this thesis was not new; as early as 1972, Sowell had warned of the potentially damaging consequences of placing black students in institutions too competitive for their individual needs.[159] But it was a thesis that took on renewed significance in the context of the 1990s as poor black graduation rates appeared to confirm the black economist's pessimistic early forecasts. For his insight, the prominent Harvard couple, the Thernstroms, praised Sowell as "the most penetrating critic of affirmative action in higher education," only puzzled as to why his warnings about the setbacks blacks would inevitably suffer as a result of affirmative action were never heeded.[160] On this subject, as with others, the black conservatives were cast by white conservatives as experts whom the nation ignored at its peril.

The implication here was that Sowell and company were correct in their assessment of black students' performance in higher education; and that had these students attended less academically demanding institutions—for example, a second-tier university or state-operated historically black college—they would have continued with their studies and graduated at a similar rate to whites. Given its widening appeal, this position demanded further attention. In the 1990s Theodore Cross, editor of the *Journal of Blacks in Higher Education,* duly provided this attention, investigating, among other things, variations in the black dropout rate across the tertiary sector and drawing from this investigation conclusions about the reliability of the black conservatives' claims.[161] Not only did his studies—which involved meticulous research—prove the black conservatives wrong, they also revealed serious flaws in these critics' approach to black intellectual life.

Cross took Sowell's comment about Harvard and the University of Texas as his starting point. He discovered that, far from being temporary tokens, African Americans at Harvard completed their degrees within six years at a rate in excess of 90 percent—significantly, only three percentage points behind whites. Cross's focus then shifted to the University of Texas. There, remarkably, the graduation rate for blacks stood at 51 percent, an astonishing 41 percentage points lower than the prestigious Ivy League college. With whites graduating Texas at 69 percent, a sizeable 18 percentage points higher than African Americans, Cross asked: "Is the University of Texas a better choice for blacks when the black dropout rate is more than six times the rate at Harvard?"[162] In exposing as flawed the assumption that African Americans at this leading institution were having their "brains beaten out" due to affirmative action, these findings provided the impetus for yet further analysis.

Aware that Sowell had failed to do his research in respect of Harvard and the University of Texas, Cross then diverted his attention to other universities, embarking on a rigorous macro study of black performance across the entire tertiary sector. The results of this study were damning not only of the black conservatives, but of all who would argue that African American students were better off enrolled at institutions with lower academic standards. Cross's work demonstrated that the high black college-dropout rate in the United States had, in fact, very little to do with what Williams called "racial double-standards in admission."[163] Black students, it turned out, graduated at a far higher rate at the more prestigious private universities—where preferential measures were firmly in place—than at the less selective state universities and black colleges, where the majority of blacks did indeed dropout.[164] In revealing that a number of these less selective institutions did not even practice affirmative action, Cross's thesis crystallized.[165] The black conservatives, it seemed, were involved in a "bait-and-switch" game of their own, presenting the poor performance of black students at the lesser universities in order to justify uprooting affirmative action for potentially the best black students at leading universities. These intellectuals' argument may have been loud and passionate,[166] but it was also one that appeared—on the available evidence—unsustainable.

The evidence, however, did not deter Williams from continuing his assault on affirmative action's "pernicious consequences" in higher education. "If we had to single out one American institution that stands at the forefront of modern-day racial discrimination, deception, and contempt for fundamental principles of liberty," he wrote, "it would be American universities."[167] For Williams, then, and indeed many black conservatives, establishing race neutrality as a procedural ideal in university admissions was an unconditional aim, never to be compromised. The notable exception was Loury, who, from the late 1990s, expressed increasing disquiet about the soundness of this position.[168] To be sure, Loury had not mutated into an uncritical supporter of affirmative action in higher education: he remained opposed, for instance, to strict quotas, concerned that they often sheltered blacks from the challenge of competing on their merits.[169] But in surveying the contemporary tertiary scene, this black intellectual had come to worry even more about the potentially devastating impact on black enrollments of renouncing *all* race-based programs in this important sphere.[170] Racial diversity on campus evidently mattered.

It mattered, Loury insisted, because nothing less than the integrity of American institutions was at stake. Without racial diversity at the most selective universities, he argued, the democratic character of the process through which the nation selected its elites could—and would—be questioned.[171] That "elite higher education was the primary place in America where access to influence and power was rationed" was clear to most. Even clearer to Loury was that blacks needed to be able to participate in these institutions if they were to achieve genuine and lasting parity in national life.[172] Thus, this MIT-trained economist rejected *ideological* allegiances to race neutrality—which, by reducing black numbers, he believed would only heighten racial awareness—in favor of the *pragmatic* need to pursue racial justice as a public good.[173] Despite some obvious flaws, Loury contended, affirmative action at universities had opened doors previously closed to blacks by prompting institutions "to look in nontraditional places and ways for prospective candidates."[174] So long as the relevant programs evolved and became truly affirmative, "lifting blacks up to standards rather than pulling standards down to meet them," they could be defended as a necessary evil to combat one of the enduring legacies of American history: racial inequality.[175]

That Loury had undergone an epiphany (of sorts) was obvious to those familiar with his history and work: intellectually, this was not the same man who, in the 1980s, had been the toast of the conservative labyrinth.[176] But in belatedly putting the case for conditional preference in university admissions, Loury was skirting around the vexed issue of role-modeling and, in one sense, reaffirming a strong—albeit more radical—commitment to an age-old conservative principle. This impressive black intellectual had long maintained that African Americans of equal ability to whites often wound up less successful because they lacked the "right networks."[177] With an eye to the affirmative action–fueled black middle class, Loury now contemplated a higher education sector free from preferences and was troubled by the potential impact on those valuable networks that had emerged. Touting the responsibility of the black elite to teach poor blacks about social and cultural capital, and also to serve as models of academic and professional achievement, Loury questioned the wisdom of renouncing the very policy that—despite its shortcomings—had gone a long way to making this role-modeling viable. In his view, black students graduating from elite institutions such as Harvard served as an example to other blacks of what was possible in America.[178]

Loury's reluctant acceptance of affirmative action in higher education appeared consistent with his emphasis on the importance of black role-modeling.[179] Steeped in pragmatism rather than idealism, this was a position that set him apart from many other black conservatives. Woodson and Steele would also promote role-model ideology, viewing black middle-class moral and economic mentoring of the black poor as essential to uplift in the long term.[180] But curiously both intellectuals rejected affirmative action, the policy that had produced the people who presumably were to serve the poor in this capacity. Sowell's and Williams's position was different again. Although rejecting role models in the formal sense of criticizing the term and lamenting its entanglement with affirmative action discourse, both men preached the importance of social capital to racial advancement, emphasizing, in particular, how a respect for entrepreneurialism and education—as well as individual determination—needed to be harnessed from within black America itself.[181] Who better to harness these values, Loury might have asked, than a black business graduate of Harvard, accepted initially as part of an affirmative action program, who had worked hard to raise his standards to the level of the best and brightest at that institution?

It was not long before the debate over race neutrality in the academy spilled over into the political domain; and yet again, black conservatives were at the forefront. In the 1990s a number of these intellectuals would explain their opposition to affirmative action in terms of Dr. King's dream of a color-blind America, where individuals were to be judged not by the color of their skin but by the content of their character. By employing the language of the black freedom movement, however, they hoped not only to campaign more effectively against compensatory justice measures for black people, but to garner some semblance of respectability for their stand within the African American community. In 1995, for instance, conservative African American businessman and former chair of the California Proposition 209 initiative,[182] Ward Connerly, chose King's birthday to announce the beginning of a nationwide crusade to destroy affirmative action, claiming that the great freedom fighter had always been a sworn enemy of social engineering measures that categorized people according to race.[183] Similarly, in 1994, the Heritage Foundation sponsored a conference entitled "The Conservative Virtues of Martin Luther King," at which leading black conservative figures presented themselves as the true heirs to the civil rights vision by lauding King's fine record as a political activist of the right.[184]

Beginning in the early 1990s, this narrow reading of King's message also found its way into the titles of several black conservative texts. First, in 1991, there was Shelby Steele's award-winning *The Content of Our Character*. Steele's book would stir other black conservatives—not generally considered intellectual—to engage King's legacy in books of their own. Alan Keyes's *Master of the Dream: The Strength and Betrayal of Black America* was followed by Ken Hamblin's *Pick a Better Country: An Unassuming Colored Guy Speaks His Mind about America* and then Gary Frank's *Searching for the Promised Land: An African American's Odyssey*.[185] In the late 1990s, King's famous words were invoked yet again with the publication of *A Dream Deferred*, Steele's second controversial book on race relations inside a decade. Seeking to recover the values they associated with the early phase of the civil rights movement (1954–1965), these authors shared two broad assumptions: first, that the noble visions of individualism and color-blindness had been corrupted by liberals and radicals after 1965; and second, that the modern conservative movement remained the best chance of recapturing the spirit of that earlier golden age.

Of the group, Ward Connerly was undoubtedly the most committed and visible proponent of these views. Although Connerly cannot be considered a black conservative intellectual for the purposes of this book—he has never adopted positions on black poverty and secondary education—no analysis of affirmative action can ignore his contribution to the black conservatives' construal of the King ideal. In numerous opinion pieces and one major publication, *Creating Equal: My Fight Against Race Preferences*, this African American entrepreneur consistently placed Martin Luther King, Jr., and his color-blind dream at the forefront of the movement to overturn racial preferences.[186] Formerly a property investor, in the 1980s and 1990s he rotated between Republican appointments in state housing agencies and business activities facilitated largely by minority set-aside programs.[187] Having received millions of dollars from California's Department of Energy (because he was a black who owned a business), this increasingly well-known figure founded the California Civil Rights Initiative (CCRI)[188]—a coalition of conservatives committed to overturning affirmative action and realizing the dream of a "color-blind society."[189] Equating his own endeavors with King's struggle for black justice and equality in the 1960s, the controversial Connerly suggested that it was really continuous blending in the melting pot that was the key to liberty in the future. Interracial marriage, he assured, would deliver the dream of "one nation indivisible" and resolve, once and for all, the nation's racial dilemma.[190]

The color-blind critique of affirmative action favored by some black conservatives in the 1990s was not entirely original; rather, its roots lay in the discourse of white conservative social science from the preceding two decades. The focus on Martin Luther King, Jr., however, was a new addition to the scholarship, and a formidable addition at that. The preeminent symbol of black dignity and strength in American history, King had proven exceptionally adept at crawling inside the "jeremiad form" throughout his career, frequently invoking God and the Constitution and Declaration of Independence to legitimize the struggles of the "Negro" people.[191] Toward the end of his life, he had attacked Black Power, both as a rallying call and a political concept, fearing that a powerful separatist movement had the potential to destroy forever his visions of racial and economic justice.[192] King, according to Steele and Connerly, was a proud American—a socially moderate individualist who had always valued personal integrity over collectivist radicalism—like them. Shrewdly appropriating these elements of the civil rights leader's legacy appeared an intellectual masterstroke for a time. It wrong-footed liberal and radical critics and forced them to reexamine the spirit of the civil rights movement and their own conceptions of what freedom might mean. But though initially puzzled by these appeals to King, the progressive response in time proved insightful and penetrating.

Liberal and radical scholars made clear their objections to what they saw as the perversion of King's dream. In *Guess Who's Coming to Dinner Now?* Angela Dillard argued that the attempt to create a right-wing intellectual tradition centered on King was a distortion sustained only by a number of out of context but judicious quotations borrowed from the great man.[193] It was interesting, she noted, that these black conservatives had ignored "their leader's" increasingly militant calls toward the end of his life for a radical redistribution of wealth in American society and failed to explain why King's dream had, in his own words, been devastatingly shattered.[194] Why had there been no mention of this other King, Dillard asked, the King who had expressed fears after 1965 that his dream had become a nightmare, the King who had never displayed much affection for the doctrine of assimilation, the King who had come to identify capitalism as a force incompatible with the attainment of true justice and equality?[195] A selective interpretation of one of the civil rights leader's speeches may have allowed Steele and Connerly to portray him as a patriotic color-blind crusader; but in seeking to cement *only* this image of King, these black conservatives appeared to freeze him in time and define him as a one-dimensional thinker. King, of course, was not a one-dimensional thinker, nor a principled opponent of affirmative action.

In recorded speeches, interviews, and books toward the end of his life, King left a distinct impression of his support for sweeping structural reforms in American society—most notably, social programs for the poor but also, very importantly, employment programs to achieve racial integration. Despite the civil rights legislation of the early to mid-1960s, King observed that little had changed. "The Negro," he believed, continued to be "walled in by color and poverty. The law pronounces him equal—abstractly—but his conditions of life are still far from equal."[196] Never one to confuse the dream with reality, he insisted that legal formalities were not enough to democratize the nation. Rather, a more interventionist approach was required on the part of government. True to his belief in genuine equality, King had foreshadowed the need for color-conscious social engineering as early as 1964:

> Whenever the issue is raised, some of our friends recoil in horror. The Negro should be granted equality they agree, but should ask for nothing more. On the surface, this appears reasonable, but is not realistic. For it is obvious that if a man enters the starting line of a race three hundred years after another man, the first would have to perform some incredible feat to catch up. . . . It is impossible to create a formula for the future which does not take into account that our society has been doing something special against the Negro for hundreds of years. How then can he be absorbed into the mainstream of American life if we do not do something special for him now, in order to balance the equation and equip him to compete on an equal basis?[197]

In 1967, in his last great work *Where Do We Go from Here: Chaos or Community?* King again appeared to express strong support for affirmative action, making clear his belief that job selection based on the principles of color-blindness and merit tended all too often to discriminate against African Americans. "The insistence on educational certificates and credentials for skilled and semi-skilled jobs is keeping Negroes out of both the private business sector and government employment. . . . Negro exclusion is not the purpose of this insistence upon credentials, but it is the inevitable consequence today. The orientation of personnel offices should be Jobs First, Training later."[198] In keeping with these observations, King called on government to create a huge human services job pool specifically to train black Americans—"the explosive outsiders of the American expansion"[199]—and to reward companies that took initiatives to employ them. Noting that in Europe employers were required to hire a certain percentage of handicapped people, King had asked, "Why not a similar requirement in America for blacks?" A racial quota system was one way the nation could atone for the injustices it had inflicted upon its black citizens.[200]

Far from a supreme individualist in the mold of contemporary black conservatives, then, King was a man steeped in African American political culture, a community leader—first and foremost—who was deeply attached to his people and committed to their liberation. Confronted daily with the gross inequities of American life, he appeared color-caring rather than color-blind, a man who understood the realities of human oppression and the need for substantive remedies to fight it on all fronts. Indeed, in the final chapter to *Where Do We Go From Here?* King essentially asked two questions: How do we help those marginalized by poverty? And how do we provide genuine opportunity for blacks to rise above the encumbrance of race? One of King's answers was class-based affirmative action; the other was race-based affirmative action. For King, it was not a case of preference for one race over the other, but of preference for integration and full democracy over division and exclusion. Programs that brought Americans together were not punitive, he insisted, but beneficial to the nation as a whole. In fact, they had the potential to carry America forward.[201]

As one scholar has noted, Martin Luther King "suffers the fate of every human being: when you are dead you belong to the ages. People can distort your positions and use them for their own purposes."[202] To be sure, King often dreamed of realizing a color-blind society in which race would have no place, but some black conservatives in the 1990s confused this philosophical prescription with the objective social reality. While King may have sacrificed his life in the pursuit of a color-blind America, he never downplayed the significance of racism as a negative force shaping black life and he certainly never counseled black people to surrender to injustice. On the contrary—and unlike black conservative intellectuals—he believed that the struggle to defeat racism and the gradual movement toward a truly color-blind society would require the employment of race-conscious social policies until discrimination had ended and black equality was a reality. In their rush to lay claim to King's mantle, Steele, Connerly, and others ignored this important point. They also failed to reconcile the other dimension to King's teachings, which emphasized that the goal of civil rights was not so much color-blindness as cultural diversity and pluralism within a tolerant, ethical, and humane social order.[203] These crucial omissions rendered these intellectuals' commitment to this variation of the color-blind critique of affirmative action unconvincing.

"Unconvincing" is a word that many scholars of the African American experience would employ to describe the *entire* black conservative critique of affirmative action. Sowell and company's opposition to the policy was not, after all, defined by a single theme: it took various forms, evolving over time. From concerns about constitutional principle and reverse racism in the 1980s to black psychology and middle-class welfare in the early 1990s, the black conservatives' discourse on preference played itself out in the American workplace and at universities, reinforced periodically by appeals to color-blindness and the legacy of Martin Luther King, Jr. It was a discourse as diverse as it was controversial, that drew its inspiration from multiple sources within both the American and African American traditions.

To speak of one black conservative view of affirmative action is therefore problematic. Some of these intellectuals—Sowell, Williams, Thomas, Parker, and Wortham—were unqualified critics of *all* preferential policies, insisting that they could never be reconciled with the American political creed. Since affirmative action was wrong in principle, they argued, it simply had to be opposed in principle. Yet these same intellectuals also pointed in their work to preferences' practical failure to assist the black community. Joined in this enterprise by Woodson, Steele, and McWhorter—who had not expressed the same ideological concerns—the broader black conservative church had embarked on a campaign to overturn affirmative action *for the sake of* African Americans. With the exception of Loury, who gradually came to view the policy more favorably, these intellectuals were united in a common purpose. But their analyses varied even so, swinging between a focus on the political and cultural consequences of affirmative action for black people to a focus on consequences psychological and economic in nature. What is more, within each of these categories, opinions had at times differed.

These differences did not necessarily indicate a subtlety of thought on the part of the black conservatives whose arguments were out of step with the established empirical wisdom of mainstream scholarship, yet lacking the hard evidence to seriously challenge that wisdom. When stripped to the bare essence, Sowell and company had opposed affirmative action on the grounds that the policy had harmed black people in general and the black poor in particular. But both positions had proven untenable, as the 1970s explosion of the black middle class clearly illustrated. Many in what Bart Landry called the "new black middle class" were once a part of the black working poor. Most of these beneficiaries of preference did not appear diminished—politically, culturally, psychologically, or otherwise (and how was diminishment to be determined anyway?). Nor had the attempt by some black conservatives to co-opt the legacy of civil rights in their fight to bring down affirmative action been particularly credible. Merit and color-blindness were fine ideals, to be sure, but in America, as Loury and others noted, there was little evidence they were anything more than this.

Arguably, the black conservatives' most significant contribution to the debate over affirmative action was to dramatize the condition of the so-called static strata of African Americans whose lives appeared to lie beyond the reach of the policy. Although some black conservatives quite erroneously blamed affirmative action for the plight of these people, their focus on the plight itself served a clear and important political function. It was, above all, a reminder to progressives that racial preferences, if isolated from the deeper crises of black America—problems concerning the family and extreme economic deprivation resulting from unemployment—could be seen as a universal remedy. Effective though the policy had been, it was certainly not a universal remedy. One had only to cast one's eyes over the racial inequality so manifest in the nation's inner cities—as the black conservatives had—to know that more was required to tackle the African American community's deeper crises. The interpretations and solutions offered by Sowell and company in their analyses of black poverty logically become this book's next focus.

Chapter 3
Partisans of the Poor?

At the dawn of the twenty-first century, nearly one-third of all African Americans were living below the poverty line, compared with 10 percent of whites. Single women headed half of all black families and more than two-thirds of all black children were born out of wedlock. Over one-quarter of African American men aged between eighteen and thirty were either in prison, on probation, or awaiting trial. And black life expectancy was lower than that of any other group in America, comparable even to that of some Third World countries.[1] Confronted with these alarming realities, scholars and activists have asked why? Why do so many black people in the United States today continue to live what Malcolm X once called the "American Nightmare"?[2]

There is no one theory that explains the foundation of contemporary black disadvantage conclusively: the fierce national debate of the past four decades has yielded multiple explanations for the various crises afflicting poor African Americans. While white right-wing commentators pointed to a black culture of irresponsibility in their analyses, liberals and radicals typically emphasized economic forces and the power of American racism. The contributions of black conservatives to the debate over racial inequality sometimes fell within the boundaries of this discourse, but at other times resisted neat categorization. Rejecting studies that attributed African American problems to white prejudice, these intellectuals preferred to focus on poor black people's deficiencies while promoting the emancipatory potential of capitalism. Lamenting, in particular, the cultural impact of the social provisions associated with Great Society liberalism, members of the cohort sometimes reached back into history, recalling a golden age of black independence before civil rights in their campaign to make self-help, once again, the panacea for the African American community. While largely united in this self-help campaign, subtle variations of interpretation nevertheless existed in the black conservatives' discourse on black poverty.

*   *   *

It is important to recognize at the outset that the roots of this debate over racial poverty pre-date the emergence of contemporary black conservatism by nearly two decades. As early as 1962, Michael Harrington had written *The Other America*,[3] a book widely credited with "discovering" the poor and providing the ideological impetus for Lyndon Johnson's War on Poverty.[4] If Harrington's generic work on poverty was the first of its kind to be so influential at the political level, soon the American intellectual market would be flooded with literature specifically addressing the causes and consequences of *black* poverty. Particularly influential in this area were the contributions of Kenneth Clark, Elliot Liebow, Ulf Hannerz, and Lee Rainwater. In their studies of black urban ghettos, these scholars provided vivid descriptions of growing cultural dysfunction among poor African Americans—rising crime, sexual exploitation, teenage pregnancy, "matriarchy," alcoholism, and drug addiction, among other things. But rather than focus unduly on what were arguably the behavioral symptoms of economic disadvantage, they believed in tackling the structural dynamics in American society that had, in all likelihood, produced these problems in the first place.[5]

Despite their intellectual sophistication, none of these scholars had as much impact in propounding this thesis as one Daniel Patrick Moynihan. In 1965, as a young Assistant Secretary of Labor in the Johnson administration, Moynihan wrote a report on the condition of African Americans entitled *The Negro Family: The Case for National Action*, warning in particular of the high incidence of divorce, illegitimacy, and female-headed households within the black community.[6] Widely known as the Moynihan Report, it ignited a fire of controversy across the nation, largely because the ideas it presented were misinterpreted by various interests and sensationalized by the media. But the future Democratic senator's findings were hardly extreme. Moynihan recognized that history and contemporary structures were almost certainly to blame for the disruption to black family life, but added that this disruption had now become "a fundamental cause of other forms of pathology."[7] The implications of his thesis were thus clear: if the problems of welfare dependency, juvenile delinquency, and poverty among African Americans were to be solved, urgent steps would need to be taken—by government and black people—to reinvigorate the black family.[8]

The Report soon became the most important frame of reference for discussions of racial inequality in American life. Moynihan's civil rights critics, ignoring the first part of his argument, denounced him as a racist denigrator of black culture and accused him of shifting the responsibility for black disadvantage away from societal institutions and onto African Americans themselves.[9] White liberals were, on the whole, less hostile but continued to insist that government, through the War on

Poverty, could successfully tackle the myriad problems of black urban life.[10] But as black rioting erupted in the nation's cities over the slow pace of change, Moynihan's thesis was (re)interpreted, most notably by conservatives, to demonstrate the futility of attempting to deliver equality to African Americans by way of social programs.[11] Since black culture, not white racism, was the cause of the rioting, black moral rehabilitation, not federal expenditure, was the solution to end rioting.[12] In 1968, as black frustration deepened and white backlash set in, Richard Nixon was elected to the presidency. The emerging conservative culturalist position on black life had a new and powerful political proponent.

There was no more forceful an intellectual proponent of this position than Edward Banfield.[13] A professor of government at Harvard, Banfield was the first scholar to claim that defective lower-class culture, alone, accounted for black poverty in the United States. Progress and prosperity continued to elude so many African Americans, he argued, because these people were impulsive and present-oriented and placed absolutely no value on hard work.[14] Unlike Clark and Moynihan, whose liberal instincts had led them to explain this culture as a product of oppressive and complex social structures, Banfield believed culture was rooted in a set of "psychological processes" and that it was these processes that produced and perpetuated poverty. Unable to identify or explain the roots of the "inferior" psychology among blacks, Banfield insinuated that genetics could be a factor.[15]

With these attitudes, it was little wonder that Banfield and other conservatives opposed government initiatives to tackle black urban misery through the War on Poverty. With legal equality for African Americans secured by the mid-1960s, pouring funds for education, job training, housing, and health care into these communities was President Johnson's liberal attempt to bolster the struggle for material equality—to salvage the salvageable among those clustered below the poverty line in American life.[16] Significantly, there was also means-tested cash assistance, or Aid to Families with Dependent Children (AFDC).[17] Tailored to meet the realities of the post–civil rights era—in particular, the problem of racial poverty—Johnson's bold agenda promised, for a time, to deliver much to the disadvantaged economically. But arguably the War on Poverty's most enduring legacy was to elicit a backlash politically. By the end of the 1960s, the fact that African Americans—constituting only 12 percent of the population—accounted for 40 percent of the nation's welfare recipients had transformed traditional anti-black attitudes into radicalized anti-welfare attitudes. With the conservative movement particularly fixated on AFDC, the image of welfare as a program that paid young, unmarried black women in dilapidated neighborhoods to have several children to different men took hold in the public consciousness.[18]

If the mid-1960s marked the zenith of a brief age of government action to assist poor African Americans, the 1970s marked a new period in which the racial liberalism of the previous decade would be overwhelmingly rejected.[19] With the connection between culture, history, and economics effectively lost, the condition of the black poor came to be seen increasingly as a problem of their own making. It was in this context in 1977 that *Time* ran a story announcing the birth of the American underclass.[20] Observing that poverty and related problems of drugs, crime, teenage pregnancy, and high unemployment had become more concentrated and severe in urban areas with highly segregated black populations,[21] the magazine's editorialists wrote: "Behind the [ghetto's] crumbling walls lives a large group of people who are more intractable, more socially alien and more hostile than almost anyone had imagined. They are the unreachables: the American underclass. . . . Their bleak environment nurtures values that are often at odds with those of the majority—even the majority of the poor. Thus the underclass produces a highly disproportionate number of the nation's juvenile delinquents, school dropouts, drug addicts and welfare mothers, and much of the adult crime, family disruption, urban decay and demand for social expenditures."[22]

Although the term "underclass" had been employed by the Swedish sociologist Gunnar Myrdal as early as 1962 to describe groups that did not share in the nation's prosperity,[23] it was the *Time* article—building on Banfield's work—that set the tone for much of the contemporary debate over race and poverty. In the 1980s it inspired Ken Auletta's important book *The Underclass* and triggered a flood of academic literature on the subject.[24]

Predictably, conservative theorists, offering behavioral explanations for the condition of the "undeserving poor," won the most acclaim in Reagan's America. Gary Gilder's *Wealth and Poverty* and Lawrence Mead's *Beyond Entitlement* were two of the conservative movement's favorite titles.[25] But both were surpassed by Charles Murray's *Losing Ground*, which became, in many ways, the New Right's unofficial handbook on race and welfare. In an earlier life, as a teenager, Murray had set fire to a cross—"the iconic act of the Ku Klux Klan."[26] Now, three decades on, he argued that the cause of poverty in the United States had actually been the fight to eradicate poverty. Far from reducing inequality, it turned out, liberal social policies had exacerbated inequality by institutionalizing perverse incentives that encouraged laziness, immorality, and general social recklessness. The dependency that had become the black poor's major obstacle to a better life could only be addressed, it seemed, by eliminating every social benefit in an effort to induce independence.[27] Apparently tough love—and fear—would succeed where government had failed.

Murray's arguments were not supported by rigorous empirical research.[28] But his thesis drew ringing endorsement from the Reagan administration and made him a celebrity in the social policy research industry virtually overnight. Whether any individual black conservative achieved Murray's intellectual fame is debatable, but the collective influence of the black conservatives made them at least as formidable politically. Having with great fanfare climbed out of "the ghetto," these intellectuals were cast as experts on the ghetto—experts who could speak not only professionally but also personally to the myriad problems of black urban life. Their controversial explanations for the proliferation of the black underclass sometimes echoed the culturalist arguments of Banfield and Murray. But the black conservatives would contribute a number of popular and penetrating theories of their own.

In terms of its scope and capacity to provoke, Sowell's scholarship on poverty stood out on the American intellectual scene. Convinced that racism could no longer explain why blacks continued to lag behind other groups in socioeconomic progress, Sowell wrote *Ethnic America* and *The Economics and Politics of Race* in the early 1980s and pointed to the importance of different cultural heritages in shaping people's destinies. In these books and in many that followed, he compared the development of various ethnic groups over time, concluding that upward mobility in the United States had typically been achieved by groups that had adopted the traditional American ethic of thrift, work, and education. But in downplaying the significance of the different histories each of these groups had brought *to* America, Sowell was forced to contend with charges of "ethnic minority stereotyping," reminiscent of those once leveled against Edward Banfield.[29]

A great admirer of Banfield's work, Sowell pleaded "not guilty" to the charges and set about demonstrating the soundness of his approach and the reliability of his findings. Nowhere was his defense of the cultural paradigm more impassioned and assured than in his discussion of the roots of contemporary African American disadvantage. Sowell's first task was to disprove the argument that white racism had produced the black underclass. If discrimination was the most powerful explanatory variable, he asserted, then by definition there would be uniform outcomes within the same minority group, for in the eyes of a racist, "one black is pretty much the same as another."[30] But this had not been the American experience: West Indian blacks had always outperformed native-born blacks economically even though to most whites the two groups were indistinguishable. In 1969, for instance, the family incomes of West Indian blacks were 94 percent of the national average while the incomes of native-born blacks constituted only 62 percent of that average.[31] During the 1970s West Indian representation in professional occupations was double that of native-born blacks and "slightly higher than that of the U.S. population as a whole." If color prejudice alone accounted for the pitiable condition of so many black people in the United States, why, Sowell challenged, this large disparity in demographic representation among black people themselves?[32]

The two black groups in question had supposedly acquired out of their respective slave experiences values and attitudes that were strikingly different. Discouraged from taking initiative and denied incentives to work hard except to escape punishment, American slaves, according to Sowell, developed foot-dragging and other "work-evading patterns"—together with a culture of "duplicity" and "theft"—that had remained ingrained long after emancipation.[33] West Indian slaves, by contrast, were socialized into a "spirit of capitalism." Afforded opportunities for economic development in more market-style surroundings, they had been encouraged to work and compete in order to get ahead: "Unlike slaves in the United States, who were issued food rations and were often fed from the common kitchen, West Indian slaves were assigned land and time to raise their own food. They sold surplus food in the market to buy amenities for themselves. In short West Indian Negroes had centuries of experience in taking care of themselves in a significant part of their lives, even under slavery, as well as experience with buying and selling. . . . They had the kind of incentives and experience common in a market economy but denied American slaves for two centuries."[34]

Pushing the cultural capital component of success might have appealed to conservative anthropologists and economists with little knowledge of the black experience in the United States. But this approach soon earned Sowell the ire of distinguished scholars in the field.[35] Pointing out that his assumptions about the American and West Indian slave systems had been refuted long ago, these scholars confirmed that foot-dragging, work-evasion, duplicity, and theft had in fact been common features of *all* slave societies, including the Caribbean.[36] And a similar observation could also be made about slave dependence and slave entrepreneurialism, since neither trait was universally present in one system nor universally absent in the other.[37] Sowell's argument, while provocative, did not appear to stand up to empirical scrutiny.

There were other problems with this Caribbean case study, for even if Sowell could establish the West Indian immigrants' superior ancestral relationship to the soil, he still had to prove its impact on a history unfolding a world away in time and place. In more than a century since slavery's demise, critics asked, had nothing of significance happened to black West Indians or Americans that could also explain the discrepancy in achievement between the two groups?[38] But the stubborn Sowell was unmoved in the face of such criticism. Culture, to him, was a static "thing" standing outside the sweep of human history, resisting change with an almost genetic immutability.[39] Although the predisposition toward certain cultural traits was not innate or inherent, as in nature, it was still somehow assumed to be transferred between members of various groups. But nowhere did Sowell explain how culture came to be self-organizing and self-producing. In failing to do so, he appeared to create what William Wilson called a "circular argument," "inferring cultural values from the behavior to be explained and using these values as the explanation of the behavior itself."[40] Such an approach was unhelpful, the historian Ian McKay noted, not only "because it deals with an imaginary world but because it offers insufficient explanations of a real one."[41]

Although Sowell's cultural thesis may have lacked intellectual originality—scholars had been discussing the economic mobility of African Americans relative to black West Indians since the 1920s[42]—its political utility to a conservative movement seeking to deny the reality of American racism remained indisputable. But in the late 1980s the thesis came under renewed attack. Two stratification analysts, Reynolds Farley and Walter Allan, scrutinized Sowell's data on post-1965 West Indian mobility and discovered that his claims had been "quite exaggerated." It turned out that West Indian representation in the professions was not double that of black Americans, "since in 1980, 14 percent of the foreign-born blacks compared with 11 percent of the native blacks held professional or executive jobs."[43] Farley's and Allan's research also revealed that, though West Indian family income was once 94 percent of the national average, that figure had fallen to 80 percent by 1980, akin to the average for African Americans.[44] Optimistic claims about West Indian entrepreneurial success could no longer be sustained, since in Reagan's America little separated these black immigrants from the native-born black population. In moderate academic circles, Sowell's reputation as an economist lay in tatters, his data seemingly more the product of his conservative imagination than objective empirical research.

If Farley and Allan had disturbed the soil around the edges of Sowell's thesis, by the 1990s a number of scholars hostile to cultural analyses had destroyed its roots. Building on the earlier works of Ira de A. Reid[45] and Stanley Lieberson,[46] Jerry Watts asked: If West Indian culture convincingly explained why West Indians were marginally better off than African Americans in the United States, how was the less-than-sterling achievement of this same culture in the poverty-stricken Caribbean to be explained?[47] The black Milton Friedman, however, remained silent. The problem with Sowell's work, Watts and other scholars suggested, was that it consistently failed to recognize "that there may be something socially significant about the immigration experience itself that selects out West

Indians who are highly motivated."[48] It was well known, for instance, that the Caribbean immigrants who docked on America's shores during the first half of the twentieth century were hardly typical West Indians. Rather, they came from an exclusive sector of West Indian society whose uniqueness and complexity the description "West Indian" never satisfactorily captured.[49] To compare the success of this privileged middle-class elite with the "failure" of poor African Americans in the Jim Crow era and to conclude, simplistically, from this that racism was not an obstacle to black advancement in the United States appeared not only unsophisticated but entirely unfounded.

After 1965, moreover, when the victories of civil rights began to improve African Americans' access to education and jobs, and the new immigration opened the nation's doors to less skilled Caribbean migrants, the long-standing disparity between the two groups had narrowed, in a further blow to Sowell's thesis. But still more could have been done to demonstrate the thesis' intellectual inadequacy. A comparative study of black and white immigrants to the United States during the first half of the twentieth century would have revealed a striking fact missing in the literature on Sowell. Although it is well known that black first-generation West Indian immigrants usually brought to America a higher level of education and skills than their white European counterparts, and achieved greater success, less known is that the second generation was actually outperformed by second-generation whites.[50] That the children of skilled, middle-class West Indians eventually found themselves behind the children of unskilled, white Europeans was arguably a testament to the strength of American racism to restrict the life chances of *all* black people.

The West Indian cultural model embraced by Sowell to deny the significance of racism in American life may have been discredited intellectually. But other black conservative explanations for contemporary racial disadvantage continued to proliferate and penetrate politically. Culture, however, remained the group's preferred analytical lens: specifically how welfare had destroyed the culture of the black poor and, in doing so, the fabric that had once sustained proud black communities. Williams, whose thinking usually mirrored Sowell's, condemned as "simply nonsense" the old "slavery damaged" argument. While some black Americans may have emerged from slavery "not ready for prime time," their circumstances over a century ago, he insisted, could not explain the crime and illegitimacy that was ravaging black communities in the modern era.[51] Pointing to Herbert Gutman's classic study *The Black Family in Slavery and Freedom, 1750–1925*,[52] Williams noted that, in the late nineteenth century, black communities were intact—"five out of six children under the age of 6 lived with both parents."[53] As late as 1940, "illegitimacy among blacks was only 19 percent" and African Americans had a "marriage rate slightly higher than whites." "If what we see today in many black neighborhoods . . . are the vestiges and legacies of slavery," Williams asked, "how come that social pathology wasn't much worse when blacks were just two or three generations out of slavery? Might it be that slavery's legacy and vestiges have a way, like diabetes, of skipping generations . . . six generations?"[54]

These were challenging questions. Seemingly oblivious to his previous position that peoples' cultural characteristics endured over centuries and determined the fate of their descendants, Sowell endorsed Williams's line of questioning with conviction. "Whatever may be the real causes of the very different patterns among blacks in the world of today must be sought in the twentieth century, not in the era before emancipation," he now wrote.[55] Gutman's statistics suggested "the broken families of today are a legacy of our own times and our own ill-advised notions and policies." A contradiction thus lay at the heart of Sowell's work. In a number of his academic books, he continued to maintain that contemporary black "dysfunction" was best understood as a cultural "legacy of slavery." But in other works, he categorically rejected this interpretation, dismissing it as yet "another distortion of history."[56] Such analytical inconsistency might simply be put down to bad scholarship, an inability on the part of the author to master complex arguments. But Sowell's idiosyncratic stance might also be understood in terms of the political dynamics operating within Reagan's America.

"We fought a war on poverty," Reagan declared, "and poverty won."[57] Conservatives had long worried about the consequences of "growing up in the stultifying atmosphere of programs that reward people for *not* working, programs that separate families and doom children to repeat the cycle in their own adulthood."[58] Their social concerns now found political expression in Reaganism. Reagan was determined to launch a full-frontal attack on the welfare system—to reduce federal expenditure, eliminate dependency, and encourage more personal and parental responsibility. To these ends, he slashed spending on food stamps, unemployment insurance, health care, education, job training, housing, and most significantly, AFDC.[59] It was increasingly clear from these actions that the Reagan administration opposed the visions and goals of 1960s liberal policy-makers, including their commitment to a guaranteed minimum income. These liberals, in devising social policy, had started with the question, "How can we help the poor?" By contrast, Reagan and his supporters asked, "How can we cut costs and get people to work?"

In his war against welfare, the new president reserved special criticism for AFDC, insisting that these handouts had destroyed the urban ghettos by causing young blacks to exploit benefits rather than work for a living. In many ways, his view of these people represented a significant departure from nineteenth-century perceptions of the downtrodden in the slums. Then conservatives had seen the poor as intemperate, shiftless, and immoral.[60] Reagan, however, saw the 1980s poor as often rational calculators of their own self-interest, strategically living off the public purse. Nowhere was his view more evident than in relation to AFDC recipients, a disproportionate number of whom were black and female. Cleverly juxtaposing race and welfare dependency, Reagan told what turned out to be an enduring political anecdote. He cited a Chicago "welfare queen" who had swindled $150,000 from government, using eighty aliases, thirty addresses, a dozen social security cards, and four fictional dead husbands. Ordinary Americans, predictably, were outraged. Reagan dutifully pledged to scale back welfare, the image of the welfare queen driving her "welfare Cadillac" forever cemented in American political mythology.[61]

Echoing Charles Murray and other New Rightists opposed to safety nets for the "undeserving poor," the black conservatives became the face of the president's campaign to cut welfare entitlements to millions of black Americans. In this conservative milieu, the "legacy of slavery" was no longer as effective an explanation for contemporary black social misery; it certainly did not carry the same political weight as explanations that blamed the very liberal social policies that Reagan was seeking to jettison. Thus, the "foot-dragging, work avoiding patterns" (and the "duplicity and theft") Sowell once cited as a "legacy of slavery" to account for modern black disadvantage were forgotten, replaced by a politically more useful discourse that impugned the welfare state as the primary generator of contemporary black ills. "The issue," Sowell wrote at the time, "is not that the government gives too much help to the poor. The problem is that government creates too much harm to the poor."[62] Directing their message squarely at poor African Americans, other black conservatives agreed with Sowell's assessment, calling for initiatives that encouraged individual self-reliance in contrast to the dependence engendered by The System as it existed.[63]

What had the welfare state done to African Americans that was so damaging—in the minds of these black conservatives—as to warrant dramatic downsizing if not immediate dissolution? These intellectuals agreed on a number of points. Not only were the relevant social programs too centralized and bureaucratic, with very little of the money filtering down to the poor, but they had increased dependency and encouraged behavior that was incompatible with mainstream work and family obligations. By "subsidizing unwed pregnancy," welfare was said to have destroyed the foundation of the black heritage—the black family—and set in motion the dialectic among personal and social forces that were at the root of modern black disadvantage.[64] Illegitimacy was cast by the black conservatives as the cause of just about all the black poor's problems: "Boys growing up without fathers are less likely to become civilized. The values in communities without fathers are adolescent values: predatory sex, violence and self-destructive behavior. Our welfare system produces what is known in the insurance industry as 'moral hazard.' Young women who lose self-control, are promiscuous and engage in early sex activity are rewarded with welfare benefits."[65] Because of welfare, young black women increasingly turned to the federal government for support instead of to the fathers of their children. And because of welfare, young black men increasingly eschewed their parental responsibilities, knowing that the state would effectively serve as their surrogate. It was little wonder, then, according to black conservatives, that the state had supplanted the family as the primary institution in the lives of disadvantaged blacks. And it was also little wonder that the accompanying proliferation of single-parent families and erosion of moral authority in the black home had led to the "re-barbarization" of neighborhoods, fueling criminal behavior in the inner city and the staggering statistics on black juvenile delinquency.[66] Williams summed up the black conservatives' view of the relationship between the welfare state and the family forcefully; as an institution, he insisted, it had "done to the black family what slavery, Jim Crowism, and the rankest racism could never have done."[67]

If the negative cultural effects of welfare were clear to all black conservatives, so too was welfare's failure to improve the economic fortunes of the black poor. These intellectuals noted that the condition of poor African Americans had deteriorated since the early 1970s—ironically after the welfare state had burgeoned to "unprecedented proportions."[68] This was never the intention, but it had certainly been the result. By changing the incentive structure and trapping the black poor in a culture of dependency, liberal policy-makers had effectively removed the motivation for these people to work hard and improve their material circumstances.[69] In contrast to white conservatives, then, who typically sought a reduction in the welfare state to meet the requirements of supply-side economics or to appease angry public sentiment, Sowell and company argued against generous welfare entitlements on the grounds that they had compromised the interests of poor black communities.

That the black conservatives as a group were fundamentally opposed to the welfare state was beyond dispute. And yet it would be wrong to suppose that these intellectuals' opposition always took the same form, since their analyses at times varied. Subscribing to Friedman's capitalist rationality, some within the cohort questioned any approach to poverty alleviation that involved a role for government. Sowell and Williams—and to an extent, Thomas, Parker, and Wortham—argued that fighting poverty with welfare instead of economic growth was destined not only to fail but to exacerbate the existing problems of the black poor.[70] Many Americans had voiced discontent with government in the 1970s and 1980s for allocating public funds excessively to blacks and allowing them a "free ride" at the wider tax-paying population's expense. While agreeing with this general sentiment, these black conservatives' criticism of government flowed primarily from their philosophical conviction that the market was the only sure road to black advancement, and correspondingly, that state interference in the market was the chief cause of black subordination.

The practical consequences of not allowing the market to function naturally, according to these intellectuals, were dramatically illustrated by the contemporary economic predicament of the most poverty-stricken wing of black America. Since the late 1960s, Williams noted, the government had spent $2.5 trillion on urban renewal and poverty programs. The results were as devastating as they were revealing: "Cities in the steepest decline are those that receive the most federal aid, have the highest tax rate, and have the highest spending per capita. Cities spending the most on education have the poorest student academic performance. If a man from Mars asked you how to identify cities that spent the most money per capita, it would be easy. Just tell the guy to look for cities with the steepest decay and decline, greatest crime rates, greatest family breakdown, most rotten schools, and filthiest streets."[71]

Parker endorsed Williams's sentiments, maintaining that it was "not the role of government at any level . . . to provide food, clothing and housing" for the poor.[72] When government transgressed its proper role as a protector of individual rights, Thomas and Wortham argued, there were bound to be negative repercussions.[73] And so there had been. While in the 1960s black poverty had been steadily declining, at the very height of the welfare state in the 1970s, these black conservatives noted that this decline had ceased and black families experienced a rise in impoverishment.[74] The problem, then, was not how government spent its money on the black poor, but that government would spend money on the black poor at all.

Casting his eyes over the past, Sowell took this critique of state intervention further. Responding to the observation that when government failed to take "responsibilities for upward black mobility and equality and justice no one did," Sowell commented, "No, I would say just the opposite. The government has been quite active in suppressing the advancement of blacks in the United States. . . . The great achievement of civil rights organizations has been getting the government off the backs of blacks, notably in the South with Jim Crow laws, but in other parts of the country with other kinds of laws and other kinds of practices. When these civil rights groups tried to get government to play a positive role, so-called, that's when they not only failed but when they've had counterproductive results."[75]

Leaving to one side the obvious point that the federal government had sometimes been a friend to black people—the abolition of slavery and segregation, for example, would surely have been impossible without it[76]—Sowell's argument was perhaps most significant in its embodiment of the aggressive antistatism that defined the American polity of the 1980s. "We cannot be tied to the old ways of solving our economic and racial problems," Reagan told a gathering of NAACP leaders in 1981.[77] "The Government can provide subsistence, yes, but it seldom moves people up the economic ladder. . . . Free enterprise is a powerful workhouse that can solve many problems of the black community that government alone can no longer solve."[78] Williams backed the president's position and, in doing so, provided insight into what an alternative approach to poverty might look like: "Many programs that people talk about wiping out appear to me to be cancers on society, and normally, when you excise a cancer, you do not worry about what you will replace it with. You just take it out. I think a lot of programs in the United States represent such cancers on our society that we need not worry about replacing."[79]

Sowell agreed: "No matter how disastrously some policy has turned out, anyone who criticizes it can expect to hear: 'But what would you replace it with?' When you put out a fire, what do you replace it with?"[80] The answer, Sowell suggested, was "with nothing." Rejecting a role for government in principle, but concerned also about its impact on the black poor in practice, some black conservatives sought a return to the imagined halcyon days of pre–New Deal laissez-faire capitalism.[81] They appeared to subscribe to Benjamin Franklin's philosophy that "the best way of doing good to the poor, is not making them easy in poverty, but leading or driving them out of it."[82]

As conservative blacks, Loury and Woodson would also express concerns about the pernicious effects of welfare on poor black Americans. But their misgivings were determined less by ideology—a rationalist aversion to all state intervention—than pragmatic frustration at the apparent failure of government to improve the conditions under which these people lived. Not so concerned with proving that Hayek and Friedman were right and that Keynes and Galbraith were wrong, these two intellectuals simply drew attention to the deteriorating condition of the black underclass and suggested the need for a new approach to attack the scourge of racial poverty. Since the late 1960s, Woodson argued, the "government-knows-best policy" had "herded low-income families into high-rise buildings that bred crime and frustration, discouraged the work ethic, fostered dependency on public assistance and stifled the initiative of small entrepreneurs with programmed-to-fail bureaucratic restrictions."[83] But rather than denouncing government—simplistically and for all time—as the greatest enemy of the black poor, he and Loury wondered what government might do (rather than not do) in the future to improve these people's circumstances. In contrast to some of their fellow black conservatives, then, both men saw a meliorative role for the state in addressing problems such as a failing economy, serious criminality, inadequate educational preparation, and social pathology.[84]

It was only important that government's involvement in the lives of the black poor be tempered by respect for the power of political measures on the one hand and the primacy of personal autonomy on the other. "The main public policy consideration," in Loury's view, was "to avoid rewarding vice (i.e. individual actions which retard [individuals'] ability to become self-supporting—like having a baby before being able to properly care for and support it), and to avoid punishing virtue (i.e. individual actions which promote independence)."[85] Woodson agreed, adding that "without abandoning programs that sustain the poor, policies that breed dependence must be shunned and those that promote development embraced."[86] Rather than enlist and remunerate bureaucrats to help the black poor, he asked, why not transfer federal monies directly to these people so they might help themselves? It was they, after all, who had "first-hand knowledge" of the problems and they who had the greatest investment in the outcome.[87] Woodson's proposal, however, seemed unworkable to Loury, who offered his own—arguably more practical—alternative to the existing welfare system. The former Harvard economist supported the retention of state supports for poor blacks but insisted on the imposition of mandatory work requirements for recipients. Such a system, he argued, would encourage in these people a sense of social obligation, thereby affirming their human dignity.[88] Unlike some other black conservatives, Loury and Woodson did not believe that government—through the welfare state—had caused the black poor's economic and cultural misery, only that it was implicated. Their response, then, was to call not for welfare's elimination but, rather, for welfare's reform. Leaving to one side their implicit observation that modern black disadvantage was more complex than some of their intellectual allies had hitherto supposed, Loury and Woodson's own interpretations of racial inequality—and how to deal with it—seemed at least to have merit. But it was not only what they said about the black poor that convinced others of the sincerity of their concern, but how they said it and to whom. While always quick to lament the erosion of morality inside the black community and to call attention to family breakdown, neither man appeared comfortable with the tough love approach championed by Sowell, Williams, Thomas, Parker, and Wortham. In Loury and Woodson's work, the black poor were presented as people with dignity who had the capacity to help themselves and lead better lives. Both claimed to be aware of an untapped reservoir of human potential in black America, having written for black publications, spoken before black audiences and—in Woodson's case—organized grassroots initiatives with and for thousands of black inner-city residents throughout the 1980s and 1990s.

Speaking and writing for white right-wing audiences only, the black conservative proponents of tough love had no such affiliations with the black community. And this detachment appeared to have bred an ugly indifference to the plight of the black poor. "Our society may be headed for a dead end in the long run," Sowell wrote belligerently, "if we don't start backing up the decent people . . . instead of embracing the punks and bums who seem to fascinate deep thinkers in the media and academia."[89] Failing to distinguish between those who had made mistakes and were now trying to improve their lives and those who might be labeled the "worst criminals," Sowell simply questioned the legitimacy of helping "black trash."[90] "One of the consequences of such notions as entitlements," he argued, "is that people who have contributed nothing to society feel that society owes them something, apparently just for being nice enough to grace us with their presence."[91] Similarly harsh sentiments were expressed by Williams, who had constructed an almost identical binary to Sowell's of a world neatly composed of decent people on the one side and "hoodlums" on the other.[92] But arguably the most astonishing stand was taken by Thomas, who would exploit his own sister to make a political point about the mindset of African Americans living on welfare. "She gets mad when the mailman is late with her welfare check," Thomas told the Fairmont Conference. "What's worse is that now her kids feel entitled to the check too. They have no motivation for doing better or getting out of that situation."[93]

It is hardly surprising that dependence on government should be deplored within the American capitalist system—a system that relies on the idea of free-floating, autonomous individuals to sustain itself. But in the 1980s and 1990s black conservatives—to varying degrees—elevated this long-standing national concern over dependence to a new level, some going as far as to equate reliance on welfare with slavery as they implored blacks to get off the "liberal plantation."[94] These intellectuals' alarm at black "intergenerational poverty" needed to be taken especially seriously, since millions of Americans now evidently believed that dysfunctional behavior was *the* defining characteristic of the black poor, seemingly transmitted from one generation to the next through the scourge of the immoral black single mother.[95] Prodded by an overly generous and undemanding liberal state, the argument went, black women had effectively chosen their own fate by preferring welfare to work and single parenthood to marriage. In Reagan's America, the political utility of these arguments was beyond dispute, adding ammunition to the president's unfolding war against the welfare state. But the question for scholars was: how reliable were these arguments intellectually?

A number of studies from the 1980s and 1990s that focused on the intergenerational poverty theory—increasingly identified with the black conservatives—found its assumptions to be flawed and its conclusions exaggerated.[96] The evidence, although scattered, was voluminous. Taken as a whole, these studies threw serious doubt on the black conservatives' thesis that black underclass (welfare-fueled) culture was the major cause of self-perpetuating poverty. Most poor blacks, it turned out, only made use of AFDC periodically, shifting between low-paid employment and government support. Their children were not disproportionately the recipients of welfare.[97] What is more, two out of three blacks were poor *before* becoming single parents and certainly all were poor before becoming eligible for public assistance.[98] When combined with the fact that states with high benefit levels tended to have lower rates of black illegitimacy than states with low benefit levels, yet further doubt was cast on these intellectuals' claim that the welfare state was responsible for the explosion of black out-of-wedlock births and female-headed families.[99] To state categorically, then, as some black conservatives did, that social provision had caused family breakdown and made the black poor poor was problematic to say the least. Given that only a small percentage of welfare recipients fit the description of "permanent welfare dependent" anyway, how could some black conservatives seriously insist that this phenomenon was a crisis tantamount to slavery?

The answer, simply, was that they could not: most black conservative critiques of dependency were too selective and ideological to be insightful in an intellectual sense. And yet despite a number of empirical refutations of their work, the "failure of welfare" argument, to which they subscribed, retained a firm grip on the public imagination. Clearly, the most vigorous and convincing response to the black conservatives (and others) who championed this position came from the distinguished sociologist William Wilson. Armed with case studies and reams of statistical data, Wilson argued in *The Truly Disadvantaged* that the deteriorating condition of black urban life was a consequence neither of liberal social policies nor of immoral black behavior, but was tied to broad structural changes in society and the economy that had taken place in the 1970s.[100] The shifting base of the U.S. economy from manufacturing to service industries, he believed, was the causal root of the black underclass, systematically reducing opportunities for black mobility by wiping out many of the blue-collar jobs that inner-city blacks had traditionally relied upon to escape poverty. Lacking the skills to compete for jobs in the new service economy, Wilson continued, young black men of the inner city were also negatively affected by two other developments: first, the suburbanization of industry, which cut them off geographically from new entry-level employment; and second, the increasing absence of community role models as large numbers of middle-class blacks moved to the suburbs as economic beneficiaries of the civil rights movement.[101] In time, Wilson's thesis was endorsed by countless other scholars of the African American experience.[102] These scholars shared his conviction that, if the behavioral patterns and impoverishment of so many black urban dwellers were genuinely to be understood, they could not be divorced from the new social and economic realities that confronted these people.

The principal shortcoming of the black conservatives' failure of welfare thesis, liberals argued, was that it did not account for the real historical processes that had shaped welfare policy and its impact. The fact that roughly 32 million jobs were lost in the 1970s as a result of shutdowns, relocations, and scaling back operations was surely significant to any assessment of black urban life and culture in the 1980s.[103] Increasingly cut off from the structures of opportunity and socially isolated in the inner cities, the black poor's worsening predicament could not legitimately be reduced to a set of welfare-fueled behavioral attributes. Their situation appeared far more complex than this. In all likelihood, for many of these people, welfare served as one of the few remaining lifelines in hard times. Although the black conservatives were certainly right to argue that transfer payments could not win a war on poverty, they were surely wrong to insist that these payments did not "sustain some boats that would otherwise sink, given the high rate of unemployment."[104]

Since Wilson and other prominent liberal scholars saw no empirical grounds for supposing that welfare had contributed to the deterioration of black inner-city life, the challenge for policy-makers, in their view, was not to let the welfare state wither away so that blacks might one day work their way out of poverty in the competitive economy. Rather, it was to rebuild the welfare state on grounds that might one day overcome the divisions of race and class at the heart of American society. Rising up to counter the black conservatives' antiwelfare treatise, these scholars advocated substantial government involvement through universal programs for education, job training, social services, and economic growth to improve conditions in the ghetto. Their argument was premised on the plausible assumption that the nation either invested in social programs in the short term, or paid for welfare and prisons in the long term. Poor blacks, they concluded, like all Americans, were desperate to work, marry, and raise children in clean and safe neighborhoods but had been prevented from doing so by impersonal forces largely beyond their control.[105]

Policy-makers were not the only ones who confronted a challenge in these difficult times; so did scholars. Their challenge, according to progressives, was to take history seriously in their assessments of the welfare state—something the black conservative proponents of tough love had hitherto failed to do. Sowell and company, for instance, seemed unable (or unwilling) to grasp that the welfare state was a compromise in American life between progressives seeking broad subsistence rights for the poor and conservatives arguing for unfettered markets.[106] That such a compromise should exhibit flaws was hardly surprising; even the radical Cornel West conceded, "the reinforcing of dependent mentalities and the unsettling of the family are two such flaws."[107] But West's acknowledgment of welfare's limitations was not an expression of support for the massive cutbacks to social provision that defined the Reagan era—cutbacks the black conservatives advocated as essential. Indeed, in the light of high and rising unemployment, he and other progressives insisted that these cutbacks would not only fail to promote the self-sufficient and stable families Sowell and company predicted, but produce even more social dislocation and more broken black families.[108] "This was so," West concluded, "because without jobs to be productive citizens," the black poor become even more prone toward dysfunction— the major proximate symptom of the structural transformation within urban economies.[109]

With the exception of Loury, the black conservatives failed to discuss this critical structural transformation in their work, probably for fear that it would diminish the political value of their tirades against the welfare state and black culture. Intellectually, this oversight was astonishing. For Sowell and Williams, as academic economists, the oversight appeared especially striking, confirmation, if any was needed, of both men's proclivity to put partisanship on the race question above scholarship. But even Loury's analysis of the effects of 1970s deindustrialization on the culture of the black urban poor failed to appreciate the importance of occupational stability and economic security to people's dignity and sense of themselves. Forging a connection between economics and culture, he believed, smacked of mechanistic determinism and did not account for the "mysteries of human motivation."[110] Perhaps. And yet as to what did account for the mysteries of human motivation—in this case, the issue of behavior in inner-city black communities—Loury was often unclear, offering vague hypotheses about spiritual matters and the declining significance of God.[111]

If the black conservatives' attitude to welfare lacked historical sophistication and social policy astuteness, their conceptualization of the black poor's "defective" culture—hardly original as we have seen—also lacked analytical clarity. A decade earlier sociologist William Ryan had denounced the Edward Banfield–driven discourse on black pathology as "blaming the victim"—an attempt at "justifying inequality by finding defects in the victims of inequality."[112] Entering the political lexicon in 1971, the phrase rather ingeniously highlighted the tendency of conservative social science to reduce complex social phenomena to an individual level of analysis, thereby deflecting attention away from the structures of inequality and onto the behavior of the people whose lives were most adversely affected by structures. In the 1980s and 1990s, a host of progressive scholars co-opted the essence of the Ryan model and deployed it with minor amendments to attack the conceptual basis of the black conservatives' emergent poverty thesis.

Whereas liberals like Wilson were mindful of a link between culture and social structure—tracing poor blacks' behavior primarily to the jobs crisis in the economy—radicals tended to reject the black conservatives' cultural focus altogether. Adolph Reed and Robin Kelley were among the most influential of these radical scholars. To them, the very concept of a ghetto underclass was unsound, blurring the analytical categories of race, class, and culture in order to shed light on the social production of something ambiguous called "dysfunction." According to Reed and Kelley, these categories (especially culture) needed to be disentangled so that the real structures that kept blacks trapped in poverty could be addressed. To complement Wilson's economics-based structural analysis, these scholars offered a race-based structural analysis and showed culture to be something more complex than the black conservatives had thought.[113]

How, they essentially asked, was the black underclass to be accurately identified? Not only was the size of this social grouping unclear, so were the various aggregations of peoples said to comprise it. "Criminals, welfare recipients, single mothers, absent fathers, alcohol and drug abusers, and gun-toting youth," Kelley pointed out, could not be neatly fitted into the one class.[114] It was absurd, for instance, to link criminality and teenage pregnancy as hallmarks of a common deviant black culture. Out-of-wedlock births, Reed added, were hardly evidence of dysfunction: "If a thirty-five-year-old lawyer decides to have a baby without seal of approval from church or state or enduring male affiliation, we do not consider her to be acting pathologically; we may even laud her independence and refusal to knuckle under to patriarchal conventions. Why does such a birth become pathological when it occurs in the maternity ward in Lincoln Hospital in the South Bronx, say, rather than within the pastel walls of an alternative birthing center?"[115] "If a woman's decision expresses pathology because she makes it in poverty," Reed continued, then underclass theorists such as the black conservatives had engaged in circular reasoning: "she is poor because she is pathological because she is poor."[116] Rather than stigmatize the black poor, this radical black intellectual called on social critics to recognize that what they understood as dysfunction was in fact observable across racial and class lines, throughout American society.[117] Kelley agreed with Reed's assessment, suggesting that if only scholars were to "flip the script" and apply the "same principles to people with higher incomes, who are presumed to be functional and normative," the absurdity of the notion of a black underclass, defined by a culture of poverty, would become apparent. Borrowing from the political scientist Charles Henry, Kelley noted the existence of a "culture of wealth" where "drug use and white collar crime" were rampant and where a "permanent cycle of divorce" and "forced separation through boarding schools" were seemingly the norm. In the light of such dysfunction, why, he wondered, was the black underclass frequently called upon to emulate the values and behavioral standards of the white middle class?[118]

Since some percentage of all Americans abused drugs, committed crime, and grew up in imperfect family settings, both Reed and Kelley concluded that it was entirely misleading to assert that cultural dysfunction had somehow produced black poverty and fueled the black underclass.[119] And since "dependence," too, was a subjective "thing"— dependence on welfare, for instance, was widely thought to breed pathology while dependence on military contracts evidenced a patriotic commitment to country—it was surely also misleading to depict this condition as in any way contributing to a culture of poverty.[120] If none of these factors could be shown to cause poverty, Reed asked, why focus on them at all "in the context of policy-oriented discussions about poverty?"[121] So long as analysts persisted in isolating the behavior of the black underclass and proposing measures to redeem the deficiencies of the individuals thought to comprise it, the result would be shallow value-judgments, inadequate policies, and persistent racial inequality. Reed's and Kelley's impassioned challenges to the reasoning embraced by black conservatives were compelling.

Ignoring this criticism, however, Sowell and company continued to present detailed depictions of an objectively existing black underclass. But while these intellectuals were able to find evidence to support their argument about the concentration of crime, welfare dependency, and homelessness in poor black communities, they could not sincerely deduce from their research that a lack of individual or cultural will explained these problems. Content to deal in generalizations, they continued simply to *assume* that dysfunction lay at the root of the problem. Without interviewing the black poor and despite rejecting these people's understandings of their own plight, the black conservatives presumed to know their social and cultural motivations. Clearly this approach was problematic—so problematic that it prompted Kelley to declare that such claims about black life had "about as much basis in hard evidence as anything coming out of the dozens, but without the subtlety, irony and humor."[122]

The black conservatives' analyses of black poverty might have been condemned by progressives for lacking rigor and depth. But the *concern* Sowell and company routinely expressed for poor blacks gave their work racial legitimacy on the political front and allowed them to promote often radical free-market approaches to assist these people. *Concern* for the black poor's pride and independence—not being treated as victims—was used to criticize enforced dependency by government, as evidenced in the notion that individual initiative and responsibility were severely undermined by government programs. Once the poor's capacity to act for themselves had been agreed upon in principle, their behavior was subjected to even greater scrutiny by black conservatives as the root cause of their condition. Soon, moreover, this concern with what the black poor had been doing *to* themselves was translated into what they needed to do *for* themselves. The black conservative cohort asserted that big government and the self-destructive behavior that had purportedly characterized black life since the 1960s needed urgently to end. But their recommendations were more explicit than this. Only a revitalized self-help agenda geared to meet the demands of contemporary American life could truly restore black dignity and confidence.

Referred to by one commentator as the "bedrock" of contemporary black conservatism,[123] "self-help" emerged as a powerful slogan during the Reagan-Bush era as the federal government retreated from its commitment to employ the state as a vehicle of support for the poor and marginalized in society. By the mid-1990s debates over self-help were ubiquitous within the African American community, as the ideological orientation and political success of Farrakhan's controversial Million Man March clearly demonstrated.[124] The central demand of the 1995 March was blunt if strikingly familiar: black men needed to atone for their sins. In the future, Farrakhan instructed, state provisions were to be rejected, black businesses supported, and greater personal responsibility exercised as part of the push for black renewal. But the march largely ignored public policy issues such as affirmative action and welfare reform. In a message that meshed perfectly with the conservative agenda of the preceding fifteen years, almost one million black men left the nation's capital effectively acknowledging that in them lay the problems of black America and only in them lay the solutions.[125] The March, one commentator noted wryly, thus acquired the dubious distinction of being the first "protest" in history in which people had gathered to protest themselves.[126]

Although the March belonged to Louis Farrakhan, its agenda arguably belonged to the black conservatives, who had peddled similar views
in the 1980s and 1990s without attracting significant black support. The
black poor ought not to wait for solutions to be "parachuted in by middle
class, professional service providers,"[127] they had argued; rather, self-help
needed to be embraced as a "philosophy of life."[128] Implicit in this call
was the judgment that disadvantaged African Americans had to assume
responsibility for improving their condition. Since poverty was "largely
a transitory experience for people . . . willing to work,"[129] the black
poor, by working or studying, would most likely overcome poverty and
get ahead. Deterministic views of human achievement were rejected by
the black conservatives, who refused to see the life chances of inner-city
black youth as inevitably shaped by ghetto conditions. It was Wortham,
undoubtedly, who best encapsulated the individualistic (or "bootstraps")
essence of their thought. "Frederick Douglass made it," she wrote, "It
stands to reason that somewhere, this day, there is a young black person
determining that he will not be the next generation of his family on
welfare. . . . The central idea of individualism is the autonomy and sovereignty of individual consciousness—that is, free will. And this is a feature
of human *nature*, independent of historical or social circumstances."[130]

Wortham's rejection of determinism and embrace of individualism
and self-help were a function of her devotion to the libertarianism of
Ayn Rand, a white intellectual. But other black conservatives endorsed
self-help by invoking the memory and wisdom of Booker T. Washington.
According to Loury, Washington understood that "when the effect of
past oppression has been to leave people in a diminished state, the attainment of true equality with other former oppressors cannot much
depend on his generosity but must ultimately derive from an elevation
of their selves above the state of diminishment."[131] Of course, by elevation Washington did not mean political elevation but economic elevation through the work ethic and the accumulation of capital. Nearly
a century later, this was essentially what contemporary black conservatives meant too. Since the 1980s these intellectuals had played down
the importance of political rights and promoted strategies of economic
self-help to improve the black social condition. Rooted in organic and
voluntary associations—the mediating structures of family, church, and
local schools—and interacting with the dynamics of the modern market
economy, these strategies were thought to have the potential to do more
than just improve the black condition: they were said to have the potential to deliver social and economic parity.

Self-help bromides were predictably invoked by the black conservatives to sell this message. "The victimizer might knock you down," Woodson maintained, "but the victim is the one who has to get himself up."[132]

In the same spirit, Loury insisted it was "absolutely vital that blacks distinguish the fault which may be attributable to racism and the responsibility for relieving that condition."[133] Since "to be dependent" was apparently "to be degraded," Williams implored contemporary blacks to heed Frederick Douglass's 1853 warning, "Learn trades or starve," and to recapture the "can-do-spirit."[134] American history was said by these intellectuals to be littered with examples of black people who, with great determination and diligence, had struggled against severe economic hardship to become self-sufficient.[135] Thomas claimed proudly that his grandfather, Myers Anderson, had been one such person, implying that young black Americans might do well to follow his example. Anderson, according to Thomas, had presided over:

an environment with very strict rules, an environment that put a premium on self-help, an environment that did not preach any kind of reliance on government—there was a feeling that you had an obligation to help other people, but it didn't come from the government. For example, we lived out in the country during the summer, and so we'd shop once a month. We had chickens and hogs and corn and beans on the farm, but the staples we had to go to the grocery to get. When we came back my grandfather would go by people's houses, and he would just drop groceries on the porch. Or if we harvested something, he'd just put it there and leave. Somebody's house burned down, he'd go and start marking it off and we'd start building another house.[136]

In addition to their emotional and philosophical attachments to self-help strategies, some black conservatives claimed to have evidence that these strategies worked in practice. In empirical terms, Sowell insisted, the verdict of history was clear: economic self-help had proven the single most effective catalyst for social mobility in democratic capitalist polities. In the United States, for example, immigrant groups that had traditionally relied on themselves—most notably the Jews and the Japanese—had prospered while those that looked to the political system for assistance—namely blacks—had struggled.[137] Sowell elaborated: "If you made a list of those groups that have risen from poverty to affluence and particularly those who've done it most rapidly or against the greatest opposition, they are the groups that have either avoided politics or are not terribly successful at politics."[138] The implication here was that African Americans would have been better off had they only eschewed politics. History appeared to reinforce this point in Sowell's view, for even where African Americans had succeeded in achieving some semblance of economic equality, he argued, it had been despite rather than because of government: "The 'self-help' approach simply recognizes that blacks do not have unlimited time or resources to put into political crusades, nor are these crusades likely to produce as much net benefit as putting time and resources into developing yourself or your community."[139]

In the light of the obvious point that the political civil rights movement had delivered more economic benefits to African Americans than any other crusade in the nation's history, how serious and significant did scholars and politicians consider Sowell's and other black conservatives' reflections on self-help to be? First, the historical significance of the term self-help needed to be unpacked. It is important to recognize that early black self-help efforts were a function of necessity in a hostile and violent racist environment marked by the absence of a developed welfare state. It is also important to recognize that, in the post-Reconstruction era, Washington's self-help agenda was sustained by white philanthropy to offset the woeful services provided blacks in the segregated South. At the very time that blacks were being implored to embrace self-help, however, the federal government was distributing a "half-billion acres of public land to speculators and monopolists" through land grants.[140] What is more, in time, politicians and business elites pounced on successful black self-help initiatives as a reason to "deny the necessity of broader public responsibility for major social needs."[141] And black economic disadvantage remained. Prior to civil rights, poverty, mitigated only by mutual aid and private charity, was a way of life for the majority of African Americans. Considering that as late as 1959 the poverty rate for blacks stood at 55.1 percent, the self-help formula championed by contemporary black conservatives to alleviate black inequality appeared somewhat unpersuasive.[142]

Although there were clear historical problems associated with these intellectuals' view of black self-help, evidence for the strategy's effectiveness was also said to be rooted in the contemporary world, with the "liberating" power of free-market economics. "I do not have faith in the market," the confident Sowell wrote, touting the "invisible hand" as the best way forward for poor blacks who would help themselves; "I have evidence about the market."[143] The private sector, if left alone, would, through the free enterprise system, significantly improve the economic circumstances of the most poverty-ridden segment of black America. In the context of the 1980s, critics argued, this black conservative position provided the ideological justification for the massive disinvestment underway in black America since the 1970s, a disinvestment that only accelerated under the Reagan administration.[144]

Free-market ideology promoted by black intellectuals was presumably supposed to make government downsizing in black urban areas more acceptable. In addition to the contraction of municipal and state tax bases due mainly to capital flight, Reagan's "New Federalism" resulted in huge cutbacks to urban governments in the 1980s, which led to the further shrinking of labor markets. Federal assistance for cities stood at $22 billion when Reagan entered office in 1980, but was slashed to $17 billion in 1987, as he was about to leave office.[145] These developments, in conjunction with deindustrialization, fueled the jobs crisis, contributing to greater impoverishment of the very group—the black poor—whose interests the black conservatives claimed to advocate.

As Reagan sought to deal with the crisis by giving large tax breaks to the rich, the conditions confronting poor blacks deteriorated even further. In the first half of the 1970s, the total number of poor black families living below the poverty line had risen from 1.3 million to 1.5 million. But in Reagan's America, the escalation of racial inequality was more dramatic. In the president's first year in office, the real median income of all black families declined by 5.2 percent compared to the 1980 figure, and the share of black families living below the poverty line moved upwards from 32.4 percent to 34.2 percent.[146] In a single year, "much of the progress that had been made against poverty in the 1960s and 1970s" had been "wiped out," according to John Herbers of the *New York Times*.[147] James McGhee of the Urban League went further, arguing that Reaganomics had blunted "the hopes and dashed the dreams of millions of the poor," while seriously threatening "the existence of an emerging, still fragile black middle class as well. . . . Programs that accomplished so much are now being eliminated one after another for seemingly ideological rather than budgetary reasons, and America is defaulting on its commitment to assure equal opportunity for all its citizens."[148]

As the federal government cut funds for cities and poor people and reduced guarantees for benefits and services, the black conservatives seemed content to exhort the black poor to somehow transcend the social and economic inequalities that had beset them. Although the black rate of unemployment slumped to 25 percent during Reagan's first term—equal to the national rate at the height of the Great Depression[149]—Steele was moved to write: "There was much that [President Ronald] Reagan had to offer blacks, his emphasis on traditional American values—individual initiative, self-sufficiency, strong families—offered what I think is the most enduring solution to the demoralization and poverty that continue to widen the gap between blacks and whites in America. Even his de-emphasis on race was reasonable in a society where race only divides."[150]

In time, other black conservatives—also seemingly oblivious to the emerging racial realities—endorsed Steele's barely credible sentiments. Submitting to the new Reagan equation in national politics, these intellectuals essentially sent out a call for a community of heroes, unable to accept the fact that state supports and self-help did not have to be mutually exclusive. Although blacks had historically been the last hired and the first fired, they were now expected not only to accept the "rules of the game" but to embrace them, since, according to black conservatives, the rules were heavily weighted in their favor. Governed by the profit motive, their assumption was that capitalists would hire anybody who was productive and willing to work for the lowest possible wage. Poor blacks should therefore work for the lowest possible wage. Although frequently disparaged by civil rights leaders and intellectuals as dead-end work, entry-level jobs, in Sowell's view, served as "useful instructors in the instrumental, or bourgeois values (diligence, discipline, punctuality), which as components of larger social processes equip the young person for social mobility."[151] Short-term sacrifice in the pursuit of long-term self-reliance was thought sufficient to ensure a practical route out of poverty.

The black conservatives' position on the minimum wage meshed perfectly with their belief in self-help and the inviolability of the free market. Parker, for example, denounced the concept of a minimum wage as "morally wrong," insisting, on principle, that in a decent society "individuals should negotiate their own individual salaries with their own employers."[152] Thomas took a different approach, drawing on personal experience to reject the need for such legislation: "I never would have had my first job if I had to make the minimum wage," he claimed, "but the benefits of the job were more than just the salary: getting up, going to work, working hard, doing a good job, not destroying my boss's equipment, just being responsible."[153] Sowell and Williams espoused similar views, but in a more scholarly fashion, drawing yet again on the theoretical assumptions popularized by their mentor, Friedman.[154] In the 1980s it was these intellectuals who were most readily identified with black conservative opposition to the minimum wage, claiming to be especially concerned about its impact on the black poor. The minimum wage law supposedly eliminated the bargaining power of unemployed black workers by denying these workers the chance to work at lower wages than whites. But it also had the effect of lowering the capitalists' profit margin, thereby causing them to expand less and resulting in fewer jobs, especially for black youth—"the least desirable people in the job market in terms of education and experience."[155]

This black conservative argument about the free market as an antidote to racism became the focus of Thomas D. Boston's *Race, Class and Conservatism*[156] and a number of more minor studies.[157] Categorically rejecting the view that blacks were unable to compete with other workers at the existing minimum wage rate, not because of discrimination, but because they lacked the requisite productive capacities, progressive scholars sought to show that racial discrimination remained a significant determinant of black life chances. If the black conservatives were correct about the color-blind nature of capitalism, how, these critics asked, did they account for the existence of racism in the private sector?[158] The answer, simply, was that they did not. Rather, they pointed to formal, legalistic equality as proof of America's achievement of racial equality in the workplace and implored their fellow blacks to develop the productive capacities necessary to make it in what was now a "free" and "fair" nation.

A 1991 study sponsored by the Urban Institute, however, demonstrated the fallacy of the notion that employment discrimination was a thing of the past. Focused on prospective employees at the lower-end of the labor market, where the issue of the minimum wage was most relevant, the authors carried out 476 hiring audits in the cities of Chicago and Washington, seeking to measure anti-black discrimination directly. In each audit, two people—one black, the other white—were hand-picked and furnished with professional and personal qualities indistinguishable in the context of a low-skilled, entry-level job-hiring decision.[159] The study found that blacks, in responding to "help-wanted" advertisements in the cities' main newspapers, confronted "entrenched and widespread" racism: "young black jobseekers were unable to advance as far in the hiring process as their white counterparts 20 percent of the time; black testers advanced farther than their white counterparts 7 percent of the time. Blacks were denied a job that was offered to an equally qualified white 15 percent of the time; white testers were denied a job when their black counterparts received an offer in 5 percent of the audits."[160] The authors went on to argue that these were only "conservative estimates," since, historically, racist employers had been reluctant to advertise in newspapers.[161]

Significantly, the Urban Institute's study was not the only study to provide evidence of existing racial discrimination at the lower end of the American labor market. In a paper entitled "We'd Love to Hire Them But . . ." sociologists Joleen Kirschenman and Kathryn Neckerman observed a similar pattern of discrimination in the city of Chicago.[162] After interviewing a sample of 185 employers, a complex and interlocking set of attitudes emerged that pointed to racism as an important factor accounting for black unemployment. According to the authors, employers repeatedly voiced racist stereotypes about blacks such as "they don't want to work"; "they are lazy"; "they steal"; "they lack motivation"; "they don't have a work ethic." Others commented, "my customers are 95 percent white . . . I wouldn't last very long if I had some black; and my guys don't want to work with blacks."[163] The Kirschenman-Neckerman study certainly offered pause for thought. Those black conservatives who dismissed the idea that racism remained a force in the labor market, retarding black mobility, appeared to be operating in an idealized free-market paradigm. All the self-help in the world could not overcome racist employment practices.

Caught in their idealized paradigm, Sowell and company often seemed oblivious to the real workings of the American political economy. In addition to denying or downplaying the significance of racism, these intellectuals failed to grasp the concept of market coercion. Having a job—any job—was tantamount to independence and self-reliance for African Americans, no matter how oppressive the work conditions or how low the pay. So important was merely having a job that even Woodson—a free-market moderate among black conservatives—dismissed as "antipoor" those who would "require all public housing residents to conform to prevailing wage laws and union rules," in competing for construction jobs. Woodson, following Sowell's and Williams's lead, insisted that this principle was antipoor because it priced the "lowest skilled of the lowest skilled"—who were disproportionately black—out of the market.[164]

To be sure, this was rigid capitalist economic theory. But one of the practical consequences of this theory was to depress the wages of all workers by introducing low-wage competitors for stable jobs during a time of declining real wages. In 1987, for example, when the black unemployment rate returned to the lower 1978 level, black earnings declined to their pre-1972 level.[165] The only change for many blacks, then, in this increasingly competitive economic environment, was that they now constituted the working, rather than non-working, poor—people who were employed full-time but whose wages left them below the poverty line. The ethnographic research of Elijah Anderson revealed that work for pay at family-sustaining wages—as opposed to some idealized ethic of work for its own sake—was a central concern of low-income blacks, male and female.[166] But the black conservatives' discourse on the virtues of work sidestepped this concern; by emphasizing employment and trivializing income, these intellectuals ignored another important source of black poverty. Indeed, to most progressive scholars, it often seemed that they were dismissive of the essence of racial oppression in America—what Stephen Steinberg described as a system of occupational segregation that restricted blacks to the least desirable job sectors or that excluded them from job markets altogether.[167]

In their discussions of the pitfalls of the minimum wage, however, the black conservatives' flawed characterization of prevailing economic conditions in America and the wider world appeared to extend further. It was often difficult to see, for instance, how low-skilled black workers could be as productive a source of labor in the wake of the technological advances and professional specialization of the 1970s. Indeed, as one critic of the black conservatives, Clay Smith, noted shortly after the Fairmont Conference: no "employer today would hire forty teenagers to perform a mathematical computation which one computer programmer can finish in a minimum amount of time, no matter how little you allow the

employer to pay the teenager."[168] But Smith expanded on this critique in
an attempt to defuse these intellectuals' calls for the adoption of a sub-
minimum wage. Building on the work of Robert Hill, who in 1981 had
authored a report on the subject for the National Urban League, this
Howard law professor argued that their proposal ignored the fact that
one-half of the teenagers employed in the United States were already in
jobs that paid at or less than the minimum wage.[169] Noting that a sub-
minimum wage had been legal since 1938, but had *not* been employed
aggressively by business to hire more teenagers, Smith questioned the
claim that such a provision would significantly reduce the disparity between the black and white rates of unemployment.[170] Since research indicated that most businesses were not usually willing to hire the black
poor "even at one hundred percent subsidies," the major beneficiaries
of Sowell and company's sub-minimum wage proposal would not, in all
likelihood, have been black teenagers but their white counterparts.[171] In
American working life, race mattered.

The black conservatives' opposition to the minimum wage placed
them squarely at odds with the vast majority of African Americans. But
their call for self-help was arguably the most warmly received of their
messages in the black community. That this should be so was hardly remarkable: black people, after all, have a rich tradition of self-help in the
United States. As Dorothy Height, president of the National Council of
Negro Women, noted in the early 1990s: "The civil rights movement of
the 1950s and 1960s was perhaps the most extraordinary example of a
mass self-help movement in American history: self-help mounted under
grave conditions to throw off the yoke of American apartheid."[172] Usually
rooted in movements for social change, self-help had literally defined
how black people managed to survive slavery, segregation, and a series
of trials and travails right through to the present day. Yet the black conservatives spoke little of the contributions of black liberal organizations
to blacks' political uplift and even less of the struggles of black radical
organizations to deliver the black poor a semblance of economic justice.
It has already been noted that Sowell and company's version of self-help
was defined along the accommodationist lines established by Booker T.
Washington in the late nineteenth century.

Some scholars saw in a number of the black conservatives' embrace of
Washington a form of pragmatism that, in the 1980s, would enable the
black community to come to terms with its increasing political margin-
alization on the one hand, and serve to inspire self-help initiatives and
black enterprise on the other.[173] But drawing on the legacy of Washington, as we have seen, did not improve the condition of the black poor, economically or otherwise. Indeed, it often seemed the Tuskegee Wizard's
ideas were promoted by these intellectuals for another, albeit related,

reason: simply to convince African Americans that depending on government to solve their problems had become futile. And this message carried significant political traction. It was against the backdrop of the public disinvestment in black America under Reagan that Loury wrote:

It makes sense to call for greater self-reliance at this time because some of what needs to be done cannot, in the nature of the case, be undertaken by government. Dealing with behavioral problems, with community values, with the attitudes and beliefs of black youngsters about responsibility, work, family, and schooling is not something government is well suited to do. The teaching of "oughts" properly belongs in the hands of private, voluntary associations. . . . It is also reasonable to ask those blacks who have benefited from set-asides for black business to contribute to the alleviation of suffering of poor blacks—for without the visible ghetto poor, such programs would lack the political support needed for their continuation.[174]

For Washington, of course, self-help was always more than an economic strategy to combat segregation and second-class citizenship; it was also about moral values and instilling the value of hard work through role-modeling. While Woodson tapped predominantly into the economics of self-help, emphasizing the need for poor blacks to become empowered through business enterprise,[175] the wellspring of Loury's approach for assisting the truly disadvantaged was to harness the talents and social capital of the emergent black middle class. Having adopted traditional values and attitudes and achieved professional success, Loury argued, these people's experiences could stand as examples for the lower class of their community who had failed to break the cycle of poverty and despair.[176] Although these intellectuals diverged somewhat in their emphases, Woodson appeared to believe his fellow black conservative's strategy for racial uplift could complement his own of trying to bring about an internal economic transformation for the poor. In the mid-1980s, according to Clarence Page, the president of the NCNE went as far as to investigate "other self-help ideas that appear to be working," such as the adoption of poor black families by a group of black professionals in California.[177]

Both Loury's and Woodson's self-help models were collectivist-oriented. Both were geared to stimulate black development and enhance black independence in the future. And both had deep roots in the black past. Their brand of communitarian conservatism—whereby Africans Americans were essentially to be engaged in the forging of community, connected by their mutual goals and obligations—differed significantly from the libertarian conservatism of the other black conservatives. The libertarians' self-help creed was predicated upon a fierce individualism, advocating only laissez-faire formulae for advancement and requiring the commitment of individual blacks only to economic and cultural assimulation. These intellectuals' understanding of community was less dense than Loury's and Woodson's, a confluence of individual interests rather than the product of people engaged in a shared project of collective development.

Both of these black conservative positions, however, were problematic. The role-model ideology supported by Loury and Woodson—which valued voluntarist activity and encouraged an elite-led campaign to uplift the black masses—tended to reinforce racial categories: the notion that blacks were responsible for blacks, Jews for Jews, Hispanics for Hispanics, and so on. Mentoring was evidently supposed to inspire poor blacks to emulate the achievements of the black middle class. But the danger with this strategy, progressive scholars argued, was that it would continue to deflect attention away from the real problem facing these people: the near-absence of adequate employment opportunities.[178] Loury's and Woodson's suggestions were potentially counterproductive in other ways too. Not only did mentoring confer moral authority on people with money, but it also assumed that such people were culturally whole (as opposed to just privileged or lucky) and therefore entitled to counsel the allegedly less-than-whole poor about the behavior and values that were required to make it. The upshot of role-model ideology, then, was to exaggerate the social importance of well-to-do blacks, whose flight from the inner cities in the 1970s was one explanation offered for the emergent black urban dysfunction of the 1980s.

Since the black libertarian conservatives were concerned less with role model ideology than with what the individual needed to do for him- or herself, criticisms of their brand of self-help differed. A number of scholars pointed out that black spokespeople across the ideological spectrum had always acknowledged the importance of individual responsibility, but had invariably felt compelled to highlight social injustices that were beyond the scope of individual remedy.[179] Too often, however, these black conservatives wrote about values and attitudes as if blacks lived in a political and economic vacuum. They did not seem to understand the distinction between feeling responsible for oneself and actually being enabled to help oneself. Achieving the latter required genuine opportunity as well as an awareness that inspirational slogans and antigovernment rhetoric could never substitute for concise social analysis and practical action. A change of life required more than a change of mind. Sowell and company's failure to examine countless instances in which black people had imitated the Protestant work ethic and still remained on the bottom rung of society's ladder was revealing.[180]

Just as Booker T. Washington's call to "cast down your buckets where you are" reflected an outdated reading of black economic opportunities in the late nineteenth century, the black conservatives' focus on self-help appeared misplaced at a time when structural forces were redefining the globe. While Washington's program of appeasement had legitimized white supremacy in the rapidly industrializing South, Sowell and company's self-help agenda provided ideological cover for the regressive shift in the entrenchment of racial inequality in modern America. During the Reagan and Bush administrations, these intellectuals' "neo-Bookerism" offset appeals for a more equitable redistribution of resources by imploring black communities that were increasingly poor to turn inward while government support and employment went elsewhere. The populist rhetoric that underpinned the black conservatives' discourse on racial poverty—where making poor blacks independent and strong, *once again*, was the stated objective—served only to mask its damaging practical consequences.

While agreeing on key themes—most notably, the adverse impact of welfare on the culture and economic condition of the black poor and the value of black entrepreneurial activity in the free market—the black conservatives were not always a monolithic voice when it came to poverty. Whereas ideology dictated Sowell's and Williams's view of the black underclass and appeared important to the less conspicuous analyses offered by Thomas, Parker, Wortham and Steele, Loury and Woodson offered perspectives that were more carefully thought out, more grounded in black history, but perspectives that were, in the end, similarly problematic. After more than a quarter century in the public spotlight, the black conservatives' views on black disadvantage—its causes and remedies—had been devastatingly critiqued by an array of progressive scholars. In the face of sustained empirical scrutiny, these intellectuals' arguments had been exposed as unconvincing, significant in their embodiment of the prevailing conservative political orthodoxy but without the necessary depth to seriously address the most pressing problems of the black poor.

At the most fundamental level, the black conservatives' approach to racial inequality was problematic because it dismissed explanations of race and class and, in doing so, diverted attention from essential public policies. Not only did their criticism of welfare suggest that it was somehow illegitimate for black citizens to view government as a vehicle for egalitarian redress, their support of self-help effectively let authorities "off the hook" by "throwing black people a few token scraps and telling them to be enterprising and solve their own problems."[181] In opposing the black conservatives' individualistic strategies for assisting the black poor, liberals and radicals reaffirmed their commitment to the state as an important site in the struggle against racial disadvantage. In the post-industrial economy, they argued, social provisions needed to be expanded to create better jobs, rebuild homes, and improve access to health care. But even more importantly, if bridging the racial divide was truly a priority, the public school system—which most poor black children attended—needed to be reinvigorated with more money and better resources to provide greater opportunities for social mobility. Harking back to the 1954 *Brown v. Board of Education* decision, this was an argument that the black conservatives extraordinarily rejected for reasons that embroiled them in a major debate over public education.

Chapter 4
Visions of School Reform

Education is one of the few bridges that exist to help lead people from poverty, homelessness, and illiteracy toward a better life.

—*Manning Marable*

For years I've said that if the Ku Klux Klan wanted to sabotage black academic excellence, they couldn't find a tool more effective than the public school systems in most major cities.

—*Walter Williams*

On May 17, 1954, the United States Supreme Court handed down the landmark ruling in *Brown v. Board of Education of Topeka* that laws mandating racial segregation in public schools were unconstitutional. The unanimous verdict, which overturned the pernicious separate but equal doctrine established fifty-eight years earlier in *Plessy v. Ferguson*, rocked the nation to its foundations, leaving a diverse array of ideological forces fighting over the social and political significance of the Court's finding. While conservatives and white supremacists of the day sought to cast *Brown* as a reckless piece of judicial activism that indulged those perfidious liberal proponents of federal excess, the black community and its white allies hailed the decision as a decisive breakthrough in the struggle for racial equality in America. The irrepressible torrent of opposition to *Brown* on the one hand, juxtaposed against the impassioned support for the Court's judgment on the other, revealed a broad appreciation, across the segregationist divide, of the power of education to shape fundamental social relations. In seeking to break the institutional back of Jim Crow in this critical sphere, the Warren Court effectively set in motion a national frame of reference for race relations in which educational philosophy and policy were deeply embedded. Modern scholars of the African American experience know all too well how pertinent this frame of reference remains today.

How could they not know? More than fifty years after the *Brown* decision, the facts of educational failure in black America are nothing if not alarming. Segregation, we are told in some quarters, has found its way back ("if, indeed, it ever left some schools") while the gap between black and white academic achievement, once in decline, has climbed sharply since the mid-1980s. Black students in the twelfth grade now typically score lower in English than white students in the eighth grade, and the same is true in history, geography, and math.[1] Among conservatives, liberals, and radicals, competing explanations for this educational disparity inevitably abound, even as all commentators—black and white, left and right—openly acknowledge the reality of a deteriorating public school system that continues to limit black opportunities. "Public Education for Blacks is a Disgraceful Disaster," declared Walter Williams.[2] "There is no dispute that the train is off the tracks, the house is on fire, and the dirty laundry is pushing out of the closet," admitted the liberally inclined Juan Williams.[3] "Progress toward improving black public education has been reversed," charged the black socialist Manning Marable. Given that education remains one of "the few bridges that exist to help lead people from poverty, homelessness, and illiteracy toward a better life,"[4] it is little wonder that the state of the schools continues to be a burning issue in the black community. How, then, is the contemporary schools crisis as it relates to African Americans best understood? Why this crisis now? And what is to be done about it?

During the three decades leading up to the fiftieth anniversary of *Brown*, black conservative intellectuals were at the forefront of the major educational debates concerning African Americans, offering myriad answers to these questions. Claiming a devotion to the verdicts of empirical evidence and maintaining that it was no longer sufficient to educate on the basis of assumptions, these intellectuals challenged the long-established civil rights wisdom on schools and attempted to show how and why such wisdom has been inimical to black interests. But far from seeking simply to discredit the left/liberal orthodoxy that stressed integration and funding as the best means of achieving equal educational opportunity, black conservatives proposed numerous school reform measures of their own. Theirs was essentially a neoliberal agenda that sought educational marketization via vouchers and private school management companies; but it was unique in that it was tailored to appeal to a black citizenry traditionally suspicious of conservative politicking. Although mysteriously ignored in much of the scholarly literature, black conservative ideas on education had a significant influence in social policy circles—particularly from the early 1980s—often with direct consequences for African American people. These ideas demand further scrutiny.

Of course, any study of black intellectual involvement in conservative educational reform must engage, at least ephemerally, with the historical realities that have defined and limited African American experiences of schooling in the United States.[5] To assess how effective black conservatives were in dismantling the arguments of their black liberal adversaries, and in setting out their own policy visions, it is necessary to situate their educational philosophy in the broader context of an era of conservative educational mobilization—mobilization that grew out of the social "backlash" against busing in the 1970s before finding formal expression in the politics of Reaganism. The Reagan Revolution of the 1980s, after all, turned into a major assault not only on affirmative action and welfare but on public education as well.[6] While usurping the color-blind discourse of liberals from the desegregation movement, conservative leaders and intellectuals worked hard to discredit efforts to improve the schools (for blacks) by making them more inclusive. They instead sought the application of market solutions to return America to the educational golden age from which it had allegedly declined. Black conservative contributions were made, and must therefore be understood, in the context of the conservative movement's drive to restore the educational equilibrium—an equilibrium that the *Brown* decision and its progeny had long threatened to upset.

Much of the significance of *Brown* springs not from the opinion itself—important though this was—but from an appreciation of what it sought to eliminate: a social, political, economic, and legal system that once classified black people as property and, after the demise of slavery, established an alternative system of domination that treated them as second-class citizens.[7] By tolling the bell for state-mandated segregation in public education, the Warren Court essentially renounced this past and created, in the words of Manning Marable, "the legal framework for a democratic, color-blind society within the structures of liberal capitalism." It was as if black children had escaped the clutches of an evil pharaoh and the dream of a promised land of justice and equality lay within reach.[8] How could African Americans not see it this way? In the black community education had long been understood as the panacea for liberation, a vehicle of hope and aspiration for a despised and downtrodden people struggling to become free.[9] NAACP chief counsel Thurgood Marshall certainly saw it this way, confidently forecasting that *Brown* would end all school segregation in the United States within five years.[10] Black Fisk University president Charles S. Johnson went even further, anticipating that the judgment would break down barriers not only in schools but in all areas of public life.[11] In the same euphoric spirit, the New York *Amsterdam News* proclaimed *Brown* "the greatest victory for the Negro people since the Emancipation Proclamation."[12] But it was that great organ of black resistance—the NAACP—that issued perhaps the boldest state-ment of all: black people, it predicted, would be "free by '63."[13]

But somewhere the myth veered off course. Southern white resistance to *Brown* mushroomed at every level in society, ensuring that the drive toward educational reform was agonizingly slow.[14] Indeed, only in the mid-1960s—after the Civil Rights Act, more Supreme Court decisions and a number of federal threats to eliminate school funding—did de-segregation become a reality in many parts of the South, and even then the gains were comparatively negligible. By this time, moreover, the educational outlook among liberals—black and white—was shifting sig-nificantly. Although the legal edifice of segregation had belatedly crum-bled, blacks, by virtue of economic subordination, continued to find themselves racially isolated at the nation's worst schools.[15] The Johnson administration's response was to introduce Head Start and Chapter 1, compensatory programs aimed specifically at providing children from disadvantaged backgrounds with educational assistance, health care, and nutrition.[16] But while generally pleased with the president's plan to allocate more resources to the nation's poorest schools, civil rights leaders' greatest concern was now on integrating them. As the decade wore on, these leaders challenged the assumption that only deliberate, state-sponsored segregation was inconsistent with law, eventually asking the Supreme Court in *Swann v. Charlotte-Mecklenburg Board of Education* to insist on the actual mixing of the races. And they were successful: the de-cision effectively obliterated the distinction between desegregation and integration. The measure of whether schools were open to children of all races was now whether they were actually attended by children of all races in roughly equal numbers.[17] In years to come, contemporary black conservatives would enter the ideological fray and seek to undermine the basis and criticize the implications of the Court's reasoning.

Far from simply ending segregation, then, *Brown* marked the begin-ning of a new phase of struggle to raise the profile of educational oppor-tunity for black children. But where the decision of May 1954 legitimized and helped shape views that were slowly emerging as a moral consensus among an increasing number of white Americans, many of these same people never accepted the rationale for the Head Start programs and forcible race mixing that came later. Nor did a young black economist by the name of Thomas Sowell. Stepping into this educational milieu in the early 1970s, the forty-something Sowell attacked these developments within black education, reserving special criticism for the new integra-tionist agenda; it was, in his view, an unjustifiably costly crusade destined to fail.[18] The black community should not rely on government to inte-grate the public schools in the hope that they would then deliver a better service to black students. Instead, Sowell contended, its leaders should focus on the "positive aspects" of segregation and acknowledge that, in the past, a great many "Negroes" had managed to thrive educationally without government. Their inspiring stories—usually centered on the historically all-black private schools—could constitute a model for contemporary black educational action.[19] In a black intellectual era defined by the struggle for integration in the public domain, this proposal made Sowell a curious black figure indeed.

The book in which these arguments were originally advanced was *Black Education: Myths and Tragedies*, a biting polemic that sharply divided academic opinion upon release. To the conservative reading *Black Education*, Sowell was "a brilliant scholar with that rare combination of qualities: passion and reasonableness";[20] but to the liberal he resembled a mixture of "precious child, brash adolescent, arrogant intellectual and premature elder statesman."[21] What, though, of the book itself? The first thing to note is that, although Sowell promised an empirical assessment of black education, he did little more than provide an experiential commentary: private accounts and reflections on those aspects of schooling in which he had been directly involved. His personal history as a black man with a broad educational experience—from the typical segregated Southern elementary school to the lecture theatres of elite northern universities—was emphasized presumably to establish his "expertise" on all matters to do with black schooling. But while laying claim to a grassroots black authenticity, Sowell failed to do his job as an economist: some of the most pressing problems confronting black inner-city schools—most notably, their declining resource base—were not explored in the book. Rather than a glaring oversight, though, this silence was an early indication of a decidedly ideological view of education in which spending was seen as antithetical to high standards.

The economist Sowell wrote little else on schools in the 1970s. But by the early 1980s his authority in this sphere was being widely touted by the Reagan administration, which offered him the important post of Secretary of Education.[22] Although he declined the position, Sowell's thinking on questions relating to integration and funding closely resembled the accepted wisdom in the Reagan White House, and he wrote determinedly in support of the new president's reform agenda throughout the 1980s. "Our educational system is in the grips of a crisis caused by low standards, lack of purpose, and a failure to strive for excellence," Reagan charged, as he launched a campaign for reform early on in his first term.[23] In the president's view, there was little doubt that civil rights enforcement had hurt basic education over the previous two decades. "The schools were charged by the federal courts with leading in the correcting of long-standing injustices in our society," he said. "Perhaps there was just too much to do in too little time."[24] Addressing a delegation of senior bureaucrats shortly after winning office, Reagan laid out his alternative schools vision: "Don't ask me to waste more federal money on education. Over the years . . . we have put in more only to wind up with less. Just discover excellent schools to serve as models for all the others."[25]

Although Sowell was certainly the most prominent African American to endorse the president's sentiments, he was soon joined on the educational front line by Walter Williams, the savaging of the public system seemingly their first priority. Encumbered by "runaway pay scales and plush pensions that teachers' unions have extracted from politicians handing out the taxpayer's money,"[26] the public schools, according to these black conservatives, had simply ceased being educators of children. Not only was illiteracy and innumeracy rampant, but the textbooks were inadequate and disciplinary standards virtually nonexistent. Invoking his thesis from the early 1970s, Sowell—supported now by Williams—endorsed Reagan's major concerns and, similarly, blamed civil rights leaders and the broader liberal establishment for the crisis. By supporting government initiatives such as Head Start and busing, the "special interests" were said to have transformed American schools from academic institutions into social welfare centers, with damaging consequences for all students. But Sowell and Williams insisted that poor black students had been the greatest victims of liberal educational "excess." Unable to read, write, and compute at even an eighth-grade level, these students were being issued fraudulent graduation diplomas, effectively setting them up for a lifetime of failure.[27] With a nod to his own professional success, Williams expressed relief that he had been fortunate enough to receive his education "before it became fashionable for whites to like black people."[28]

As with the controversies surrounding affirmative action and welfare, Sowell and Williams, in criticizing the thrust of liberal reform within public education over the preceding two decades, initially found themselves out of step with majority black sentiment. Most African Americans supported busing to deliver greater educational equity, and since a disproportionate number of them had benefited (and/or seen their children benefit) from Head Start and Chapter 1, these programs were especially popular with black people.[29] Outside the black community, however, Sowell's and Williams's views on schools were far from controversial: the silent majority, after all, had spoken by this time and the role of the liberal in education was increasingly under attack. Millions of ordinary people derided programs like Head Start, and especially busing, as reverse discrimination, a violation of individualism and thus contrary to the American way.[30] Under Reagan, funds for federal compensatory education programs were slashed, busing condemned, and the abolition of the Department of Education mooted in a clear sign of the president's intention to effect a radical overhaul of the public system.[31] Sowell and Williams would champion this educational agenda in the interests of the black poor in contrast to most scholars, who saw them being even more disadvantaged as a result of it.

Considering that Reagan was a man who believed that the federal government caused rather than solved problems, one might not have expected the government he led to create a movement that would bring about major changes in American education. But that is precisely what his administration did. Early on in his presidency, Reagan convened the National Commission on Excellence in Education (NCEE) and directed it to examine and report on the quality of schools across the nation within eighteen months. The Commission worked diligently and produced a unanimous and influential report—*A Nation at Risk: The Imperative for Educational Reform*—documenting the woeful state of public schools and the potential consequences for the national economy. Described by its authors as "an open letter to the American people," the report warned:

Our Nation is at risk. Our once unchallenged preeminence in commerce, industry, science, and technological innovation is being overtaken by competitors throughout the world. This report is concerned with only one of the many causes and dimensions of the problem, but it is one that undergirds American prosperity, security, and civility. . . . If an unfriendly foreign power had attempted to impose on America the mediocre educational performance that exists today, we might well have viewed it as an act of war. As it stands, we have allowed this to happen to ourselves. . . . We have, in effect, been committing an act of unthinking, unilateral educational disarmament.[32]

The NCEE, however, believed that the decline in the quality of education could be arrested if there was committed leadership and a public resolve to do so. To reverse what it described as an "act of unthinking, unilateral educational disarmament,"[33] then, the Commission issued a set of recommendations that it felt could realistically be implemented by the administration. At the most basic level, it called for the adoption of more "rigorous and measurable standards" in public education—tougher high-school graduation requirements, improved educational curricula, higher standards for incoming teachers, longer school days and years, and more homework for students.[34]

These recommendations drew sharp criticism from a number of liberal commentators who saw *A Nation at Risk* as creating a misleading impression of doom rather than an objective appraisal of American schooling in the early 1980s. But according to most educational experts, the report and its findings were long overdue.[35] Significantly, the conservative response was varied. While pleased that the NCEE had confirmed the flaws within public education and called for a return to traditional pedagogy, they nevertheless expressed dissatisfaction at its failure to offer market-based reforms as a solution.[36] Despite its origins within the Reagan administration, the National Commission on Excellence in Education did not appear to regard such reforms as sufficiently important to include them among the topics it explored. In fact, the Commission appeared to believe in the American public education system's ability to act on its recommendations and—with additional resources—reform itself.

That *A Nation at Risk* stimulated much soul-searching and debate is beyond dispute. Widely circulated and often cited by the president, it inspired a torrent of literature aimed at improving the schools and came to be seen more generally as a wake-up call for the nation. But although Reagan endorsed the report, he chose to highlight his own priorities in order to support his case for "an end to federal intrusion."[37] Conservative proposals for change emphasizing consumer choice and economic competition predictably came to dominate in the 1980s. To considerable acclaim, prominent public intellectuals such as James Coleman and Thomas Hoffer called for the introduction of school vouchers—not additional funding and greater equity—as the most effective means to restore American education.[38] Over time, their work served as inspiration and firepower to a generation of leaders and commentators who had lost faith in the civic purpose of public schooling and were now committed to its destruction. Contemporary black conservatives were among this generation. How better to raise doubts within the black community about the efficacy of the public system than to reach back into history and denigrate *Brown*, so long the celebrated symbol of this system? And who better, symbolically, to instigate such an attack than a handful of African American intellectuals sympathetic to conservative causes? These intellectuals' critiques of *Brown* would address not only the rationale behind the decision, but also the decision's allegedly harmful impact on the very people it was supposed to help: black people.

The campaign by black conservatives to discredit *Brown* can be seen to have begun in earnest with the publication of *A Nation at Risk* and to have continued ever since. Over the years, these intellectuals' criticisms of the Warren Court proceeded along two distinct lines—one philosophical, the other practical. First, Sowell and company poured scorn on the rationale behind the decision, interpreting *Brown* as "a classic example of a correct result reached by lousy reasoning."[39] The Court had erred, they argued, in striking down segregation not "as a matter of simple justice" but rather on the basis of "psychological evidence, compassion, and a failure to connect segregation with the evil of slavery."[40] This philosophical criticism of the decision led to a more substantive practical one. *Brown*, the black conservatives insisted, had simply failed—failed to desegregate public education and deliver improved black academic standards, failed even to remedy any psychological feeling of inferiority black schoolchildren might have had. Brown's only "achievement," they believed, was to compel (through the logic of its philosophical reasoning) "busing and other policies that were irrelevant to parents' concerns for a decent education"—policies that, in the end, had turned out to be far more damaging to black education than segregation itself.[41] Condemning desegregation and integration as shams at worst and unattainable dreams at best, these black intellectuals called on the African American community to recommit itself to the idea of black educational excellence within all-black settings.

What was going on here? How could a group of intellectuals seemingly so concerned with blacks' assimilation into the American mainstream wind up insisting that blacks renounce an integrationist vision of education in favor of a separatist one? Scholars of the African American experience and of conservative political thought have, for too long, ignored or trivialized the black conservatives' remarkable anti-*Brown* stance. This historiographical silence is curious indeed. Leaving to one side the obvious point that the black conservatives' own success in America would have been unthinkable without the Warren Court's momentous decision, three important and interrelated questions emerge. What was the intellectual basis of these intellectuals' opposition to *Brown?* How credible and influential were their arguments? And what, ultimately, was the significance of such a controversial educational outlook in the context of the contemporary American political culture?

The first thing to note is that the black conservatives' rejection of *Brown* was defined, from the beginning, by their objections to sociologist Kenneth Clark's theory concerning the destructive educational effects of segregation on black children.[42] With his famed study of black and white dolls, Clark had sought to demonstrate to the Court that black children were damaged by the stigma imposed on them by the state when it confined them to separate schools because of their race. Segregation, he argued, was an expression of white prejudice about black inferiority that had filled the black student with "basic feelings of inferiority, conflict, confusion, resentment, hostility towards himself, hostility towards whites." For these reasons, the question of funding was deemed irrelevant: racially separate schools were "inherently unequal." The upshot of Clark's thesis, then, was clear: if black children were to be lifted from the educational doldrums, segregation in public education needed to be struck down without delay.[43] Significantly, this black academic was not alone in putting this argument at the time; in fact, more than 90 percent of social scientists surveyed as early as 1948 declared segregation to be wrong and harmful to black children.[44]

Although all the black conservatives criticized the Clark thesis, some black conservatives judged the acclaimed sociologist's research more harshly than others. Of the group, Clarence Thomas and Thomas Sowell were certainly the two most vocal critics of the view that "separate educational facilities are inherently unequal." Pointing to several all-black schools that produced high levels of academic achievement before the official desegregation of public education began in the 1950s, they insisted that there was "absolutely no reason to think that black students cannot learn as well when surrounded by members of their own race as when they are in an integrated environment."[45] Indeed, "it so happened," Sowell wrote on the fiftieth anniversary of the *Brown* decision, "that within walking distance of the Supreme Court"—where the psychological roots of black underachievement had been discussed and apparently established—"there was an all-black high school, Dunbar, that had produced quality education for more than 80 years." "Back in 1899," he continued, "this school outscored two out of three white high schools in Washington on standardized tests."[46] And there were other such schools. That Frederick Douglass in Baltimore, Booker T. Washington in Atlanta, P.S. 91 in Brooklyn, and McDonough 35 in New Orleans achieved similar academic levels suggested to Sowell that "some systematic social process was at work, rather than anything as geographically random as outstanding individual ability."[47] Whatever the social process at work, these schools' success demonstrated that it was not being racially separate that made black education inferior.[48]

While Sowell sought to expose the *academic* fallacies of the social science behind *Brown* by pointing to "Patterns to Black Excellence" that predated the decision, Thomas chose to direct his critique, appropriately, at the judicial system. "It never ceases to amaze me," Thomas wrote, "that the courts are so willing to assume that anything that is predominantly black must be inferior. First the Court has read our cases to support the theory that black students suffer an unspecified psychological harm from segregation that retards their mental and educational development. This approach not only relies upon questionable social science research rather than constitutional principle, but it also rests on an assumption of black inferiority."[49]

Dismissing the arguments of the doomsayers who had dwelled for too long on the "dubious" psychological dimensions of black underachievement, Thomas—building on Sowell's work—emphasized, instead, how black schools could "function as the center and symbol of black communities and provide examples of independent black leadership, success and achievement."[50] The *Brown* decision, in his view, had been condescending (and racist) to African Americans by suggesting that black students would do better simply by sitting next to whites in classrooms.[51] One of the most disastrous consequences of this reasoning was the way it had undermined African American institutions by forcing black people into white ones with little regard for the dignity and worth of the African American experience. Too many black institutions had been weakened and too much black social capital lost, Thomas concluded, for the decision to be considered an unmitigated good in the manner it had been embraced by the majority of Americans.[52]

The Sowell-Thomas position on *Brown*—which was emblematic of the broader black conservative one—was best seen as paradoxical. In some respects, they and other black conservatives made a legitimate point about black institutions and pride, for many Americans are still too ready to assume that anything predominantly black must be inferior. By documenting patterns of black excellence in some all-black schools prior to 1954 and pointing to the existence of strong, nurturing black institutions in the same era, Sowell and Thomas showed this view to be false. Clearly, black schools were not inferior because black children attended them. As John McWhorter also pointed out, some of these schools were indeed models of scholarly achievement, regularly producing PhDs and eminent figures.[53] Even as they lacked the most basic resources, these exceptional institutions played a vital role in educating African Americans in the segregation era. In reminding Americans of this fact, black conservatives provided a useful, if hardly original, contribution to the debate over *Brown*.

On the whole, though, the black conservatives' criticisms of the *Brown* decision appeared unconvincing. At the most basic level, these intellectuals displayed an inability or unwillingness to think within the context of time or, to put it another way, they were asking Americans to conceive of a past altogether different from the one many had actually known. "Decline from Segregation" narratives, according to Adolph Reed, were dangerous on two levels, falsifying the black past and serving hostile interests in the present. The "cheery tones of personal triumph" that lay within these narratives, he insisted, tended all too often to "wash brightly over the backdrop of codified racial subordination."[54] That blacks had responded courageously in the face of centuries of racist institutional oppression was a fact well documented by historians. Acknowledging the significance of black resilience in this environment, however, was very different from the nostalgia expressed by black conservatives for the environment itself. As numerous historians—liberal and conservative—have shown since *Brown*, the conditions of educational segregation were in no way positive, nor was the resulting subjugated status of African Americans an unintentional one: separate was not, and never could be, equal. The historical achievements pointed to by Sowell and others may have demonstrated that *some* blacks were able to achieve academic success against the odds. But rather than undercutting assumptions about the negative consequences of segregation, these examples revealed one of the unintended positive consequences of a system that worked—for the most part, effectively—to keep black people in their place. One must not forget—black conservative rhetoric notwithstanding—that black educational outcomes were miserable, more or less across the board.[55]

In framing their critique of the Clark thesis adopted by the NAACP in *Brown,* black conservatives failed to recognize what would be required to get the Supreme Court to declare segregation in America unconstitutional. In 1954 such a declaration was certainly not inevitable. Rather than a challenge to the racial composition of the learning environment because of concerns about black psychology, historical scholarship has consistently demonstrated that the *Brown* case was primarily a push for equal access to educational resources. It was a recognition that black schools were inferior, not because they were all black, but because they were overcrowded and underfunded, with too few effective teachers to teach the children who arguably needed education the most. If African Americans could get themselves into schools with the children of the whites who controlled the educational purse strings, it was thought, the result would be vastly improved black education and later, racial integration into the mainstream of American life. Without rich and plentiful resources, though, black children would continue to be severely disadvantaged.[56]

Attuned to these political realities of the day, most scholars now acknowledge that Clark's social science research is best understood as an effort to bolster the Court's ruling in the light of what was certain to be a decision of momentous proportions and consequences.[57] To maintain that the Warren Court could have overlooked this research and still made their finding revealed a certain degree of historical naivety on the part of black conservatives. For these same intellectuals to then chide blacks for needing to "sit next to whites" to overcome a sense of inferiority reflected not only a bizarre and rather mischievous reading of history, but also a fundamental misunderstanding of arguably the central goal of *Brown* and its progeny: educational equity.

It would be entirely misleading, however, to see the black conservatives' philosophical objections to *Brown* as original; in reality, their skepticism had roots in the African American past. Black attitudes toward racial separation in the United States have always been complex. Since emancipation, virtually all blacks opposed the stigma that was involved in segregation because it was used as a tool to prevent their access to a better life. But this position did not automatically translate into a deep commitment to integration as an end in itself.[58] In fact, the emergence and development of a unique African American community, replete with its own culture, was an achievement of which many blacks came to be proud. At different times and with varying degrees of intensity, this pride found political expression in the ideology of black nationalism. Of course, the black nationalist tradition within black political culture was—and remains—tremendously varied; but one broad impulse has always defined it. Deeply pessimistic about the ability or willingness of white society to transform itself to include "people of color," black nationalists urged African Americans to reject white society and define themselves within the context of their own independent communities.[59]

Scholars of the African American experience have largely ignored connections between black conservatism and black nationalism. The reasons for this oversight remain unclear. It was certainly difficult to know what to make of Sowell's and Thomas's adherence to what is perhaps best described as a complicated variant of black nationalism in their analyses of *Brown*. Their insistence that blacks should not pursue integration but welcome all-black institutions; that blacks should assert that they derive no special benefit from the company of whites; and that black schools may provide African Americans with superior educational opportunities were all positions curiously resonant of a black nationalist worldview with respectable (if problematic) roots on the American left. Thomas, for his part, often couched his opposition to *Brown* in terms of a black nationalist worldview, praising Malcolm X for being "hell on integrationists" and asking, "Where does he say you should sacrifice your institutions to be next to white people?"[60] Leaving to one side the obvious point that Thomas and other black conservatives—in attending universities such as Yale, Harvard, and Stanford and then going on to prestigious positions in the mainstream—have themselves long been "next to white people," this apparent ideological intersection of left and right is worth pursuing.

In 1987, for example, in a manner similar to that of black conservatives, the well-known black nationalist scholar Harold Cruse complained that *Brown* wrongly presumed "that separateness is inherently to mean inferiority." "Intrinsically," Cruse insisted, "it means no such thing. Legally imposed segregation was what rendered separateness implicitly inferior. Remove the legal sanctions, and separateness has the potential of achieving equality in its own right."[61] Six years later Alex Johnson, writing in the *California Law Review*, declared that *Brown* was a mistake and that integration had failed American society.[62] In time, the New York University law professor Derrick Bell, a NAACP Legal Defense Fund attorney in the 1960s, echoed Johnson's assessment. Bell argued that, in the 1950s and 1960s, he and other lawyers failed to realize that "racism is permanent in this country" and that excessive faith in integrationist ideals could actually harm black students' education.[63]

Seemingly united in pessimism about the black future, and disregarding educational realities from the black past, the black right and black left sometimes converged in their assessments of *Brown*. Surveying the contemporary educational landscape, conservatives and nationalists both concluded that the interests of black people might have been better served through self-organization. The key difference between them, however, was that while the conservatives called for self-organization with limited or no commitment to funding public education, the nationalists demanded more resources for the nation's most disadvantaged schools (in which African Americans were, of course, overrepresented) to offset the myriad effects of poverty. In essence, then, black conservatives opposed the intellectual justification for *Brown* but without offering African American children realistic alternatives for advancement within the existing public system.

If the first phase of the black conservative critique of *Brown* focused unpersuasively on the "philosophical flaws" of the decision, the second phase addressed its "practical failure" to achieve the ends its early supporters had predicted. With the benefit of more than three decades hindsight, these intellectuals repeatedly emphasized that black liberals at the time had been naïve to forecast a *Brown*-induced black educational nirvana. In reality, Sowell and company argued, the costs accompanying the shifts from segregation to desegregation to integration had far outweighed any benefits for blacks. This broadly held view, however, masked subtle variations in emphasis among the black conservatives.

Since these intellectuals reserved most of their criticism for busing, the details of this policy and the history behind it need to be reiterated. In the 1970s, as the educational condition of most black students remained separate and unequal despite *Brown*, civil rights leaders and progressive scholars expressed increasing support for a policy of transporting children by bus to schools outside their neighborhoods in order to achieve racially integrated schools.[64] Racial imbalance was not, of course, confined to the South's educational institutions. It was observable across the land, wherever blacks and whites were segregated residentially—which is to say, in practically every one of the nation's cities. But whereas *Brown* had required only state neutrality toward students of different races, judicial decisions in the late 1960s and early 1970s would require nothing less than "affirmative state action to desegregate school systems." Since racial fairness was henceforth to be measured statistically, the race of each student became the decisive factor in educational placement decisions. Schools that were primarily black—even in states with no history of formal segregation and in which resistance to *Brown* was never an issue—were presumed to be educationally inferior as well as legally suspect.[65]

Conceived to eliminate continuing racial isolation—as distinct from segregation—in American public schools with a view to maximizing integration and enhancing black opportunities, busing encountered fierce resistance from the outset. Much of the scholarship that has addressed the policy has focused on the nature of white opposition—usually in Boston—and either trivialized or ignored the significant black opposition.[66] In the 1980s and 1990s black conservative intellectuals would become the face of this black opposition, presenting a number of challenging arguments in favor of the policy's abandonment. Whereas white resistance to busing was focused almost exclusively on the harm it was inflicting on white children, these intellectuals' resistance was more multifaceted: to varying degrees, their critiques combined support for whites' constitutional rights on the one hand with concern for the policy's harmful impact on black children on the other.

Sowell began his criticism of busing by endorsing the sentiments of the white majority. "Kipling's doctrine of the white man's burden," he noted, had effectively been "transformed into a judicial doctrine of the white child's burden"—"a doctrine that came very close to fighting racism with racism."[67] Predictably, but not altogether implausibly, Sowell laid the blame for this sticky situation on the social science rationale that had informed the *Brown* decision. "If it was separation that made schools inferior," he wrote, "then only integrated schools could provide equality in education."[68] *Brown* may not have prescribed compulsory busing for racial balance. But the logic of its argument, according to Sowell, had led inexorably to that conclusion. This "tortuous evolution" of the law after 1954 was said by the black Milton Friedman to be a nagging reminder of the wisdom of Sir Walter Scott: "Oh, what a tangled web we weave, / When first we practice to deceive!"[69] Psychological reasoning, without basis in law, had been used deceivingly in *Brown*, Sowell asserted, to force the educational hand of Southern segregationists. But as time passed that reasoning came to take its own course and to exact its own toll on the school systems and social fabric of the whole nation.[70]

Stressing that she was neither against "Negroes" nor for "Negroes,"[71] Wortham—in contrast to Sowell—wrote little about the educational significance of *Brown* for African Americans, and nowhere attempted to blame the decision for the ensuing controversy surrounding busing. Her only concern was what this controversy meant for Americans' individual freedoms. "Why," Wortham asked, "is it that children, because of their race or ethnic group, alone, are not allowed to attend the neighborhood schools of their choice, but forcefully transported to distant schools . . .

despite the fact that 74 percent of Americans opposed court-ordered busing?"[72] Woodson's opposition to the policy was altogether different from Wortham's. Seemingly less concerned by the white ill-will it had generated, he criticized busing out of a belief that it ran counter to poor blacks' best educational interests, impugning civil rights leaders in the process: "I didn't fight for integration, I fought against segregation. Their embrace of integration and busing really turned me off. . . . They seemed to be impressed with issues that were important to middle or upper-income blacks, but did little for lower-income blacks."[73]

Consistent with his view that social policy which implied that poor blacks needed to be "rescued by outsiders" was patronizing, Woodson suggested that ordinary black people were really the best qualified to recognize and overcome their own educational difficulties. But busing, he believed, had broken up the natural, organic ties in black neighborhoods that ultimately offered the solution to these difficulties.[74] Thomas, in time, expressed similar reservations about the policy's practical effectiveness, but (unlike Woodson) added to these reservations a more principled criticism. "I do not believe an institution can change its numbers, change its quotas, change its courses, or reduce its standards and make us better," he wrote.[75] But even if blacks could be made better, Thomas continued, busing would have to be opposed on the grounds that it was a clear violation of individual rights, of "what was best in the American political tradition."[76]

If Thomas's view of forced integration was a simple fusion of the perspectives offered by Wortham and Woodson, Loury's analysis of the subject was altogether more sophisticated, socially astute, and politically quite convincing. But it too was an analysis not without flaw. Unlike his fellow black conservatives, Loury acknowledged that good intentions— namely, the desire to equalize educational resources for white and black children—had motivated the "1970s-style judicial activism on behalf of the cause of integration."[77] But this approach, he felt, simply had not worked. The so-called flight of middle-class white families from urban districts subject to desegregation mandates had "made it all but impossible to achieve anything beyond token integration in many places."[78] What is more, in the 1990s, the educational achievement gap between white and black children was continuing to widen. Since results had not matched expectations, the message from Loury was clear: "achieving true equality of opportunity for the poorest public school students" meant "securing for them better teachers, smaller class sizes, longer school hours and greater support services."[79] The racial composition of the schools mattered little. Given the widely acknowledged failure of integration to effect the transformation in black education that many had predicted in the 1970s, the distinguished black economist's thesis seemed correct in principle. But the real question remained: how was his vision to be realized in practice?

The answer, simply, was that it was very difficult to see how it could be realized. In Loury's work, there was no acknowledgment of the fact that public school systems were administered on tax dollars and that, traditionally, those tax dollars have been spent in the places where people with the most political and economic influence could derive the most benefit from them. Nor was there any acknowledgment of the implications of this reality: that tax dollars for public education were spent disproportionately in areas dominated by whites, not in the inner cities inhabited disproportionately by poor people of color.[80] As flawed a policy as busing may have been, its supporters recognized this fundamental truth. As the liberal black lawyer Percy Sutton remarked, somewhat ironically, before the largely conservative Fairmont Conference: "I always felt that if a white child was to sit in school next to me, white people look out for their children and society looks out for white people, so I would have a better chance. And if it takes busing to create the phenomenon of Black children sitting next to white children, we are going to have to put up with busing."[81]

Busing was an attempt to solve instantly problems of prejudice and discrimination deeply rooted in American history. But it was a policy that was misguided, and destined to fail, for several reasons. First, parents understandably wanted to send their children to school in their local communities. Many had purchased housing in secure neighborhoods expressly for this purpose and naturally frowned upon having their children bused to other parts of town to attend what were, clearly, inferior schools. Put simply, parents assumed that they should have a degree of flexibility about where their children were to be educated. Accustomed to dealing with a school system that was administered democratically, in consultation with local residents, with busing they found themselves *subject* to one presided over by federal court judges who were both far removed from the educational realm and protected by lifetime tenure. "I want my freedom back," said one Boston parent after court-ordered busing began there. "They took my freedom. They tell me where my kids have to go to school. This is like living in Russia. Next they'll tell you where to shop."[82]

If these white parents resented their children being used as part of a social experiment to integrate public schools, in the 1980s black conservatives criticized busing not only for fear of further inflaming their resentment, but also because they believed the policy had delivered (and would continue to deliver) counterproductive results to black students. Busing may not have caused blacks' educational dilemmas, they reasoned, but it had certainly not solved these dilemmas and it may even have exacerbated them. Due to the flawed reasoning behind the *Brown* decision, the legacy of school desegregation in the United States had been one of missed opportunities. With the exception of Loury—who in the late 1990s had offered a laudable but seemingly impractical vision for public schools—these intellectuals did not see a stronger government education system as important to improving black life chances. Government was the problem, in their view, not the solution. The controversy over busing suggested to them that the key to enhancing black educational opportunity was not state-imposed integration but rather market-driven parental choice.

The debate over school choice certainly accelerated during the 1980s. But the rationale for publicly funded vouchers was not new, having originally been proposed by Thomas Paine at the time of the Revolutionary War.[83] This fact is little known, arguably because the roots of the modern debate lay not with Paine but with Milton Friedman. In 1955 Friedman had written a seminal essay, "The Role of Government in Education," and made an impassioned case for the adoption of a more market-driven system of schooling in the United States.[84] One year after the *Brown* decision, the reasoning behind his thesis was clear. Since market forces were a more efficient means of allocating resources, he argued, allowing them to reign free would enhance competition and innovation, and foster an educational environment in which "providers" were more responsive to the needs of "consumers." Friedman insisted that the society as a whole would benefit if his proposal were adopted. Shortly after the publication of "The Role of Government in Education," "choice" became the focus of considerable academic attention.[85] But nationally, at the political level, the idea failed to penetrate. In the 1960s and early 1970s government-mandated integration remained the official approach for delivering democratic educational access and standards.

Beginning in the mid-1970s, however, frustration at the failure of integration to improve the public schools made people of all political stripes more receptive to the idea of pursuing private alternatives.[86] By the 1980s, as calls to maximize parental choice grew louder, increasing numbers of African American parents also joined the chorus, recognizing that their children were disproportionately the greatest victims of the sub-standard system.[87] For once, black community sentiment mirrored black conservative ideology. Seeking to capitalize on this grassroots discontent, Sowell and company shrewdly positioned themselves as the most committed defenders of poor blacks' educational interests. In the black conservative discourse on choice that emerged, the language of neoliberalism—parental empowerment, accountability, and individual freedom—was reappropriated and combined with ideas of collective black freedom and a concern for the most disadvantaged African American children. This hybrid discourse, which blended meanings from multiple political sources and agendas, was to have a significant impact on the wider schools debate.

Although all black conservatives promoted choice as the best alternative to the educational status quo, divisions soon emerged within the group over what choice actually meant. Strict free-marketers such as Sowell and Williams dreamed, like their mentor Friedman, that the introduction of choice would revolutionize the system by transferring the administration of public schools to a market-driven network of essentially private schools. Such a system was desirable, they insisted, not only because private schools were "less expensive" and "more efficient" than public schools, consistently producing better results, but also because it would mean a weakened state, as the responsibility for education was wrested from government and placed in the hands of individual citizens.[88] In time, Wortham endorsed Sowell's and Williams's sentiments: "We need to do more than merely call for reforms in the public education system. We need a different system altogether—a system that fosters choice, competition and efficiency. . . . [In public education] there is little systematic incentive for educators to provide the quality education that consumers want and that a democratic society and the high technology of the computer age require. We are not likely to improve the quality and efficiency of education under such conditions."[89]

Rather than provide detailed descriptions of what a revised private system would look like, however, these three intellectuals initially focused most of their attention on the implications of choice for public education. Those public officials who had "taken our money, betrayed our trust, failed our children and then lied about the failures with inflated grades and pretty words"[90] would, it was predicted, "lose the monopoly power they now hold over a captive audience."[91] With vouchers in hand, millions of poor parents—a disproportionate number of whom were black—would simply withdraw their children from defective government schools and send them to private schools, thereby hastening the public system's demise.

Whereas Sowell, Williams, and Wortham supported the demise of public education (it seemed) largely for ideological reasons, the moderate black conservatives, Woodson and Loury, adopted a more judicious approach. It was arguably they, more than the free-market purists, who embodied the will of so many black parents, whose major concern was not ideology, but rather ensuring the best educational opportunities for their children. Rather than dwell excessively on government's failure to provide these opportunities, Woodson and Loury sought to channel these people's growing indignation into a more constructive dialogue about the possible make-up of an alternative schools model. Woodson, for instance, agreed with Sowell, Williams, and Wortham that a better-funded public system would not "do the trick." "If you keep giving money to the same doctor," he explained, "and the patient continues to get worse, you'd better seek a second opinion."[92] But both Woodson's and Loury's understanding of that second option—choice—differed from their three fellow black conservatives. By enabling children to attend the school their parents favored within their local district, choice, they predicted, would facilitate greater access not only to private institutions but also potentially to the best public ones as well.[93]

These black conservatives' halfway-house position between the Friedmanite free-market conservatism of a Thomas Sowell and the economic liberalism of civil rights leaders was noteworthy. But although not committed to the destruction of public education, Loury's and Woodson's primary objective was still to put the "time-tested practicality and efficiency of private schools to work for black students and their parents."[94] What is more, they maintained, like other black conservatives, that a voucher system offered the best hope of realizing this objective. How specifically though would such a system assist the black poor? Ultimately, these intellectuals argued, it would confer upon poor black parents the same freedom of choice about how to educate their children as the well-to-do possessed. Of the black conservatives, it was arguably Parker who put this case best: "At the present time, only affluent and middle-class Americans have freedom of choice. They can send their children to public schools or can send them to private schools. Only the poor, a disproportionate number of whom are members of minority groups, are compelled to use the public schools. I support a voucher system which would give the poor the same freedom of choice about how to educate their children that only the prosperous now have."[95]

What Woodson called "parent-selected education,"[96] other black conservatives insisted would inevitably lead increasing numbers of black children away from the decrepit public system and into private schools, where discipline was strong and values were taught. Harking back to the community control movements of the 1960s, the NCNE president even suggested that choice might provide opportunities for low-income black parents to establish and administer their own—predominantly black—neighborhood schools.[97] Such developments within the black community were to be welcomed, he continued, because "when you empower people and give them a sense of ownership, they become responsible and learn how to make decisions."[98] Educational self-determination, then, according to Woodson, had the potential to unleash dormant social capital that could be deployed to tackle the myriad other problems confronting the black poor.[99] These were confident claims indeed.

Sowell's and Williams's claims often seemed even more self-assured. Occasionally moving away from their attacks on the public educational establishment, they too would focus on what choice and private schooling could do for the most disadvantaged blacks. Woodson, to support his case, had appropriated the activist rhetoric of the 1960s, speaking of the need to fight poverty by "empowering those at the bottom."[100] But Sowell peered further into the past, citing numerous examples of outstanding achievement in all-black private schools before public education was even open to African Americans.[101] Eschewing a historical focus, Williams based his case for blacks' private schooling on a surveying of the contemporary environment. As a group, he observed, blacks had received a "grossly inferior education," but there were notable exceptions, mostly in nongovernment schools: "Los Angeles' Marcus Garvey School's black elementary school students achieve higher scores than their white counterparts. Students at Marva Collins' Westside Preparatory School exceed the achievement of their Chicago government school counterparts by a wide margin. Eighty percent of Philadelphia's Ivy Leaf School students score at or above the national norm on standardized tests and some even score two, three, and four years above."[102]

Thus, the challenge for policy-makers, this black economist insisted, was to enhance the opportunity for students to leave public schools doing a poor job at a high cost and to enroll at private schools such as Marcus Garvey and Marva Collins, who were doing a good job at a low cost. Since real-estate prices prohibited poor blacks from moving to the better areas where the better schools tended to be located, Williams asked, why not enable students' attendance with vouchers?

Extraordinarily, no specific attempt has been made during the past quarter century to evaluate the merits and flaws of the black conservatives' support for school choice. Perhaps one reason for the dearth of literature in this area is that vouchers, while consistently surfacing as a reform concept in discussions of public education, have yet to be nationally tested in the United States.[103] In the absence of a widely operative choice model and a clearly defined body of scholarship, definitive judgments about the value of these intellectuals' proposals are difficult. But placing proposals for vouchers in their historical context is surely an important first step to considering the significance—and possible implications—of such a system for the modern African American community. One might ask: has the ceding of regulation from democratic institutions to the marketplace previously enhanced or impeded blacks' educational development?

The black conservatives, however, in making their case for vouchers in the 1980s and 1990s, appeared somewhat reluctant to engage with history or, to put it another way, they showed themselves to be rather poor historians. Convinced that only choice could salvage black education in the present, these intellectuals conveniently overlooked that freedom-of-choice movements had seriously thwarted black education in the past. In his analysis of the drive to democratize schools after *Brown*, law professor James Ryan emphasized this point strongly. "It is certainly true that Southern states and school districts relied on school choice to avoid integration. So-called freedom-of-choice plans . . . offered students a choice among public schools that was free in theory but not in reality."[104] Of course, tuition grants became one of the most powerful tools of white resistance to blacks' drive for a better education in the post-*Brown* era, shaping the policy image of the Court's decision in what turned out to be a decade-long struggle for the soul of Southern education.[105] If the Supreme Court supported a parent's constitutional right to choose where to educate their children, the argument went, how could the Court, in good faith, oppose school-choice programs, even if these programs maintained racial segregation and bolstered white supremacy?

Despite the various official justifications for choice that appeared in the 1950s and 1960s, unofficially choice meant racial discrimination in support of the all-white schools that were established by Southern officials to preserve Jim Crow education.[106] This context was important, modern critics of choice insisted, not because the contemporary and historical proposals were the same, but rather because it confirmed that the American past was replete with examples of organized interests capturing the terms "freedom" and "choice" and using them to advance their own agenda.[107] "In a country founded on freedom of choice," Sowell argued in the 1980s, "it is amazing how many battles still have to be fought over that issue."[108] But since "freedom" and "choice" were clearly not always what they seemed, unpacking this terminology as the black conservatives deployed it had the potential to shed some light on their educational agenda for African Americans. As time passed, moreover, these intellectuals' claims could also be measured against studies that—while not addressing their work directly—focused on the likely consequences of the choice vision they so enthusiastically promoted.

Although championed by black conservatives as a remedy for the disparities between rich white students and poor black students, there was little empirical evidence to suggest that the school choice programs of the past quarter century had any such educational impact. In fact, much of the evidence that did exist cast serious doubt on this claim. The nation's two largest voucher schemes of the past fifteen years—the Milwaukee Parental Choice Program and the Cleveland School Voucher Program—were practical cases in point, confirming in the 1990s a number of the theoretical concerns about choice raised by scholars in the 1980s.[109] Far from validating Sowell and company's thesis that deregulation would improve poor blacks' academic standards, "neither program," according to social critic Leon Beauchman, could "document any meaningful change in student performance."[110] Progressive analysts would not have been surprised. Choice was destined to fail, they had long argued, because its supporters ignored the sociological reasons behind educational disadvantage in the first place.

It seemed that the black conservatives were particularly guilty in this respect. Although unanimously committed to a voucher system—subtle variations of emphasis notwithstanding—these intellectuals never spelled out any specific policy detail, and they neglected to engage with the myriad counterarguments advanced by school choice's opponents. Sowell and company claimed, for instance, that vouchers would allow poor black parents to exercise the same level of choice in school selection as privileged whites. And on the face of it, this theory appeared plausible. But vouchers' critics would point to a number of experiments with choice over the years to show that such a view lacked practical credibility. As it turned out, poor black students were often filtered out under voucher systems by the tendency of the private schools to recruit middle-class children and high scholastic achievers in order to boost their test scores and enhance their prestige.[111] Complex admission procedures that required a level of expertise to negotiate also served as a significant barrier for these students and their parents, who usually had little formal education themselves.[112] When combined with the geographical isolation of poor blacks in relation to these schools—typically located in far-away sections of the cities or in the distant suburbs—and the extensive travel time and transportation costs that would be required for them to attend, it was disingenuous to suggest that choice programs would simply neutralize distinctions of race and class and equalize educational opportunities.[113] Yet this is precisely what the black conservatives did suggest.

These intellectuals' support for choice might have been more convincing had they actually provided details of *how* such a system would overcome barriers seemingly so ingrained in the nation's social and economic fabric. For example, did Sowell and company support programs that extended vouchers to all students, regardless of family income? Or were their proposals more tightly focused, means-tested, and specifically targeted to help low-income families? Since the brightest black students would, in all likelihood, be skimmed off to attend private schools under a voucher system, what were the black conservatives' plans for the poorest black students left behind in faltering inner-city public schools? Logic dictated, after all, that there were not enough places in private schools for all black children of the inner city. And logic also dictated that, without the presence of any high-achieving students, inner-city schools would become even less conducive to learning, dooming the most disadvantaged blacks to an even worse education.[114] On these questions and issues, however, the black conservatives remained silent.

One issue on which the black conservatives were rarely silent was in expressing faith in the capacity of black parents to make the right educational decisions for their children if given the chance. "Considering the many disasters in the public schools created by experts over the past ten or twenty years," Sowell wrote, "it is hard to imagine how these parents could do worse."[115] The appropriate question for these intellectuals, however, was: which parents? After all, a major theme in the work of black conservatives over the past quarter century was how the disintegration of the black family since the mid-1960s—under an avalanche of drugs, crime, and welfare—had deprived millions of black children of effective parents. With the exceptions of Loury and possibly Woodson, these intellectuals never sought to understand the complex set of structural factors that had consigned so many of their fellow African Americans to lives of poverty and despair, preferring to believe that these people and their families were culturally dysfunctional. Yet, astonishingly, when the issue of vouchers arose, black conservatives claimed to recognize the intimate and responsive nature of the black family, temporarily forgetting the crack-addicted, welfare-dependent single mothers against whom they had previously railed and championing the ability of black mothers and fathers to exercise choice responsibly. Another serious inconsistency thus lay at the heart of Sowell and company's educational advocacy, one which scholars have curiously hitherto failed to note.

Black conservatives were not only concerned with educational structure in seeking to improve the quality of schooling for black children. Increasingly, these intellectuals were also concerned with the educational content to which these children were exposed. One of the salutary effects of the civil rights struggle had been to revitalize the public school curriculum, which had previously ignored or distorted the contributions of blacks and other minorities in American history. Beginning in the mid-1970s, school textbooks began to change and a racially and ethnically more inclusive story of the national past came to be told.[116] America's cultural heritage, it turned out, "did not begin and end with the intellectual and aesthetic products of Western Europe."[117] The celebrated melting pot in which a diverse array of ethnic antecedents were mixed together into an egalitarian and harmonious blend of cultures had never really existed. Rather, racism had been functional in America since the arrival of the first victims of the Atlantic slave trade in Virginia in 1619, defining and circumscribing the lives of millions of people of color and denying their humanity. But the oppressed people of color, according to the new textbooks, had refused to accept their lot. In fact, they had resisted the power and violence directed against them, utilizing their individual talents and channeling their collective energies to help shape the contours of American society. In the new multicultural age, their stories became central to the broader national narrative. Variety had indeed become the spice of life.[118]

These developments within public education were subjected to particularly rigorous scrutiny in the 1990s as the meaning of terms like "diversity" and "multiculturalism" were debated more widely across the American society. Neither term, as it turned out, enjoyed significant mainstream support, and both raised the ire of a conservative establishment already hostile to the perceived assault of political correctness on their national identity. If book titles such as *Alien Nation, The Closing of the American Mind, The Unmaking of Americans,* and *The End of American Identity* conveyed a sense that the nation was imploding under pressure from "multicultural man," Dinesh D'Souza's *Illiberal Education* told of the terrible consequences of attempts to mitigate the impediments of race, class, and gender through the education system. By enshrining difference, he argued, educators had effectively institutionalized lower standards, as well as new forms of discrimination and inequality.[119] D'Souza's thesis might have seemed overblown. But its impact in the public domain, where *Illiberal Education* was read widely, could not be denied.

It would be quite wrong, then, to present the black conservatives' campaign against multiculturalism in the educational sphere as groundbreaking; it was not. Nor was the campaign monolithic. But these intellectuals' writings on the subject were still influential, even as they displayed subtle variations and conflicting emphases. Led by Sowell, most black conservatives criticized the painstaking efforts to expand the understanding of American history into a richer and more varied narrative account. Rather than establishing a mature cultural pluralism, they argued, the new educational environment had enshrined a particularist model of multiculturalism, whose proponents believed not in a shared common culture, but in accentuating the differences of minority peoples for political purposes. "Self-esteem programs and multicultural diversity now dominate the agenda in educational circles,"[120] Sowell charged, as he condemned teachers for seeking to "reshape the social mindsets" of American children.[121] In time, Williams endorsed Sowell's assessment, insisting that "multiculturalism and diversity are a cancer on our society."[122] Perhaps nowhere was this cancer of essentialist revolt against the melting pot more striking than in the rise of the contentious Afrocentrist movement within the black community in the early 1990s. But nowhere was the reaction to multiculturalism's radicalization as fierce as the critique of Afrocentrism propounded by some black conservatives.

Before evaluating the merits, flaws, and significance of the black conservative attack on Afrocentrism, it is important to establish a working definition of Afrocentrism itself, and to consider its educational aims and impact. At the most fundamental level, Afrocentrism is an intellectual movement that rejects western scholarly standards and embraces an alternative black reality. Its proponents celebrate the discoveries, customs, and histories of African peoples as original, unique, and even superior to those of white Americans, juxtaposing the "prejudice" and "bigotry" of "Eurocentrism" with the need to develop a counter-hegemonic "black worldview."[123] As the prominent Afrocentrist Molefi Asante put it: Afrocentrism implies a "rejection of white values. . . . Afrocentrists study every thought, action, behavior, and value, and if it cannot be found in our culture, it is dispensed with quickly."[124] Such open disregard for accuracy is not difficult to explain, since the nurturing of black self-esteem—not objective inquiry—is the ultimate goal of this form of black consciousness. Serious questions would arise, however, when Afrocentrist pedagogy found its way into the educational curriculum at some of the nation's public schools.

Since most black conservatives typically emphasized a universalist American vision over a parochial race-based one as the best way forward for black people in the United States, an educational curriculum incorporating Afrocentric perspectives was never going to sit comfortably with them. This is perhaps an understatement. The news that students were learning that black children had unique intellectual habits and that standard assessment methods were "culturally biased" irritated these intellectuals. Reports that Egypt was being depicted—incorrectly—as the black cradle of civilization and that the great philosophical, cultural, and even scientific advances in world history were being attributed—again, incorrectly—to black Africans, evoked similar frustration. But it was upon learning that some children in predominantly black kindergartens were being taught to count in Swahili that black conservative anger erupted. A furious Thomas Sowell wrote: "The self-esteem doctrine is just one in a long line of educational dogmas used to justify or camouflage a historic retreat from academic education."[125] Steele, for his part, used the controversy to speculate, once more, on the perils of African Americans embracing a rigid black ethnic consciousness. Afrocentrism was, Steele argued, "more trap than liberation" because "no black identity, however beautifully conjured," will spare blacks the challenge of having to compete with others to achieve upward mobility in American life.[126]

While Woodson expressed similar concerns that Afrocentrism's exclusionary philosophy would jeopardize black mobility by imperiling the assimilative function of schools,[127] it was Wortham who offered the most intellectually dense black conservative critique of the phenomenon. "Afrocentrists harm black children," Wortham argued, "when they teach them that they cannot have pride in themselves unless they first have pride in their African origins."[128] What black children really needed, she continued, was "not immersion in the history of ancient Africa"—with traditions, beliefs, and values largely extraneous to the modern world—but "education in what is necessary for success in modern America."[129] Black children needed to know, in other words, that America was their country too. Real self-esteem would come with this realization, Wortham predicted, not with fanciful depictions of old Mother Africa as the center of everything.[130] For this black sociologist, then, Afrocentrism was essentially a flight from the reality of one's own being, a form of escape motivated by a deep-seated fear of individual freedom.

These black conservative criticisms of Afrocentrism can be seen to have at least some merit. The Afrocentrists' rather desperate effort to instill pride and self-esteem in black students by encouraging them to seek comfort in the myths of a glorious black past could not possibly deliver the educational skills that more African Americans required if they were to become successful participants in the mainstream. Therapy through mythology could never be an adequate substitute for rigorous educational training. As the black liberal scholar K. Anthony Appiah noted: "I'm skeptical about the usefulness of teaching people stuff that I have grounds for believing to be false. It can't be a very good thing to have people's egos constructed around something which, once they escape from the Afrocentric school into the large world, will be represented to them—and correctly so—as false."[131]

The black conservatives' principled rejection of the Afrocentrists' blind loyalty to race was also commendable; self-criticism was, as Martin Luther King, Jr. once noted, a most admirable quality.[132] But too often the black conservatives replaced the Afrocentrists' blind loyalty to race with a similarly debilitating blind loyalty to individualism and nation. Celebrating blackness—whether rooted in Africa or America or both—was dangerous, they insisted, because it put black people out of step with the majority of Americans. But Sowell and company's commitment to traditional Americanism was similarly dangerous, in Cornel West's view, leading "not to a deepening and enriching of black intellectual exchange, but rather to a defense of new kinds of restrictions in the name of a neo-nationalism already rampant in America."[133] The search for identity and authenticity was evidently not confined to the supporters of Afrocentrism and other forms of militant black consciousness.

While usefully identifying the flaws within Afrocentrism, black conservatives might have extended their analysis of the phenomenon further. At no time, for example, did Sowell, Steele, Woodson, or Wortham ask, "why Afrocentrism now?" Seemingly content to attribute its presence to the willingness of politically correct elites to tolerate the intolerance of black racists for the sake of diversity, these intellectuals missed a valuable opportunity to probe Afrocentrism's deeper social and political meaning. Was it not significant that this educational movement had emerged after twelve years of Republican rule, when many white Americans appeared—in Manning Marable's judgment—to have "retreated from an honest dialogue about the pervasiveness of racial inequality in American life?"[134] With the civil rights movement over and the dream of integration fading, was it not possible that the Afrocentric perspective offered an increasingly disconsolate black population a degree of certainty about their past—however misguided—which they could draw on to deal with their sense of contemporary insecurity? Rather than simply condemn as "mad" or "bad" those blacks who were taken in by the movement's extravagant claims, surely it was better to seek to understand the social landscape that had made its emergence possible. In the end, though, in failing to consider these questions, black conservatives did little more than explain the rise of Afrocentrism in terms of black individual and cultural debility.

As was so often the case, Loury was the one black conservative who bucked this trend, offering a qualified defense of Afrocentric schooling. Although one certainly could not approve of every item in Afrocentrist curricular proposals, these proposals had arisen, he believed and therefore needed to be understood, in terms of "the existential condition of blacks in this nation of immigrants."[135] Forcibly cut off from their pre-American history and long barred from interpreting the nation's past, Afrocentrism was one part of a much larger process of black people embracing their racial identity and asserting their educational selves in modern America. Rather than obsess about the more outrageous claims made by supporters of this phenomenon, scholars, in Loury's view, should have recognized its fringe status and focused instead on the positive educational developments of the multicultural age.[136] For the schools to give more attention, for example, to the heroism of the Underground Railroad than to the building of the transcontinental railroad was something to be celebrated rather than deplored.[137] Loury believed that curricular change of this kind democratized the past and, in doing so, served the broader public good.

This analysis from the late 1990s would set the black MIT-trained economist even further apart—intellectually—from the conservative movement, straining relations with many on the black right. That this should be the case was hardly surprising. While some black conservatives' reservations about Afrocentrism had been reasonable enough, their dismissal of all forms of multiculturalism was at times bizarre. Sowell, in particular, argued that past ethnic immigrants did not have multiculturalism to ease their entry into the mainstream, as if this was an argument against introducing more pluralistic educational approaches in contemporary America.[138] Loury, in contrast, recognized that schools were not isolated from the mainstream, that they were—and are—products of the attitudes and values that define the wider society. To insist that educators avoid multicultural issues in an America that was becoming increasingly nonwhite was effectively to support a return to the "good old days" when the contributions of people of color were systematically ignored. To denounce Afrocentrism as an abuse of history and a misuse of education was one thing. But for black conservatives to propose an alternative educational model that functioned in much the same way—only in reverse—was hypocritical indeed.

In their controversial 2003 book *No Excuses*, Stephen and Abigail Thernstrom identified the racial gap in academic achievement as the "central civil rights issue of our time," warning that if America did not close the gap, racial inequality would remain a wound unhealed.[139] To be sure, black conservatives had devoted considerable attention to the causes of poor black educational performance since the early 1980s, repeatedly indicting liberal analyses of and prescriptions for the problem. Suspicious of *Brown* and hostile to busing, these intellectuals rejected the view that the failure to achieve integration might account for the continuing low level of black achievement. They also rejected the view that better-funded public schools would assist the most disadvantaged black students as they struggled to meet the academic challenges before them. Instead, the black conservatives championed a radically revised agenda of school "choice" to lift the black poor from the educational doldrums. In Reagan's America, in particular, nothing less than a market-based model of education would suffice.

Although broadly united on educational matters, divisions within the cohort were still discernible. The black conservatives opposed integration and busing for different reasons; they were not always united on what to do about public education; and their conceptions of what form a voucher system should take varied. Sowell, Williams, and Wortham, for instance, grounded their analyses of all aspects of the schools system in an idealized free-market paradigm. Education for them was a wholly economic concept in which unattached individuals were to be free to make rational choices in an unfettered marketplace. While not ignoring economic issues, Thomas and Woodson—with Sowell's support—focused their analyses on matters cultural, claiming to be especially concerned at how liberal approaches to schooling, which privileged integration, were undermining black communal autonomy. It was Loury, however, who was again the most independent thinker within the group, carving out distinctive positions on a number of educational issues and not being afraid to embrace progressive ideas when he saw fit.

In the 1980s and 1990s, when the social analyses of black conservatives were arguably enjoying their widest circulation, there was little doubt that American public education—particularly as it related to poor blacks—was urgently in need of reform. But rather than call for a massive injection of resources to boost the ailing system as *A Nation at Risk* had recommended, most black conservatives sought to undermine the system by attacking its most celebrated symbol—*Brown*—and challenging the attempts of reformers to make it more inclusive. Sometimes—on the busing controversy, for example, or the debate over curricula—these intellectuals made valid arguments. But their arguments concerning the public school system on the whole lacked credibility, since their ultimate goal was to destroy, or at least to significantly weaken, this very system.

Of course, the black conservative intellectuals promoted a system of educational choice as an alternative to the status quo. Although it was certainly an exaggeration to describe this system—as one critic did—as "nothing more than a 1950s tuition grant clothed in a corporate blue suit rather than a pearly white sheet,"[140] it was almost certainly not an exaggeration to suggest that such a system would only further stratify schools by socioeconomic status and academic achievement. In fact, numerous studies had shown that vouchers, while enhancing opportunities for the best students, would significantly diminish the nation's broader commitment to educating *all* students, particularly those drawn from the ranks of the "disadvantaged." That being the case, it was sometimes difficult to see how the black conservatives could so confidently square their support for choice with their professed concern for arguably the most disadvantaged people of all: the black poor.

Conclusion

From the time of their emergence at the dawn of the Reagan era, black conservative intellectuals were an integral part of the wider conservative movement's drive to overturn racial liberalism and recapture the nation's traditional soul. To suggest that these intellectuals stirred emotions along the way—in speaking to the conservative thrust in domestic politics on behalf of black people—would be a gross understatement, obscuring just how contested their presence in modern America proved to be. Yet, for too long, the virulent nature of the commentary focused on this phenomenon centered on the black conservatives' presence *alone* and served to thwart meaningful assessment of their thought and praxis. Typically, these intellectuals were treated as an undifferentiated mass; they were good or bad, right or wrong, depending on the political leanings of the observer. Rarely were they complex individuals whose lives and ideas warranted critical, merit-based scrutiny.

Black Conservative Intellectuals in Modern America has sought to contribute to a small but emerging body of literature that, beginning with Angela Dillard's seminal work *Guess Who's Coming to Dinner Now?* resolved to take the intellectual essence of black conservatism more seriously. Identified with the various struggles against affirmative action, welfare, and public education, the black conservatism of the 1980s and 1990s can be seen as a curious blend of classical conservatism and classical liberalism. Rising from humble origins, Sowell and company shared a suspicion of state power, a preference for liberty over equality and an unyielding faith in the political project that is America—all hallmarks of traditional conservatism, to be sure. But unlike traditionalists who embraced established hierarchies, these intellectuals—drawing on their own life experiences—preferred rugged individualists (and communities) that transcended hierarchies, pitching their message of uplift to the most disadvantaged segments of the black community. Theirs was a message designed to appeal simultaneously to Republican political powerbrokers in Washington, business directors on Wall Street, and (perhaps even) to some blacks on the margins of society who wanted desperately to believe in the promise of America.

It needs to be emphasized, above all, that contemporary black conservatism, as it emerged and took shape after 1980, was not a single, coherent system of ideas, but rather an eclectic mixture of themes and policies brought together more by the contingencies of circumstance than by logic or the requirements of a sophisticated political philosophy. That there was no one black conservative uniform that fit all members of the cohort should now be clear. Even as they agreed on the undesirable nature of affirmative action, the pernicious consequences of welfare, and the need for drastic educational reform to improve the black condition, these intellectuals' analyses of these subjects varied—sometimes subtly, at other times more strikingly. It is quite astonishing, given the black conservatives' prominence in modern America, that the diversity and complexity that often characterized their thought was left unexplored for so long.

Exposition of the diversity and complexity within black conservative ranks offers a more sophisticated assessment of the controversial phenomenon they came to represent. Assessment of the strengths and weaknesses of different black conservative interpretations of affirmative action, welfare, and public education demanded location in historical context and alongside respected scholarship in all three fields. The results were mixed. The arguments of some black conservatives were, of course, more convincing than those of others; but, on the whole, these intellectuals failed to come to grips with the nuances of race and class in American society that, together, continued to limit opportunities for millions of African American people. Typically, these intellectuals' analyses were reactive rather than proactive, denouncing liberal and radical strategies to deal with racism and poverty while offering few credible suggestions of their own.

It appears clear, then, that the eminence of black conservatives in American political discourse during the past three decades had more to do with their ideological utility—with the novelty of their voices as non-liberal blacks—than with the potency of their arguments, which appeared to falter (so often) under an intellectual microscope. This is not an ad hominem attack, but merely an observation about the deep structures of racial awareness that—because of history—continue to define American institutions and public interactions. To suggest, as some did, that black conservatives were merely counterfeit heroes and that black conservatism in the United States should not exist was surely to contravene the spirit of the civil rights movement, which was fought and won partly to give all black people (even would-be conservative ones) choices. But to suggest that the black conservatives were color-blind visionaries who offered a realistic program for contemporary black advancement was equally misguided. In reality, black conservative intellectuals in modern America were neither counterfeit heroes nor color-blind visionaries.

Notes

Introduction

Note to epigraph: Thomas Sowell, quoted in H. Allen, "Hot Disputes and Cool Sowell," *Washington Post*, October 1, 1981, C1.

1. Kelly Miller, *Radicals and Conservatives and Other Essays on the Negro in America* (New York: Schocken Books, 1968), 25.

2. Ibid.

3. The inclusion of Clarence Thomas in a book entitled *Black Conservative Intellectuals in Modern America* may initially raise some eyebrows, because many would not consider Thomas to be an "intellectual" in the traditional academic sense. Yet Thomas was certainly a (if not *the*) critical "public figure" in black conservatism's rise to prominence in the 1980s, not only—I would point out—because of his various high-profile appointments, but also because of his pre–Supreme Court writings on race and class that arguably did display an *intellectual* flavor. These writings, and Thomas's other contributions in popularizing contemporary black conservative thought, simply cannot be ignored by a book dedicated to exploring the nature and significance of this thought.

4. Walter Friedman, "The African-American Gospel of Business Success," in *Black Conservatism: Essays in Intellectual and Political History*, ed. Peter Eisenstadt (New York: Garland Publishing, 1999), 133.

5. Clarence Page, *Showing My Color: Impolite Essays on Race and Identity* (New York: Harper Collins, 1996), 205.

6. Thomas Sowell, "Politics and Opportunity: Background," in *The Fairmont Papers: Black Alternatives Conference*, ed. Institute for Contemporary Studies (San Francisco: Institute for Contemporary Studies, 1980), 3–4.

7. Remarks of Edwin Meese in Institute for Contemporary Studies, ed., *Fairmont Papers*, 159–60.

8. Hanes Walton Jr., "Remaking African American Public Opinion: The Role and Function of the African American Conservatives," in *Dimensions of Black Conservatism in the United States: Made in America*, ed. Gayle T. Tate and Lewis A. Randolph (New York: Palgrave, 2002), 149–50; Georgia A. Persons, "The Election of Gary Franks and the Ascendancy of the New Black Conservatives," in *Dilemmas of Black Politics: Issues of Leadership and Strategy*, ed. Georgia A. Persons (New York: Harper-Collins, 1993), 198–201. See also John S. Saloma, *Ominous Politics: The New Conservative Labyrinth* (New York: Hill and Wang, 1984).

9. Quoted in Robert C. Smith and Hanes Walton Jr., "U-Turn: Martin Kilson and Black Conservatism," *Transition* 62 (1993): 213.

10. See, for further discussion, Amy E. Ansell, "The Color of America's Culture

Wars," in *Unraveling the Right: The New Conservatism in American Thought and Politics*, ed. Amy E. Ansell (Boulder, Colo.: Westview Press, 1998), 173–91.

11. Amy E. Ansell, *New Right, New Racism: Race and Reaction in the United States and Britain* (New York: New York University Press, 1997), 74–141.

12. Robin Kelley, *Yo' Mama's Disfunktional: Fighting the Culture Wars in Urban America* (Boston: Beacon Press, 1997), 3.

13. Manning Marable, *Race, Reform and Rebellion: The Second Reconstruction in Black America 1945–1990* (Jackson: University Press of Mississippi, 1991), 197.

14. Smith and Walton, "U-Turn," 209.

15. Marable, *Race, Reform*, 182.

16. Manning Marable, *Beyond Black and White: Transforming African-American Politics* (New York: Verso, 1995), 28.

17. Jill Lawrence, "Kerry Slow to Energize Black Vote," *USA Today*, October 19, 2004, http://www.usatoday.com/news/politicselections/nation/president/2004-10-19-kerry-black-vote_x.htm.

18. Peter Eisenstadt, ed., *Black Conservatism: Essays in Intellectual and Political History* (New York: Garland Publishing, 1999), ix–xxxii.

19. Cornel West, *Race Matters* (Boston: Beacan Press, 1993), 74.

20. Richard Hofstadter, *Anti-Intellectualism in American Life* (New York: Vintage Books, 1963), 25.

21. Joseph G. Conti and Brad Stetson, *Challenging the Civil Rights Establishment: Profiles of a New Black Vanguard* (Westport, Conn.: Praeger Publishers, 1993), x.

22. Until quite recently, the historical contributions of early conservative black spokespeople were virtually forgotten, their accommodationist ideas renounced and effectively dumped onto what John David Smith called "the trash heap of black historiography." John David Smith, *Black Judas: William Hannibal Thomas and the American Negro* (Athens: University of Georgia Press, 2000), xxiii. There were, of course, minor exceptions—most notably, some biographical studies of Booker T. Washington—but as late as 1984, political scientist Vernon E. Mc-Clean could proclaim that "there had never been a study of black conservatism in America." V. McClean, "Historical Examples of Black Conservatism," *Western Journal of Black Studies* 8, no. 3 (1984): 148. This long neglect of what the political scientist Michael Dawson identified as one of the "six historically important black political ideologies," can in part be explained by history itself. In the 1960s and 1970s, with the black freedom struggle in full swing and interest in the history of black resistance flourishing, there was a clear trend among liberal and radical scholars to redress the imbalances and injustices of the past by celebrating the achievements of African American heroes. In this environment, not surprisingly, what Dawson identified as the five other "historically important black political ideologies"—Radical Egalitarianism, Disillusioned Liberalism, Marxism, Feminism, and Nationalism—captured the spotlight, the determination of their followers to "speak truth to power" perfectly attuned to the times. Michael C. Dawson, *Black Visions: The Roots of Contemporary African American Political Ideologies* (Chicago: University of Chicago Press, 2003), 2. Although the publication of two edited book collections in the past ten years has gone some way to rectifying this historiographical silence, the history of black conservatism has continued, for the most part, to be overlooked by scholars more concerned with the politics of liberation. For the most comprehensive assessments of early black conservatism, see Eisenstadt, ed., *Black Conservatism*; Gayle T. Tate and Lewis A. Randolph, eds., *Dimensions of Black Conservatism in the United States: Made in America* (New York: Palgrave, 2002).

23. In an article in the *Australasian Journal of American Studies,* I adopted this phraseology to convey what had been, until recently, the general state of the debate. See Michael L. Ondaatje, "Counterfeit Heroes or Colour-Blind Visionaries? The Black Conservative Challenge to Affirmative Action in Modern America," *Australasian Journal of American Studies* 23, no. 2 (2004): 31–50.

24. M. Jones, "The Political Thought of the New Black Conservatives: An Analysis, Explanation and Interpretation," in *Readings in American Political Issues,* ed. Franklin D. Jones and Michael O. Adams (Dubuque, Ia.: Kendall-Hunt, 1987), 23.

25. Marable, *Beyond,* 93.

26. William J. Wilson, *The Declining Significance of Race: Blacks and Changing American Institutions* (Chicago: University of Chicago Press, 1978).

27. Julianne Malveaux, "Class Matters for Economic Prosperity," *Black Issues in Higher Education* 19, no. 10 (2002): 32. For similar examples, see Harry Edwards, "Camouflaging the Color Line: A Critique," in *The Caste and Class Controversy,* ed. Charles Vert Willie (New York: General Hall, 1979), 98–103; Charles Payne, "On the Declining—And Increasing—Significance of Race," in *Caste and Class Controversy,,* 117–39; Charles Vert Willie, "The Inclining Significance of Race," in *Caste and Class Controversy,,* 145–58. Indeed, when Wilson won a prestigious award from the American Association of Sociologists for *The Declining Significance of Race,* the Association of Black Sociologists filed a formal complaint against the decision, denouncing the book as a "misrepresentation of the black experience": *Caste and Class Controversy,,* 177–78.

28. The Association of Black Sociologists declared: "In the past reactionary groups have seized upon inappropriate analyses as a basis for the further suppression of blacks. We would hope that this is not the intent of the recent recognition that has been given to Professor Wilson's book." Ibid., 177–78. So relentless was the criticism of Wilson by black scholars that even President Reagan came to believe that he was a black conservative. An invitation was promptly extended to the Chicago sociologist to visit the White House. Shocked, Wilson called the president's advisers and informed them that a terrible mistake had been made. Joe Klein, "The True Disadvantage," *New Republic* 215, no. 18 (1996): 32–33. Although the "left's" view of *The Declining Significance of Race* was based on a fundamental misunderstanding of Wilson's thesis, the title—undoubtedly formulated with an eye to selling books—did not help matters. A simple question mark at the end would arguably have conveyed more accurately the book's fundamental premise and averted much of the confusion and controversy that ensued.

29. Angela D. Dillard, *Guess Who's Coming to Dinner Now? Multicultural Conservatism in America* (New York: New York University Press, 2001), 1.

30. See, for example, Thomas Hazlett and Manuel Klausner, "Reason Interview: Thomas Sowell," *Reason* 12, no. 8 (1980): 44–51; James W. Singer, "With a Friend in the White House, Black Conservatives Are Speaking Out," *National Journal,* March 14, 1981, 435–39; Murray Friedman, "The New Black Intellectuals," *Commentary* 69, no. 6 (1982): 46–52; Reverend E. V. Hill et al., "Black America Under the Reagan Administration: A Symposium of Black Conservatives," *Policy Review* 34 (1985): 27–41.

31. Friedman, "New Black Intellectuals," 51. For further discussion of the view that blacks were "turning conservative," see W. Greider and H. Logan, "Why Blacks are Turning Conservative," *Conservative Digest,* October 1978, 29–31.

32. See, for example, Roger Wilkins, "Sowell Brother," *Nation,* October 10, 1981, 333; Jerry G. Watts, "The Case of a Black Conservative: Thomas Sowell:

Talent and Tragedy," *Dissent* 29, no. 2 (1982): 301–13; Manning Marable, "Black Conservatives and Accommodation: Of Thomas Sowell and Others," *Negro History Bulletin* 45, no. 2 (1982): 32–35; Manning Marable, "Black Reaganism: A Rogue's Gallery," *Washington DC Afro-American*, April 24, 1982; Roger Wilkins, "Not by Bootstraps Alone: Why the Black New-Cons Are Wrong," *Village Voice*, February 4, 1986; James Jennings, "The New Black Neo-Conservatism: A Critique," *Trotter Review*, fall 1987, 15–21.

33. C. Rowan, "Backlash Against Sowell," *Business Week*, November 30, 1981, 119.

34. Alphonso Pinkney, *The Myth of Black Progress* (Cambridge: Cambridge University Press, 1984), 17.

35. Houston A. Baker, Jr., "Caliban's Triple Play," in *Race, Writing and Difference*, ed. Henry Louis Gates, Jr. (Chicago: University of Chicago Press, 1986), 387.

36. A couple of early studies in the discipline of political science found little evidence of a support base for black conservatism among African Americans. See Charles Hamilton, "Measuring Black Conservatism," in *The State of Black America*, ed. James Williams (New York: National Urban League, 1982), 113–40; Richard Seltzer and Robert C. Smith, "Race and Ideology: A Research Note Measuring Liberalism and Conservatism in Black America," *Phylon* 46, no. 2 (1985): 98–105; R. Gomes and L. Williams, "Black Public Opinion: Rumors of Conservatism," *Humanity and Society* 11, no. 1 (1987): 40–57.

37. Hill testified that Thomas frequently told dirty jokes, bragged about the size of his penis, begged her for dates, and recapped pornographic videos he had rented the night before, including one titled *Long Dong Silver*. She also claimed that, at one point, Thomas accused her of leaving pubic hairs on his can of Coca-Cola. For further discussion, see Jayne Mayer and Jill Abramson, *Strange Justice: The Selling of Clarence Thomas* (Boston: Houghton Mifflin, 1994), 95–97.

38. For Douglass as a "black conservative," see Steve Macedo, "Douglass to Thomas," *New Republic*, September 30, 1991, 23–25; Matthew Rees, "Black and Right," *New Republic*, September 30, 1991, 21. For Malcolm as a "black conservative," see Juan Williams, "Was Malcolm X a Republican?" *Gentlemen's Quarterly*, December 1992, 190–95. Some years later, in response, Columbia University Law Professor Patricia J. Williams wrote: "Clarence Thomas is to Malcolm X what Unforgettable. The Perfume. By Revlon. is to Nat King Cole." Patricia J. Williams, *The Rooster's Egg: On the Persistence of Prejudice* (Cambridge, Mass.: Harvard University Press, 1995), 125. For King as a "black conservative," see Clint Bolik, "Blacks and Whites on Common Ground," *Wall Street Journal*, August 5, 1992, A14.

39. John E. Jacob of the National Urban League, quoted in C. Foote, Jr., "Doubting Thomas: A Test for Black Conservatism," *Black Enterprise* 22, no. 3 (1991): 13.

40. Neil A. Lewis, "From Poverty to the U.S. Bench," *New York Times*, July 2, 1991, 1; Ruth Marcus, "Self-Made Conservative: Nominee Insists He Be Judged on Merits," *Washington Post*, July 2, 1991, A1.

41. "Uncle Thomas: Handkerchief Head Negro," *Emerge*, November 1993.

42. Rowan, quoted in L. Gordon Crovitz, ed., *Clarence Thomas: Confronting the Future* (Washington, D.C.: Regnery-Gateway, 1992), 14.

43. June Jordan, *Technical Difficulties: African American Notes on the State of the Union* (New York: Vintage Books, 1994), 206, 217.

44. Malveaux, quoted in David Brock, "Strange Lies," *American Spectator*, January 1995, 76.

45. Karen Baker-Fletcher, "The Difference Race Makes: Sexual Harassment

and the Law in the Thomas/Hill Hearings," Journal of Feminist Studies in Religion 10 (1994): 7–15. Lincoln Caplan, "The Accidental Jurist," *Playboy*, January 1995, 140–42, 182–84.

46. Scott D. Gerber, "Judging Thomas: The Politics of Assessing a Supreme Court Justice," *Journal of Black Studies* 27, no. 2 (1996): 225.

47. Robert Chrisman and Robert L. Allen, eds., *Court of Appeal: The Black Community Speaks Out on the Racial and Sexual Politics of Clarence Thomas vs. Anita Hill* (New York: Ballantine Books, 1992); Timothy M. Phelps and Helen Winternitz, *Capitol Games: Clarence Thomas, Anita Hill and the Story of a Supreme Court Nomination* (New York: Hyperion, 1992); Crovitz, *Clarence Thomas*; Toni Morrison, ed., *Race-ing Justice, En-gendering Power: Essays on Anita Hill, Clarence Thomas, and the Construction of Social Reality* (New York: Pantheon Books, 1992); David Brock, *The Real Anita Hill: The Untold Story* (New York: Free Press, 1993); Mayer and Abramson, *Strange Justice*; John Danforth, *Resurrection: The Confirmation of Clarence Thomas* (New York: Viking, 1994); Anita Faye Hill and Emma Coleman Jordan, eds., *Race, Gender and Power in America: The Legacy of the Hill-Thomas Hearings* (New York: Oxford University Press, 1995); Norman L. Macht, *Clarence Thomas* (New York: Chelsea House Publishers, 1995); Sandra L. Ragan, Dianne G. Bystrom, Lynda Lee Kaid, and Christina S. Beck, eds., *The Lynching of Language: Gender, Politics and Power in the Hill-Thomas Hearings* (Urbana: University of Illinois Press, 1996); Ronald S. Roberts, *Clarence Thomas and the Tough Love Crowd: Counterfeit Heroes and Unhappy Truths* (New York: New York University Press, 1995); Geneva Smitherman, ed., *African Americans Speak Out on Anita Hill-Clarence Thomas* (Detroit: Wayne State University Press, 1995). None of these books, however, saw the Thomas confirmation as a compelling vantage point from which to explore the essence of contemporary black conservatism.

48. See, for example, the case of Angela Wright, a black Republican political appointee whom Thomas had hired in 1984 to be the EEOC's director of public affairs. She later documented, clearly, the harassment she too had experienced at the hands of Thomas. Mayer and Abramson, *Strange Justice*, 131–36.

49. Thomas Sowell, "Clarence Thomas Vindicated," *Forbes* 151, no. 10 (1993): 70. See also Jacob Cohen, "Book Review—The Real Anita Hill: The Untold Story," *National Review*, July 5, 1993, 47–50; George F. Will, "Anita Hill's Tangled Web," *Newsweek*, April 19, 1993, 74.

50. For further discussion, see "The Trashing of Professor Anita Hill," *Journal of Blacks in Higher Education*, no. 32 (2001): 135. See also David Brock, *Blinded By The Right: The Conscience of an Ex-Conservative* (Melbourne: Scribe Publications, 2001), 87–120.

51. West, *Race Matters*, 35–49.

52. Ibid.

53. Ibid., 36.

54. Ibid., 42.

55. Ibid., 37.

56. Ibid., 38.

57. I have taken this phrase from West's chapter on black conservatism in his 1993 bestseller, *Race Matters*. For examples of the new and more sophisticated literature on this subject, see Ronald E. Childs, "Afrocentrism vs. Black Conservatism: Searching for Some Common Ground," *Ebony Man*, January 1993, 58–62; Martin Kilson, "Anatomy of Black Conservatism," *Transition* 59 (1992): 4–19; Smith and Walton, "U-Turn," 209–16; Martin Kilson, "The Gang That Couldn't Shoot Straight," *Transition*, issue 62 (1993): 217–25; Errol Smith, "Time to Repackage

Black Conservatism," *Headway* 8, no. 10 (1996): 17; Earl Sheridan, "The New Accommodationists," *Journal of Black Studies* 27, no. 2 (1996): 152–71; Deborah Toler, "Black Conservatives," *The Public Eye* 7 (1997): 1–30; Edward Ashbee, "The Politics of Contemporary Black Conservatism in the United States," *Politics* 17, no. 3 (1997): 153–59; Mark McPhail, "(Re)constructing the Color Line: Complicity and Black Conservatism," *Communication Theory* 7 (1997): 162–75.

58. See West, *Race Matters*, 73–90.

59. See, for example, Toler, "Black Conservatives," 1–30; Kelley, *Yo'*, 90–91.

60. See, for example, Childs, "Afrocentrism," 58–62.

61. For further discussion, see West, *Race Matters*, 36–43, 53–70; Manning Marable, "Clarence Thomas and the Crisis of Black Political Culture," in *Racing Justice, En-gendering Power: Essays on Anita Hill, Clarence Thomas and the Construction of Social Reality*, ed. Toni Morrison (New York: Pantheon, 1992), 61–85; Sherri Smith, "The Individual Ethos: A Defining Characteristic of Contemporary Black Conservatism," in *Dimensions of Black Conservatism in the United States: Made in America*, eds. Gayle T. Tate and Lewis A. Randolph (New York: Palgrave, 2002),119–20; Henry Louis Gates, Jr., "The Black Leadership Myth," *New Yorker*, October 14, 1994, 8.

62. West, *Race Matters*, 53.

63. Ibid., 68.

64. For a more detailed discussion, see Trevor W. Coleman, "Assault from the Right," *Emerge*, February 1994, 49–52.

65. For a discussion of these leaders' reactionary extremism, see, for example, "The Fallout from Khalid Abdul Muhammad's Speech at Kean College," *Journal of Blacks in Higher Education*, no. 3 (1994): 84–85; Adolph Reed, "False Prophet I: The Rise of Louis Farrakhan," *Nation*, January 21, 1991, 37; Adolph Reed, "False Prophet II: All for One and None for All," *Nation*, January 28, 1991, 86.

66. Under Gingrich's "Contract" there were to be significant reductions in funds allocated for education and health care, as well as urban policy and employment initiatives. See Republican Action Committee, *Contract with America* (Washington, D.C., 1994). An analysis of the "contract"—and black conservative support for it—can be found in Wade Henderson, "Contract with America," *Emerge*, March 1995, 48–51.

67. See, for example, A. Williams, "Black Conservatives: We Are the Future," *USA Today*, November 22, 1994, 10A. David McClean, "Black Conservatism and Its Critics," *Transition*, issue 62 (1993): 203–8; Dinesh D'Souza, *The End of Racism: Principles for a Multiracial Society* (New York: Free Press, 1995), 521.

68. Conti and Stetson, *Challenging*.

69. Ibid., 1–19.

70. Lawrence Mead, professor of politics at New York University, quoted on the book's jacket.

71. Conti and Stetson, *Challenging*, 4–5.

72. Ibid., 227–30.

73. Ibid., ix.

74. Nikki Giovanni, *Racism 101* (New York: William Morrow, 1994), 52.

75. Kilson, "Anatomy," 14–16.

76. Hanes Walton Jr., "Defending the Indefensible: The African American Conservative Client Spokesperson of the Reagan-Bush Era," *Black Scholar* 24, no. 4 (1994): 46.

77. Ibid.

78. Richard Herrnstein and Charles Murray, *The Bell Curve: Intelligence and Class Structure in American Life* (New York: Free Press, 1994).

79. D'Souza, *End of Racism*.

80. Thomas Sowell, "Upstream Issues: Bell Curve," *American Spectator* 28, no. 2 (1995), 32. See also Sowell quoted at http://www.simonsays.com/content/book.cfm?tab=25&pid=407016&agid=16.

81. Walter Williams, "Deliberations on the End of Racism," *Academic Questions* 9, no. 4 (1996): 69–76.

82. Adolph Reed, "The Descent of Black Conservatism," *Progressive*, October 1997, 18–20.

83. See, for example, Ron Dungee, "The Two Faces of Clarence Thomas and Ward Connerly: See If You Can See the Damage That You Have Done," *Journal of Blacks in Higher Education*, no. 23 (1999): 140; "Ward Connerly is Pushing Blacks Down Into Second- and Third-Tier Colleges," *Journal of Blacks in Higher Education*, no. 35 (2002): 14–17.

84. Muhammad, quoted in "Fallout from Khalid Abdul," 84. Also quoted in John Perazzo, "How the Left Trashes Black Conservatives," *FrontPageMagazine.com*, July 10, 2002.

85. Page, *Showing My Color*, 206.

86. Ibid., 199, 214.

87. See, for example, the 1982–84 *National Black Survey*, which identified poverty, civil rights, and education as the three most important issues for black Americans. A decade later, a Joint Center/Gallup Poll likewise found that for blacks, the most important issues in the 1992 election were unemployment, civil rights, and "helping the poor." In 1992, the "moral/religious decline in society" was seen as the most important national problem by less than 1% of black people. Edward Ashbee, "The Republican Party and the African-American Vote since 1964," in *Black Conservatism*, ed. Eisenstadt, 251.

88. Page, *Showing My Color*, 194–95.

89. Dillard, *Guess*.

90. Ibid., 17.

91. Ibid., 24–29.

92. Tate and Randolph, eds., *Dimensions of Black Conservatism*.

93. James Jennings, "Beyond Black Neoconservatism and Black Liberalism," in *Dimensions of Black Conservatism in the United States: Made in America*, ed. Gayle T. Tate and Lewis A. Randolph (New York: Palgrave, 2002), 229.

94. How, for example, had Sowell and company explained the contemporary "schools crisis," particularly as it related to African Americans, and what were their solutions to this crisis? What, moreover, were these intellectuals' principal objections to affirmative action? While there was no chapter that examined black conservatives' assessments of public education, chapter 5 looked cursorily at affirmative action—but only as it applied to black women. Sowell and company's writings on this policy, however, have gone far beyond this, and deserved much greater attention.

95. Godfrey Mwakikagile, *Black Conservatives: Are They Right or Wrong?* (Palo Alto, Calif.: Fultus Corporation, 2004).

96. West, *Race Matters*, 53.

97. Manning Marable, "Bush's Blacks: Race Traitors (Part 1)," *Along the Color Line*, September 2002,

http://www.manningmarable.net/works/pdf/sept02a.pdf; Manning Marable,

"Bush's Blacks: Race Traitors' (Part 2)," September 2002, http://www.manning-marable.net/works/pdf/sept02b.pdf.

Chapter 1. Profiles of an Intellectual Vanguard

1. Glenn Loury, "Wounds of Race," *New Republic,* September 4, 1989, 6.

2. Marc Fisher, "The Private World of Justice Thomas," *Washington Post,* September 11, 1995, B1.

3. Promptly aligning himself with the conservative wing of the Court, he handed down some of the most controversial judgments in recent memory, seemingly destined to be condemned by progressive critics as a puppet of the arch-conservative Justice Scalia. See, for example, Susan N. Herman, "Clarence Thomas," in *The Justices of the United States Supreme Court: Their Lives and Major Opinions 1789–1995,* ed. Leon Friedman and Fred L. Israel (New York: Chelsea House Publishers, 1995), 1829–58; Leon A. Higginbotham, "Justice Thomas in Retrospect," *Hastings Law Journal* 45 (1994): 1405–33; Julian Abele Cook, Jr., "Thurgood Marshall and Clarence Thomas: A Glance at Their Philosophies," *Michigan Bar Journal* 73 (1994): 298–302; Jeffrey Toobin, "The Burden of Clarence Thomas," *New Yorker,* September 27, 1993, 46–49. Yet Thomas appeared similarly destined to be praised by members of the American "right," who pointed to his "excellent legal mind" and principled commitment to moral causes. See, for example, Alex Epstein, "Justice Thomas's Less-Travelled Road to the Right," *Atlanta Journal-Constitution,* July 9, 1995, B1; Thomas Sowell, "Few Critics Have Read His Opinions," *Atlanta Journal-Constitution,* June 27, 1995, A8.

4. Clarence Thomas, "Civil Rights as a Principle Versus Civil Rights as Interest," in *Assessing the Reagan Years,* ed. David Boaz (Washington, D.C.: Cato Institute, 1988), 391–402. In a 1987 interview with Juan Williams, Thomas commented: "I would be lying to you if I said that I didn't want sometimes to be able to cheat in favor of those of us who were cheated. But you have to ask yourself whether, in doing that, you do violence to the safe harbor, and that is the Constitution, which says you are to protect an individual's rights no matter what. Once you say that we can violate somebody else's rights in order to make up for what happened to blacks or other groups in history, then you are setting a precedent for having certain circumstances in which you can overlook another person's rights." Juan Williams, "A Question of Fairness," *Atlantic Monthly,* February 1987, 79.

5. Thomas, quoted in Ted Jou, "The Minority in the Middle: Thurgood Marshall, Clarence Thomas, and Sandra Day O'Connor's Race Jurisprudence," *California Institute of Technology,* fall 1995, 19, http://www.ugcs.caltech.edu/~tjou/words/law/MiddleMinority.pdf. Thomas also wrote: "If I type one word in my word processor in favor of this policy, I break God's law": Marable, "Bush's Blacks: Race Traitors (Part 1)" (see intro., n. 98).

6. Bill Kauffman, "Interview: Clarence Thomas," *Reason,* November 1987, http://www.reason.com/news/printer/33217.html.

7. Remarks to Equal Employment Opportunity Commission staff in 1983, quoted in "Justice Clarence Thomas: Classic Case of an Affirmative Action Baby," *Journal of Blacks in Higher Education,* no. 18 (1997): 36.

8. Clarence Thomas, "Letter to the Editor," *Wall Street Journal,* February 20, 1987, 23.

9. Thomas, quoted in Williams, "Question of Fairness," 72.

10. Ibid., 72–73.

11. See, for example, Hermon George, Jr., "Clarence Thomas: Loyal Foot Soldier for Reaganism," *Black Scholar* 22, no. 1 (1991): 32.

12. Thomas, quoted in Williams, "Question of Fairness," 72.

13. Thomas, quoted by William McGurn, "The Trials of Clarence Thomas," *National Review*, August 12, 1991, 36.

14. Clarence Thomas, "Climb the Jagged Mountain (Excerpt of Speech at Savannah State College)," *New York Times*, July 19, 1991.

15. Clarence Thomas, "Why Black Americans Should Look to Conservative Policies," speech quoted by Lewis, "From Poverty," 1.

16. It was as "insane," Thomas argued, for blacks to expect help from the federal government for years of discrimination as it was to expect a mugger to nurse his victim back to health. Thomas, quoted in Steven A. Holmes, "NAACP Report Faults Thomas View on Equality Issues," *New York Times*, July 31, 1991, A1.

17. C. Higgins, "Interview with Clarence Thomas, Chairman, EEOC: We Are Going to Enforce the Law!" *The Crisis* 90, no. 2 (1983): 51, 56.

18. Jane Mayer and Jill Abramson, "The Higher Education of Clarence Thomas," *Journal of Blacks in Higher Education*, no. 6 (1994): 96. See also Marable, *Beyond*, 93 (see intro., n. 17).

19. Mayer and Abramson, "Higher Education," 96.

20. Ibid.

21. Ibid., 97. See also Marable, *Beyond*, 93; Karen P. Wanza, "The Three Ring Circus of Clarence Thomas: Race, Class and Gender," *Black Scholar* 22, no. 1 (1991): 107; "Justice Clarence Thomas," 35; Andrew Peyton Thomas, *Clarence Thomas: A Biography* (San Francisco: Encounter Books, 2001), 140–42.

22. Thomas's academic performance at Yale was disappointing: he finished near the bottom of his class, for instance, in a first-year course on politics and civil rights, subjects for which he claimed a special affinity. For further discussion, see Mayer and Abramson, "Higher Education," 100.

23. Ibid., 97.

24. For a discussion, see Thomas, *Clarence Thomas*, 143–44.

25. Mayer and Abramson, "Higher Education," 100.

26. For a discussion, see George, "Loyal," 32–33.

27. Clarence Thomas, "Why Black Americans Should Look to Conservative Policies," *The Heritage Foundation*, August 1, 1987, http://www.heritage.org/Research/PoliticalPhilosophy/HL119.cfm?renderforprint=1. See also Neil A. Lewis, "Thomas' Journey on Path of Self-Help," *New York Times*, July 7, 1991, 12.

28. Juan Williams, "Black Conservatives Center Stage," *Washington Post*, December 16, 1980, A21.

29. For a discussion, see George, "Loyal," 33; Ronald Walters, "Clarence Thomas and the Meaning of Blackness," *Black Scholar* 22, no. 1 (1991): 105.

30. He was, by this time, speaking regularly before audiences at the Heritage Foundation, the American Enterprise Institute, and the Cato Institute, and writing frequently for conservative publications such as the *Lincoln Review* and *Policy Review*.

31. "There is room at the inn," Thomas told the People of Color Rally in Cincinnati. "And I am here to sound the welcome bell." Bush would go on to defeat the Democratic hopeful Michael Dukakis in a landslide victory, prompting Thomas's biographer Andrew Thomas to write: "Once again, as throughout his political career, Thomas had picked the right horse. His years of loyal service and his new, self-constructed conservatism positioned him well for opportunities

that were sure to arise in the incoming administration." Thomas, *Clarence Thomas*, 312–13.

32. In nominating Thomas, Bush commented: "I have followed this man's career for some time, and he has excelled in everything that he has attempted. He is a delightful and warm, intelligent person who has great empathy and a wonderful sense of humor. He's also a fiercely independent thinker with an excellent legal mind, who believes passionately in equal opportunity for all Americans. He will approach the cases that come before the court with a commitment to deciding them fairly, as the facts and law require." Bush, quoted in Thomas, *Clarence Thomas*, 345.

33. "A Justice Until 2030?" *New York Times,* July 2, 1991, 16.

34. Marable, *Beyond,* 94.

35. Kevin Merida and Michael A. Fletcher, *Supreme Discomfort: The Divided Soul of Clarence Thomas* (New York: Doubleday, 2007).

36. In a 1987 interview with *Reason* magazine, Thomas remarked of Sowell: "I consider him not only an intellectual mentor, but my salvation as far as thinking through these issues." Kauffman, "Interview."

37. Dillard, *Guess,* 1 (see intro., n. 30).

38. A senior research fellow at Stanford's Hoover Institution, Sowell has written more than 30 academic books. His best-known works include: *Black Education: Myths and Tragedies* (New York: David McKay, 1972); *Race and Economics* (New York: David McKay, 1975); *The Economics and Politics of Race* (New York: William Morrow, 1983); *Civil Rights: Rhetoric or Reality?* (New York: William Morrow, 1984); *A Conflict of Visions* (New York: William Morrow, 1987); *Race and Culture: A World View* (New York: Basic Books, 1994); *The Vision of the Anointed: Self-Congratulation as a Basis for Social Policy* (New York: Basic Books, 1996); *The Quest for Cosmic Justice* (New York: Free Press, 1999); *Inside American Education* (New York: Free Press, 2003); *Affirmative Action Around the World: An Empirical Study* (New York: Yale University Press, 2004).

39. His columns continue to appear in more than 150 newspapers across America. Articles by Sowell can be found in publications such as *Commentary, National Review, Forbes, Public Interest, Policy Review, Reason,* and *Human Events.*

40. As one favorable (anonymous) reviewer of Sowell's work pointed out in 1981: "He likens using racism to explain poverty to using oxygen to explain burning buildings: racism, like oxygen, is too general. It's everywhere." See "Thomas Sowell," *National Review,* October 16, 1981, 1213.

41. See, for example, Thomas Sowell, "Culture—Not Discrimination—Decides Who Gets Ahead," *U.S. News and World Report,* October 12, 1981, 74.

42. Ibid., 74.

43. Thomas Sowell, *A Personal Odyssey* (New York: Free Press, 2000), 288.

44. Thomas Sowell, *Ethnic America: A History* (New York: Basic Books, 1981).

45. Jerry G. Watts, "Review of Thomas Sowell The Economics and Politics of Race: An Economic Perspective," *Journal of Black Studies* 18, no. 4 (1988): 471. Reviewed on the front page of the literary sections of the *New York Times* and the *Washington Post,* as well as in *Time, Newsweek, Fortune,* and the *Wall Street Journal,* the book propelled Sowell into the spotlight and onto high-profile television programs such as *Firing Line, Meet the Press,* and *The Phil Donahue Show.*

46. Adam Meyerson, "Conservatives and Black Americans: Overcoming the Barriers," *Policy Review* 30 (1984): 41.

47. Sowell, *Personal,* 66–105; Thomas Sowell, "Blind Alley of Racial Paranoia," *Washington Times,* January 22, 1991.

48. Sowell, *Personal*, 117.

49. Ibid., 125.

50. Milton Friedman, foreword to *Markets and Minorities*, by Thomas Sowell (New York: Basic Books, 1981), vii–viii.

51. Sowell, *Personal*, 224–73.

52. Watts, "Case of a Black Conservative," 301 (see intro., n. 33).

53. Singer, "With a Friend in the White House," 435 (see intro., n. 31); Sowell, *Personal*, 279. When the Reagan transition team leaked this information to the media, it drew a hostile response from the liberal black leadership at the NAACP: "We would view with considerable concern the appointment of Tom Sowell to HUD or, for that matter, to any other cabinet position. . . . He would play the same kind of role that historically the house niggers played for the plantation owners. He could mete out the straight discipline. No matter how inhumanely administered, it would be presumed more acceptable because the hands of the disciplinarian are black." Sowell responded in characteristically aggressive fashion: "I think the NAACP are the classic house niggers. Their support comes from the white liberals . . . and they are constantly taking positions the very opposite of the black community on crime, on quotas, on busing." Quoted in Watts, "Case of a Black Conservative," 303.

54. Thomas Sowell, "Blacker Than Thou," *Washington Post*, February 14, 1981, 23.

55. For a discussion of this childhood in Harlem, see, for example, Sowell, *Personal*, 13–52.

56. Ibid., 186–88.

57. For Sowell's praise of Washington, see, for example, Thomas Sowell, "Up From Slavery," *Forbes*, December 5, 1994, 84–93. For the similarly strong admiration he expressed for Schuyler, see Thomas Sowell, "The First Black Conservative?" *National Review*, August 20, 2001, 45–46.

58. S. Smith, "Contemporary Black Conservative Rhetoric: An Analysis of Strategies and Themes," Ph.D. diss., Pennsylvania State University, 1997, 119.

59. Conti and Stetson, 87 (see intro., n. 22).

60. Stephen Steinberg, "No Compassion for the Wretched," *Journal of Blacks in Higher Education*, no. 10 (1995–96): 110.

61. Adolph Reed, "Steele Trap," *Nation* 252, no. 8 (1991): 274.

62. Ibid., 274.

63. Adam Shatz, "Glenn Loury's About Face," *New York Times Magazine*, January 20, 2002, 18.

64. Hill et al., "Black America," 28 (see intro., n. 31).

65. Glenn Loury, "Essays in the Theory of the Distribution of Income," Ph.D. diss., Massachusetts Institute of Technology, 1976.

66. For a discussion, see, for example, Glenn Loury, "Economics, Politics and Blacks." *Review of Black Political Economy*, 12, no. 3 (1983): 43–54; Glenn Loury, "Black Survival in America," *Black Enterprise* 13, no. 10 (1983): 33; Glenn Loury, "Responsibility and Race," *Lincoln Review* 4, no. 2 (1983): 9–14. See also Glenn Loury, "Beyond Civil Rights," *New Republic*, October 7, 1985, 22–25.

67. Shatz, "Glenn Loury's," 18.

68. Befriended by the major neoconservative intellectuals of the Reagan era—including Norman Podhoretz, William Bennett, and Irving and William Kristol—he spoke regularly to audiences at the American Enterprise Institute, the Hoover Institution, and the Heritage Foundation. Ibid., 18.

69. Civil rights leaders, Loury charged repeatedly, were not so much concerned

with the problems and challenges confronting poor blacks as with establishing the necessity of their political agenda. See, for example, Glenn Loury, "Responsibility and Race," *Vital Speeches,* April 15, 1983, 398–400; Glenn Loury, "Who Speaks for American Blacks?" *Commentary,* January 1987, 34–38; Glenn Loury, "Individualism before Multiculturalism," *Public Interest* 121 (1995): 92–106.

70. Self-help, he insisted, while critical, was "not a substitute for government provision but rather an essential complement to it, ensuring that state-funded assistance is more effective, and that it is seen as legitimate by the political majorities that must approve it." Glenn Loury, *One by One from the Inside Out: Essays and Reviews on Race and Responsibility in America* (New York: Free Press, 1995), 80–81. Glenn Loury, "Two Paths to Black Progress," *First Things,* no. 26 (1992): 18–24.

71. See, for example, Loury, "Two Paths," 18–24; Glenn Loury, "The Saliency of Race," in *Second Thoughts About Race in America,* ed. Peter Collier and David Horowitz (New York: Madison Books, 1991), 75–80.

72. Glenn Loury, "Linking Public and Private Efforts in Overcoming Poverty," in *Welfare Reform: Consensus or Conflict?* ed. James S. Denton (Lanham, Md.: University Press of America, 1988), 17–22.

73. Ibid., 19.

74. See, for example, Loury, "Two Paths," 18–24.

75. Glenn Loury, "God and the Ghetto," *Wall Street Journal,* February 25, 1993, A14.

76. Glenn Loury, "A Prescription for Black Progress," *Christian Century,* April 30, 1986, 434.

77. Glenn Loury, "The Moral Quandary of the Black Community," *Public Interest* 79 (1985): 11.

78. Indeed, during the 1980s, Loury frequently charged that contemporary civil rights leaders *talked* much about racism but did little of substance to help the black poor. See, for example, Loury, "Prescription," 438. Loury wrote: "The task of narrowing class schisms within the black community should have priority. Blacks must not be afraid to make judgments about faults and failings in their community. Blacks must abandon the pernicious and self-destructive tendency arbitrarily to empower the 'man' with ultimate control over their destiny. This is almost criminal abdication of responsibility. Precisely because racism is a fact of life not likely to disappear soon, *all* blacks are 'in the same lifeboat.' This being the case, it is in the individual black's interest to contribute times and resources to the advancement of those least well off in the community. It is politically and morally irresponsible to sit back in disgust, as so many veterans of past struggles are fond of doing, constantly decrying the problems, doing little or nothing to solve them, shouting epithets and threats at whites who grow weary of being generous and understanding, while the black poor sink deeper and deeper into despair."

79. And rebuke Loury they did! Martin Kilson denounced the new black conservative powerhouse as "just another pathetic mascot for the right" who "pompously hands down critical prescriptions from on high about stuff he doesn't know anything about. He's a hustler, an intelligent hired hand." Quoted in Mark Megalli, "The High Priests of the Black Academic Right," *Journal of Blacks in Higher Education,* no. 9 (1995): 73. The then Harvard law professor Derrick Bell agreed: "Even given the fact that all blacks have to engage in some hypocrisy just to survive in our racist society, Loury has gone beyond the call of duty." Quoted in Robert Boynton, "Loury's Exodus: A Profile of Glenn Loury," *New Yorker,* May 1, 1995, 33. Invited to speak at a meeting of the National Urban Coalition in

the mid-1980s, Loury reduced Coretta Scott King to tears. "We appreciate your ideas," the coalition's president Carl Holman said in response, "but you have to be more careful about who it is you say these things to." Quoted in Shatz, "Glenn Loury's," 19. For Loury's discussion of the "loyalty trap," see Loury, *One by One,* 183–94.

80. Yet, only eighteen months before, at a symposium of black conservatives, Loury had remarked in response to a question on school prayer and discipline in schools: "I don't pretend to be an expert on education." Hill et al., "Black America," 38.

81. Quoted in Boynton, "Loury's Exodus," 33.

82. During this time, Loury wrote frequently for black publications and spoke at meetings of the NAACP and the National Urban Coalition. For articles in black publications, see, for example, Loury, "Black Survival," 33; Glenn Loury, "New Dividends Through Social Capital," *Black Enterprise* 15, no. 12 (1985): 36–37. For evidence of Loury's appearances before civil rights groups, see Smith, "Contemporary Black Conservatism," 148–56.

83. King, Loury argued, "constantly evoked an image of Americans as decent, magnanimous, moral, righteous—as a freedom-loving people whose great fault lay in failing to achieve in reality the nobility implicit in their civic creed. . . . This America of King's, of course, was deeply flawed, but he chose to emphasize its potential for redemption. . . . His method of non-violent direct action, relying as it did on compromise and cooperation with whites of good will, and rooted as it was in the compelling clarity of the simple justice which he sought, complemented this vision." Glenn Loury, "A Call to Arms for Black Conservatives," in *Critical Issues: A Conservative Agenda for Black Americans,* ed. Joseph Perkins (Washington, D.C.: Heritage Foundation, 1987), 15–16.

84. Loury, "Who Speaks," 37.

85. On this theme, see also Loury's early criticism of Sowell. "There is much truth to what Sowell is saying. But if you mainly say that the problem is self-inflicted or caused by government efforts to help, it smacks of blaming the victim." Cited in "The Backlash Against Sowell," *Business Week,* November 30, 1980, 120.

86. Loury, "God," A14.

87. Lewis A. Randolph, "Black Neoconservatives in the United States: Responding with Progressive Coalitions," in *Race and Politics in the United States,* ed. James Jennings (New York: Verso, 1997), 154–55.

88. Boynton, "Loury's Exodus," 34.

89. For a discussion, see Jenny Attiyeh, "Black Scholar Renounces Conservative Crown," *Christian Science Monitor,* September 5, 2002, 18.

90. Loury, quoted in Randolph, "Black Neoconservatives," 155.

91. See, for example, Walter Williams, "Giving Up and Claiming Victim Status," *National Minority Politics* 7, no. 1 (1995): 17.

92. After the Heritage Foundation helped launch his career as syndicated columnist in 1980, 160 newspapers nationwide have published this black conservative's thoughts in a weekly column. And by the 1990s, Williams had also been "made into" somewhat of a media celebrity. A regular guest on "Nightline," "Firing Line," "Face the Nation," "Free to Choose," "Crossfire," "Lehrer," and "Wall Street Week," he was also a very popular occasional guest-host of the "Rush Limbaugh Show." For details, see Williams's homepage: http://www.gmu.edu/departments/economics/wew/vita.html.

93. Quoted in Conti and Stetson, *Challenging,* 86–87.

94. For "Welfare as 20th Century Slavery," see "Uncovering the Black Conservative Movement," excerpts from J. Roberts, *Uncovering the Right on Campus* (New York: Center for Campus Organizing, 1997). For defense of the South, see Walter Williams, "The Civil War Wasn't About Slavery," *Jewish World Review*, December 2, 1998, http://www.jewishworldreview.com/cols/williams120298.asp. For Williams's view on the Confederate flag, see Walter Williams, "Misplaced Priorities," *Jewish World Review*, November 17, 1999, http://www.jewishworldreview. com/cols/williams111799.asp.

95. See the following books by Walter Williams: *America: A Minority Viewpoint* (Stanford, Calif.: Hoover Institution Press, 1982); *The State Against Blacks* (New York: McGraw Hill, 1982); *All It Takes Is Guts* (Washington, D.C.: Regnery Gateway, 1987); *South Africa's War Against Capitalism* (New York: Praeger Publishers, 1989); *Do the Right Thing: The People's Economist Speaks* (Stanford, Calif.: Hoover Institution Press, 1995); *More Liberty Means Less Government: Our Founders Knew This Well* (Stanford, Calif.: Hoover Institution Press, 1999). For his shorter discussions of capitalism's "egalitarianism" see the following by Williams: "Capitalism Has Been Boom to Common Man," *Human Events* 53, no. 37 (1997): 11; "Capitalism Fosters Equal Opportunity," *Human Events* 51, no. 17 (1995): 15.

96. See, for example, Williams, *America*, 29–30; Williams, *State Against Blacks*, 33–51, 67–98. More recently, see Williams, "Capitalism Fosters," 15; Williams, *More Liberty*, 42–44, 57–59.

97. See, for example, the following by Williams: *Do the Right*, vii–viii; *America*, 29–30; "What Kind of Guys Were the Founders?" *George Mason University Department of Economics*, January 14, 1998, http://www.gmu.edu/departments/ economics/wew/articles/archives/1995–1998archive.html. http://www.gmu. edu/departments/economics/wew/articles/archives/1995–1998archive.html

98. See Williams's following articles: *Do the Right*, 14–15; *More Liberty*, 51–54; "Big Government Handicaps Black Progress," *Human Events* 56, no. 38 (2000): 19; *State Against Blacks*, xiv; "Government Sanctioned Restraints that Reduce Economic Opportunities for Minorities," *Policy Review* 2 (1977): 7–30.

99. Williams, *Do the Right*, 44.

100. Indeed, this was how Williams saw himself too. "If I am pushed to label myself," he wrote, "I am probably . . . in the solid tradition of our Founding Fathers, such as Patrick Henry or Thomas Paine—those men who made the ringing declarations: 'Give me liberty or give me death,' and 'Live free or die.'" Williams, *America*, 29–30.

101. Taxation, for instance, was simply a form of theft. Ibid., 29. See also Williams, *State Against Blacks*, 32; and his more recent "Government's Legitimate Role in a Free Society," *USA Today Magazine* 129, no. 2670 (2001): 14–16; and *More Liberty*, 85–86.

102. Williams, *Do the Right*, vii–viii; Williams, *More Liberty*, vii–viii.

103. Walter Williams, "A Tragic Vision of Black Problems," *American Quarterly* 47, no. 3 (1995): 409. For similar sentiments, see also his "We Can Be Proud," *Lincoln Review* 6, no. 1 (1985): 53–55; "After Civil Rights," in *Second Thought About Race in America*, ed. Peter Collier and David Horowitz (New York: Madison Books, 1991), 29–31; *Do the Right*, 24–25, 32–34; "Civil Rightspeak," *New Perspectives* 18 (1986): 15–17. The American people, Williams argued, could feel justly "proud" at how they had handled their racial problems: "We Can," 55.

104. Williams, *More Liberty*, 48–50.

105. Walter Williams, "How I Achieved the American Dream," *Human Events* 53, no. 16 (1997): 19. For further detail about Williams's roots and life journey,

see Williams, *Do the Right*, xi–xii; Friedman, "New Black Intellectuals," 51 (see intro., n. 31); Sara Pentz, "TNI's Exclusive Interview with Dr. Walter E. Williams," March 2006, http://www.objectivistcenter.org/ct-1742-TNIMarch06.aspx.

106. For details, see Williams, *More Liberty*, xii; Walter J. Bowie, "It's Not Racism, It's Us," *Lincoln Review* 9, no. 1 (1988): 41.

107. Walter Williams, "Passing of a Giant," *Human Events*, December 6, 2006, 60. See also Williams, *More Liberty*, xii.

108. Singer, "With a Friend," 435–36.

109. See, for example, Williams, *State Against Blacks*, 22.

110. See, for example, Shelby Steele, "Affirmative Action: The Price of Preference," *Wilson Quarterly* 10 (1987): 77–91; Shelby Steele, "On Being Black and Middle Class," *Commentary* 85 (1988): 33–41; Shelby Steele, "I'm Black, You're White, Who's Innocent? Race and Power in an Era of Blame," *Harper's*, June 1988, 45–53; Shelby Steele, "The Recoloring of Campus Life: Student Racism, Academic Pluralism, and the End of a Dream," *Harper's*, February 1989, 47–55.

111. Shelby Steele, *The Content of Our Character: A New Vision of Race in America* (Chicago: St Martin's Press, 1990). The book was awarded the prestigious National Book Critics Award, establishing Steele's credentials as an authoritative voice in contemporary racial discourse.

112. Steele, quoted in Megalli, "High Priests," 72. For further discussion, see, for example, Steele, "Affirmative Action," 77–91.

113. Shelby Steele, "Defining the Problem," *Mother Jones*, January–February 1993, 6.

114. Shelby Steele, "Thinking Beyond Race," *Wilson Quarterly* 14 (1990): 62–68; Shelby Steele, "The Memory of Enemies: On the Black Experience in America," *Dissent* 37 (1990): 326–32.

115. In fact, Steele directly attacked modern black leadership for not addressing the psychological dimensions to black oppression. He wrote: "Today black leadership is both self-serving and short-sighted. They are unwilling to see that the power they have wielded in American society for the last 25 years has been the power of victimization. We are victims and therefore entitled to redress. These leaders are addicted to the power and concessions they have gained by playing white guilt over past black victimization and do not see the importance of breaking the link between our power and our victimization." Shelby Steele, "Booker T. Washington was Right," *New Perspectives Quarterly* 7 (1990): 23–24.

116. "What I am for," Steele argued, "is actual development programs where values are imparted, where skills are taught, where we are developed and brought up so that we can become competitive with other groups in a very highly competitive, global world." Steele, quoted in Megalli, "High Priests," 73. See also Julianne Malveaux, "The Race is On: A Conversation with Shelby Steele and Julianne Malveaux," *Transition*, no. 56 (1992): 170.

117. See the blurb on *The Content of Our Character*: "Steele's skill compares with that of James Baldwin, Richard Wright or Frederick Douglass." (Chicago Tribune)

118. Quoted in Malveaux, "Race is On," 166.

119. See, for example, the following by Shelby Steele: "A New Black Vanguard," *Wall Street Journal*, February 29, 1996, 18–19; "How Liberals Lost Their Virtue over Race," *Newsweek*, January 9, 1995, 41; "Rise of the New Segregation," *USA Today Magazine* 121, no. 2574 (1993): 53–55; "Defining the Problem," 6; "The New Sovereignty: Grievance Groups Have Become Nations Unto Themselves," *Harper's*, July 1992, 47.

120. For details, see Steele's homepage at the Hoover Institution: http://www.hoover.org/bios/steele.html.

121. Shelby Steele, "New Black Vanguard," 18–19. For the agenda of the Center for New Black Leadership, see http://www.ashbrook.org/events/lecture/1998/reynolds.html.

122. Shelby Steele, *A Dream Deferred: The Second Betrayal of Black Freedom in America* (New York: Henry Holt, 1998).

123. See Steele's thesis statement in the preface: "These essays contend that the liberalism that grew out of the sixties was such a politics—that its first and all-consuming goal was the expiation of American shame rather than the careful and true development of equality between the races. Shame pushed the post-sixties United States into an extravagant, autocratic, socialistic, and interventionist liberalism that often betrayed America's best principles in order to give whites and American institutions an iconography of racial virtue they could use against the stigma of racial shame." Ibid., xiii.

124. Malveaux, "Race Is On," 173. Steele commented: "Well, I'm a civil rights baby, I grew up in the movement. I sat there and saw my father get his jaw broken trying to integrate a park in South Side Chicago."

125. Ibid., 166. Here, Steele revealed that, in his scholarship, he had written "a lot on African writers, a couple of things on Ralph Ellison, some on the New Black Theatre, and some criticism."

126. Steele dated this "discovery" to a radio program he heard on the Martin Luther King Jr. holiday in 1986. But "long before this afternoon," he wrote: "I had begun to feel that public discussions of the race issue had become virtually choreographed. Blacks were expected to speak in tones of racial entitlement, to show a modified black power assertiveness—not as strident as the sixties black power rhetoric, but certainly not as ameliorative as the integrationist tone of the civil rights era. Racism had to be offered as the greatest barrier to black progress, and blacks themselves had still to be seen primarily as racial victims. Whites, on the other hand, had to show both concern and a measure of befuddlement at how other whites could still be racist. There also had to be in whites a clear deference to the greater racial authority of blacks, whose color translated into a certain racial expertise. If there was more than one black, whites usually receded into the role of moderators while the black 'experts' argued. This is still the standard media formula, the ideal public choreography of black and white." Steele, *Content of Our Character*, ix.

127. Malveaux, "Race is On," 173.

128. Ibid., 174.

129. For further discussion, see Shelby Steele, "Ghettoized by Black Unity," *Harper's*, May 1990, 20–23; Shelby Steele, "The Age of White Guilt and the Disappearance of the Black Individual," *Harper's*, November 2002, 33–42.

130. See, for example, Martin Kilson's criticism of Steele: "Steele's stuff is simpleminded, one-dimensional psychological reductionism. It's slick sophistry, a largely conceptual argument with very limited reference to empirical data and events." Quoted in Sylvester Monroe, "Up From Obscurity," *Time*, August 13, 1990, 45. Adolph Reed's attack on Steele went further, declaring his analysis to be "innocent of social and political complexity. It builds castles of psychobabble on platitudes and banal autobiographical anecdote." Reed, "Steele," 274. Steele had absolutely "nothing to offer," insisted NAACP Executive Director Benjamin Hooks, "except a conservative viewpoint in a black skin." Monroe, "Up From," 45.

131. "By making himself his own laboratory," one conservative supporter noted, "he cuts at familiar issues in a very unfamiliar way." Quoted in Monroe, "Up From," 45. "One of the most important things he is doing is questioning Pavlovian racial responses," added another. "What's important is not that other people agree with what he says. It's that serious discussion is brought to the discourse dominated by slogans and clichés." Monroe, "Up From," 45.

132. See Langston Hughes, *Montage of A Dream Deferred* (New York: Henry Holt, 1951).

133. Page, *Showing My Color*, 196 (see intro., n. 6); Conti and Stetson, *Challenging*, 160.

134. Robert Woodson, "Conservatives Have Lost the Battle of Public Perception," *Headway* 8, no. 5 (1996): 7. "The whole self-help movement," Woodson later affirmed, "owes a debt of gratitude to Peter Berger and his work." Robert Woodson, *A Summons of Life* (Cambridge: Ballinger, 1981), xi.

135. For a brief but useful overview of the NCNE, see "Bob Woodson's NCNE," *Human Events* 50, no. 10 (1994): 10. See also the National Center for Neighborhood Enterprise website, http://www.ncne.com.

136. Clint Bolick, *In Whose Name? The Civil Rights Establishment Today* (Washington, D.C.: Capital Research Center, 1988), 43.

137. Woodson once remarked: "I think of myself as a pragmatist because I'm more concerned with concrete prescriptions than with labels. My views contain certain elements of liberalism, conservatism, black nationalism, and American patriotism." Quoted in Lee Daniels, "The New Black Conservatives," *New York Times Magazine*, October 4, 1981, 23. He also commented: "I don't care about what's right or who's left. I care about what works." Quoted in Page, *Showing My Color*, 210. And he claimed: "During the 1960s, people called me a black nationalist or separatist, but today they call me a conservative." Quoted in Hill et al., "Black America," 30.

138. Lois Benjamin, *The Black Elite: Still Facing the Color Line in the Twenty-first Century* (Chicago: Rowman and Littlefield Publishers, 2005), 188.

139. Singer, "With a Friend," 439.

140. See, for example, the following statement of Woodson's: "The NAACP, the Urban League, they're all the same. . . . These people have been pushing programs and solutions that are in essence dependency-producing programs. . . . The reality is that those civil rights organizations have a vested interest in these programs now. They survive off them. They and their friends largely run the organizations that receive the federal funds to distribute and administer the aid and implement the programs. Their friends run the programs." Quoted in E. Harris, "Selling Dependency," *National Review* 44, no. 11 (1992): 40.

141. Robert Woodson, *Orlando Sentinel*, January 18, 1989.

142. Robert Woodson, "Saving the Poor from the Saviors," *Destiny*, June 1991, 35.

143. On the surface, Woodson's proposals sounded very similar to the Community Action Programs that emerged as part of Lyndon Johnson's War on Poverty, before they were "corrupted by bureaucrats, professional providers, and machine politicians." Page, *Showing My Color*, 197. Rather than "accept solutions [provided] by middle class professional service providers," Woodson argued, "black America must recognize and expand on indigenous self-help neighborhood efforts. The originators of these self-help programs have unique, first-hand knowledge concerning the problems and resources to be found within their communities." Robert Woodson, *On the Road to Economic Freedom* (Washington, D.C.: Regnery-Gateway,

1987), 23. For further discussion, see Robert Woodson, "New Politics in Action: Beyond the Welfare State," in *Left and Right: The Emergence of a New Politics in the 1990s?* ed. Heritage Foundation and Progressive Foundation (Washington, D.C.: Heritage Foundation and Progressive Foundation, 1992), 46.

144. See, for example, Robert Woodson, "Cutting Off the Race Industry's Fuel Supply," *Headway* 10, no. 3 (1998): 25; Robert Woodson, "Stop Desecrating King's Legacy," *Wall Street Journal*, February 25, 1998, A22.

145. Peter L. Berger and Richard John Neuhaus, *To Empower People: The Role of Mediating Structures in Public Policy* (Washington, D.C.: American Enterprise Institute for Public Policy Research, 1977).

146. See, for example, Robert Woodson, "Empowering Poor Neighborhoods," in *A Conservative Agenda for Black Americans*, ed. Joseph Perkins (Washington, D.C.: Heritage Foundation, 1987), 49–60.

147. See, for example, Woodson, "New Politics," 47.

148. See, for example, its transformation of one "project" in Washington, D.C., the 464-unit Kenilworth-Parkside public housing complex, which had been plagued by soaring teenage pregnancy, crime, vandalism, and a 76 percent welfare dependency rate. Using strategies developed over many years, Woodson's organization intervened with a program of jobs, training, education, and other support that led to a complete revitalization of the complex and to a turnaround in the lives of many young people who most would simply have written off. For further details, see Woodson, *On the Road*, 24.

149. Page, *Showing My Color*, 210.

150. "Second Thoughts," *Wall Street Journal*, February 3, 1988.

151. See, for example, the following by Woodson: *The Triumphs of Joseph: How Today's Community Healers Are Reviving Our Streets and Neighborhoods* (Washington, D.C.: Free Press, 1998); "Government Can't Cure Poverty," *USA Today Magazine* 126, no. 2632 (1998): 18–19; "Misconceptions About Race and Poverty," *Headway* 9, no. 4 (1997): 25–26; "Government Should Play a Supporting Role," *National Minority Politics* 7, no. 8 (1995): 7–9.

152. See, for example, Robert Woodson, "Stabilizing and Revitalizing Urban Neighborhoods," *Journal of Negro Education* 58, no. 3 (1989): 403–6.

153. Woodson, "Conservatives Have Lost," 8.

154. See, for example, John McWhorter, *Authentically Black: Essays for the Black Silent Majority* (New York: Gotham Books, 2004).

155. For a discussion, see Booknotes Interview: http://www.booknotes. org/Program/?ProgramID=1716.

See also Dudley Barlow, "Book Review: Losing the Race," *Education Digest* 66, no. 6 (2001): 75; Leo Reisberg, "A Professor's Controversial Analysis of Why Black Students Are Losing the Race," *Chronicle of Higher Education* 46, no. 49 (2000): PA51.

156. McWhorter's father was a college administrator and his mother taught social work at Temple University. And as a child McWhorter was confident: "When I was five years old I thought I was smarter than my teachers—my white teachers—and I would tell them so." For further details of McWhorter's childhood and personal life, see the following interview: Cathy Young and Michael W. Lynch, "Internal Constraints," *Reason* 33, no. 5 (2001): 36.

157. For details, see McWhorter's homepage: http://www.manhattan-institute. org/html/mcwhorter.htm.

158. John McWhorter, *Losing the Race: Self-Sabotage in Black America* (New York:

Harper Perennial, 2001); John McWhorter, *Winning the Race: Beyond the Crisis in Black America* (New York: Gotham Books, 2005).

159. George F. Will, "The Ultimate Emancipation," RaceMatters.org, 2001, http://www.racematters.org/ultimateemancipation.htm.

160. McWhorter, *Losing*, xi.

161. McWhorter, quoted in Young and Lynch, "Internal," 36.

162. Ibid.

163. McWhorter challenged conservatives who argued that the nation could have forgone affirmative action because blacks were advancing fast enough before its introduction. He felt that, due to racism, the policy was justifiable in the 1960s. Ibid.

164. For discussion, see McWhorter, *Losing*, 229–35.

165. Ibid.

166. See, for example, John McWhorter, "Why I'm Black, Not African American," *Los Angeles Times*, September 8, 2004, http://www.manhattan-institute.org/html/_latimes-why_im_black.htm. What is more, in the preface to *Losing the Race*, McWhorter placed himself in the fine tradition of black intellectuals who have dedicated their work to the uplift of the race. "I have written this book under the conviction that it doesn't have to be this way, and that more to the point, it absolutely must not. Getting back on the track that our Civil Rights leaders set us upon . . . will require some profound adjustments in black identity, which today would feel nothing less than alien to most African Americans under the age of seventy. Nevertheless, these adjustments are not only possible, but most importantly are the only thing that will cut through the circularity and fraudulence infusing so much of interracial relations in American today, and bring African Americans at last to true equality in the only country that will ever be their home."

167. McWhorter, *Losing the Race*, 32.

168. Thomas Sowell, "Seasonal Reading Selections," *Washington Times*, December 23, 2000, A10; Walter Williams, "Scholastic Expectations," *Washington Times*, November 18, 2000, A12.

169. Clarence Thomas, "Why Black Americans Should Look to Conservative Policies," Heritage Foundation, August 1, 1987, http://www.heritage.org/Research/PoliticalPhilosophy/HL119.cfm?renderforprint=1.

170. Ibid.

171. These words—part of the Lincoln Institute's mission statement—can be found on the back of each copy of the *Lincoln Review*.

172. Parker, quoted in Hill et al., "Black America," 29.

173. Parker, quoted in Stephen Goode, "The Conscience of a Black Conservative," *Insight on the News* 17, no. 7 (1991): 38.

174. Ibid., 37.

175. J. A. Parker, *Angela Davis: The Making of a Revolutionary* (Washington, D.C.: Arlington House, 1973), 7.

176. Parker, quoted in Hill et al., "Black America," 29.

177. Parker, *Angela Davis*.

178. Goode, "Conscience," 37.

179. Ibid., 37.

180. Parker, quoted in Hill et al., "Black America," 29.

181. Goode, "Conscience," 38–39.

182. Parker, quoted in Hill et al., "Black America," 32.

183. Hill et al., "Black America," 34. Parker appeared not to see the irony in this observation (in terms of his own appointments).

184. Ibid., 34. See also J. A. Parker and Allan Brownfeld, "Returning to the Goal of a Color-Blind Society," *Lincoln Review* 2, no. 2 (1981): 3–22.

185. Goode, "Conscience," 39.

186. J. A. Parker, "Disinvestment Would Hurt Black South Africans, The Very People It Is Meant To Help," *Lincoln Review* 5, no. 3 (1985): 3.

187. Ibid., 1–8.

188. For evidence of her nonconformism, see her interaction with students in Anne Wortham, *Restoring Traditional Values in Higher Education: More than Afrocentrism* (Washington, D.C.: Heritage Foundation, 1991), 15.

189. See, for example, the following by Anne Wortham: *The Other Side of Racism: A Philosophical Study of Black Race Consciousness* (Columbus: Ohio State University Press, 1981); "The New Ethnicity Versus Individualist Pluralism," *Lincoln Review* 4, no. 3 (1984): 19–30; "Afrocentrism Isn't the Answer for Black Students in American Society," *Education Digest*, November 1992, 63–66; "Victimhood Versus Individual Responsibility," *Lincoln Review* 11, no. 2 (1993–94): 13–25.

190. Wortham, *Other Side*, xi.

191. "Racism," she wrote, "is usually viewed as a collective illness, as a doctrine conditioned in one by his culture and shared by him with his contemporaries, but the cause of racism—a symptom of one's lack of self-esteem—is individual. That the self-esteem of a great many in a society is ravaged by fears, doubts, and envy that it gives rise to and then is swallowed up by their race consciousness is what makes a social disease of racism. If racism were in fact caused by 'society' or one's 'culture,' no one could escape it. But there is ample evidence that not all men are race conscious and that those who are have chosen to be so." Ibid., 5.

192. Ibid., xii. At no time did Wortham fall back on collective racial identity. Her use of the outdated word "Negro" in her 1981 work *The Other Side of Racism* arguably revealed her detachment from black community norms and standards.

193. Anne Wortham, "Martin Luther King's Flawed Dream," *World and I* 13, no. 6 (1998): 66–71.

194. Wortham, *Other Side*, 317.

195. Ibid., 240.

196. Ibid., 151–246.

197. Thomas Sowell, "Follow the Money," *Forbes* 152, no. 2 (1993): 64.

198. See, for example, Elizabeth Wright, "The True Legacy of Malcolm X: Are We Ready for His Message," *Issues and Views*, winter 1989, 1–4; Elizabeth Wright, "Without Commerce and Industry, The People Perish: Marcus Garvey's Gospel of Prosperity," *Issues and Views*, spring 1991, 16–18.

199. For a discussion, see Lewis A. Randolph and Robert E. Weems Jr., "The Ideological Origins of Richard M. Nixon's Black Capitalism Initiative," *Review of Black Political Economy* 29, no. 1 (2001): 49–61.

200. C. Mobley, *The Case of the Black Conservatives and Political Leadership: Do They Lead, Follow, or Are They In the Way?* paper prepared for delivery at the Annual Meeting of the American Political Science Association Convention, Chicago, 1995, quoted in Ashbee, "Politics of Contemporary Black Conservatism," 158 (see intro., n. 58).

Chapter 2. Affirmative Action Dilemmas

Note to epigraphs: Lyndon B. Johnson, "Commencement Address at Howard University," The Lyndon B. Johnson Library and Museum, June 4, 1965, http://www.lbjlib.utexas.edu/johnson/archives.hom/speeches.hom/650604.htm.

Chairman of the Democratic Leadership Council, July 2005, quoted in Stephen F. Hayes, "Lieberman v. Gore: On Affirmative Action, This Ticket Is Far Apart," *National Review Online,* August 8, 2000.

1. For a comprehensive overview of the Kennedy administration's position on affirmative action, see, for example, Terry H. Anderson, *The Pursuit of Fairness: A History of Affirmative Action* (Oxford: Oxford University Press, 2004), 59–66; Robert J. Weiss, *"We Want Jobs": A History of Affirmative Action* (New York: Garland Publishing, 1997), 52–55. For a brief overview, see, for example, Steven M. Cahn, ed., *The Affirmative Action Debate* (New York: Routledge, 1995), xi; Joanne Barkan, "Affirmative Action: Second Thoughts," *Dissent* 45 (1998): 5; Charles T. Banner-Haley, *The Fruits of Integration: Black Middle Class Ideology and Culture 1960–1990* (Jackson: University Press of Mississippi, 1994), 60; Bryan K. Fair, *Notes of a Racial Caste Baby: Color Blindness and the End of Affirmative Action* (New York: New York University Press, 1997), 118–19.

2. Anderson, *Pursuit of Fairness,* 66.

3. For further discussion, see Francis J. Beckwith and Todd E. Jones, eds., *Affirmative Action: Social Justice or Reverse Discrimination?* (New York: Prometheus Books, 1997), 10–11; Stephen Thernstrom and Abigail Thernstrom, *America in Black and White: One Nation Indivisible* (New York: Simon and Schuster, 1997), 172–73; Darien A. McWhirter, *The End of Affirmative Action: Where Do We Go From Here?* (New York: Carol Publishing Group, 1996), 34–35.

4. Quoted in Harry S. Ashmore, *Civil Rights and Wrongs: A Memoir of Race and Politics 1944–1994* (New York: Pantheon Books, 1994), 187–88. Indeed, affirmative action came to be "defended by government policy makers [at this time] as a transitional step towards the ultimate goal of a color-blind society and as a necessary means of enforcing equal opportunity laws." Herman Belz, *Equality: A Quarter Century of Affirmative Action Transformed* (New Brunswick, N.J.: Transaction Publishers, 1991), 234.

5. For further discussion, see Paul Seabury, "HEW and the Universities," *Commentary* 53 (1972): 39; Hugh Davis Graham, *The Civil Rights Era: Origins and Development of National Policy, 1960–1972* (New York: Oxford University Press, 1990), 448; Anderson, *Pursuit of Fairness,* 118–26.

6. For further discussion, see Dereck T. Dingle, "Whatever Happened to Black Capitalism?" *Black Enterprise* 21, no. 1 (1990): 161–68; Robert E. Weems and Lewis A. Randolph, "The National Response to Richard M. Nixon's Black Capitalism Initiative," *Journal of Black Studies* 32, no. 1 (2001): 66–83. Anderson, *Pursuit of Fairness,* 119. For a more comprehensive overview of Nixon's record on civil rights, see Dean J. Kotlowski, *Nixon's Civil Rights: Politics, Principle, and Policy* (Cambridge, Mass.: Harvard University Press, 2001).

7. In 1971, for example, in *Griggs v. Duke Power,* the Supreme Court ruled that "practices, procedures, or tests neutral on their face and even neutral in terms of intent, cannot be maintained if they operate to freeze the status quo of prior discriminatory employment practices." Affirmative action was thus declared constitutional. David Frum, *How We Got Here: The 70s; The Decade that Brought You Modern Life (For Better or Worse)* (New York: Basic Books, 2000), 242–43.

8. In their 1967 work *Black Power*, Stokely Carmichael and Charles Hamilton provided the original—and arguably most detailed and compelling—explanation of what constituted "institutional racism." They wrote: "Racism is both overt and covert. It takes two, closely related forms: individual whites acting against individual blacks, and acts by the title white community against the black community. We call these individual racism and institutionalized racism. The first consists of overt acts by individuals, which cause death, injury or the violent destruction of property. . . . The second type is less overt, far more subtle, less identifiable in terms of *specific* individuals committing the acts. But it is no less destructive of human life. The second type originates in the operation of established and respected forces in the society, and thus receives far less public condemnation than the first type." Stokely Carmichael and Charles Hamilton, *Black Power: The Politics of Liberation in America* (New York: Random House, 1967), 4.

9. For a discussion, see John David Skrentny, *The Ironies of Affirmative Action: Politics, Culture and Justice in America* (Chicago: University of Chicago Press, 1996), 223–24.

10. Stephen Steinberg, "The Role of Racism in the Inequality Studies of William Julius Wilson," *Journal of Blacks in Higher Education*, no. 15 (1997): 117.

11. For a discussion, see Anderson, *Pursuit of Fairness*, 150–55.

12. In 1965, 4.9 percent of college students were black. In 1979, 9.9 percent of college students were black. Thernstrom and Thernstrom, *America in Black and White*, 389.

13. This budding group Bart Landry called the "new black middle class." Bart Landry, *The New Black Middle Class* (Berkeley: University of California Press, 1987). For a comprehensive analysis of the gains made by the black middle class during the 1970s, see Marable, *Race, Reform*, 150–54 (see intro., n. 14).

14. See, for example, Herbert Hammerman, *A Decade of New Opportunity: Affirmative Action in the 1970s* (Washington, D.C.: Potomac Institute, 1984).

15. Graham, *Civil Rights Era*, 282–87; Barry L. Goldstein, "The Historical Case for Goals and Timetables," *New Perspectives* 16, no. 1 (1984): 20.

16. For further discussion, see Raymond S. Franklin, *Shadows of Race and Class* (Minneapolis: University of Minnesota Press, 1991), 1–21; Herbert Hill and James E. Jones, eds., *Race in America: The Struggle for Equality* (Madison: University of Wisconsin Press, 1993), 345–69; J. Blaine Hudson, "Affirmative Action and American Racism in Historical Perspective," *Journal of Negro History* 84, no. 3 (1999): 260; Hugh Graham, "The Origins of Affirmative Action: Civil Rights and the Regulatory State," *Annals of the American Academy of Political and Social Science* 523 (1992): 50–62.

17. Quoted in Howard Ball, *The Bakke Case: Race, Education, and Affirmative Action* (Lawrence: University Press of Kansas, 2000), 8.

18. For further discussion, Jeremy Rabkin, *Judicial Compulsions* (New York: Basic Books, 1989), 147–81; Graham, "Origins of Affirmative Action," 50–62.

19. For a discussion of "public opinion and affirmative action" in the 1970s, see Frederick R. Lynch, *Invisible Victims: White Males and the Crisis of Affirmative Action* (New York: Greenwood Press, 1989), 17–20. See also Marylee C. Taylor, "White Backlash to Workplace Affirmative Action: Peril or Myth?" *Social Forces* 73, no. 4 (1995): 1385–414.

20. In 1978, white applicant Alan Bakke sued the University of California for denying him admission to medical school while admitting "less qualified" blacks under an affirmative action program. While finally admitting Bakke and rejecting "quotas" for minorities, the Supreme Court nevertheless permitted race to

be taken into account in admissions to promote diversity in the student body. In doing so, it effectively authorized affirmative action within tight constraints. For a detailed overview of the Bakke case, see, for example, Ball, *Bakke Case*; McWhirter, *End of Affirmative Action*, 88–95; Anderson, *Pursuit of Fairness*, 150–55, Thernstrom and Thernstrom, *America in Black and White*, 413–18; Daniel C. Maguire, *A New American Justice: Ending the White Male Monopolies* (New York: Doubleday, 1980), 39–46; Carol M. Swain, *The New White Nationalism in America: Its Challenge to Integration* (Cambridge: Cambridge University Press, 2002), 264–68; Peter Wood, *Diversity: The Invention of a Concept* (San Francisco: Encounter Books, 2003), 99–145. For shorter summaries, see Weiss, *We Want Jobs*, 217–18; Jim D. Newman, "Affirmative Action and the Courts," in *Affirmative Action in Perspective*, ed. Fletcher A. Blanchard and Faye J. Crosby (New York: Springer-Verlag, 1989), 35.

21. For a discussion, see Frederick R. Lynch and William R. Beer, "You Ain't the Right Color, Pal," *Policy Review* 51 (1990): 64–67; Seymour Martin Lipset and William Schneider, "The Bakke Case: How Would It Be Decided at the Bar of Public Opinion?" *Public Opinion* 1 (1978): 38–44.

22. For further discussion, see Eric Porter, "Affirming and Disaffirming Actions," in *America in the Seventies*, ed. Beth Bailey and David Farber (Lawrence: University Press of Kansas, 2004), 66.

23. See, for example, Nathan Glazer, *Affirmative Discrimination: Ethnic Inequality and Public Policy* (New York: Basic Books, 1975); Daniel P. Moynihan, "The New Racialism," in *Coping: Essays on the Practice of Government*, ed. Daniel P. Moynihan (New York: Random House, 1973); Charles Murray, "The New Discrimination: A Conservative Digest Poll," *Conservative Digest*, February 1978, 13.

24. See also O. Hatch, "In the Mainstream: Affirmative Action Blatant Illegal Racism," *Conservative Digest*, July 1980, 14; K. Phillips, "The New Racism," *Conservative Digest*, March 1978, 15; Barry R. Gross, *Discrimination in Reverse: Is Turnabout Fair Play?* (New York: New York University Press, 1978); John C. Livingston, *Fair Game? Inequality and Affirmative Action* (San Francisco: W. H. Freeman, 1979), 48–63.

25. For further discussion of the Reagan administration's approach to civil rights and affirmative action, see Robert R. Detlefsen, *Civil Rights Under Reagan* (San Francisco: Institute for Contemporary Studies, 1991); Norman C. Amaker, *Civil Rights Under the Reagan Administration* (Washington, D.C.: Urban Institute Press, 1988); Reginald C. Govan and William L. Taylor, eds., *One Nation, Indivisible: The Civil Rights Challenge for the 1990s* (Washington, D.C.: Citizens' Commission on Civil Rights, 1989); Nicholas Laham, *The Reagan Presidency and the Politics of Race: In Pursuit of Colorblind Justice and Limited Government* (Westport, Conn.: Praeger Publishers, 1998).

26. Derrick Bell, *And We Are Not Saved: The Elusive Quest for Racial Justice* (New York: Basic Books, 1987), 14.

27. See, for example, Thomas Sowell, "Affirmative Action: A Worldwide Disaster," *Commentary* 88 (1989): 30–31; Wortham, *Other Side*, 19 (see chap. 1, n. 89). For further discussion of the early black conservative position on "reverse racism," see Conti and Stetson, *Challenging*, 64–65 (see intro., n. 22).

28. See, for example, Sowell, "Affirmative Action," 30–31; Conti and Stetson, *Challenging*, 64–65.

29. See, for example, Sowell, *Ethnic*, 223 (see chap. 1, n. 44); Sowell, "Affirmative Action," 21.

30. J. A. Parker, "Editor's Comment," *Lincoln Review* 3, no. 1 (1982): 6.

31. Thomas, quoted in "Lasting Stigma: Affirmative Action and Clarence Thomas' Prisoners' Rights Jurisprudence," *Harvard Law Review* 112, no. 6 (1999): 1335; see also Williams, "Question of Fairness," 79 (chap. 1, n. 4).

32. Anne Wortham, foreword to *Civil Wrongs: What Went Wrong With Affirmative Action*, by Steven Yates (San Francisco: Institute For Contemporary Studies, 1994), xi–xv.

33. Sowell, *Civil Rights*, 69 (see chap. 1, n. 38).

34. Sowell, quoted in Conti and Stetson, *Challenging*, 64.

35. Thomas Sowell, "Are Quotas Good for Blacks?" *Commentary* 65, no. 6 (1978): 43.

36. Ibid., 43. See also the following by Sowell: "The New Racism on Campus," *Fortune*, February 13, 1989, 115–20; *Ethnic America*, 223 (see chap. 1, n. 44); *Economics and Politics*, 169–70 (see chap. 1, n. 38); *Civil Rights*, 32–35; *Pink and Brown People and Other Controversial Essays* (Stanford, Calif.: Hoover Institution Press, 1981), 1; *Preferential Policies: An International Perspective* (New York: William Morrow, 1990), 141–42.

37. See, for example, Sowell, *Preferential Policies*, 13–116; Sowell, *Civil Rights*, 34–35.

38. Williams, *South Africa's War*, 67–95 (see chap. 1, n. 95); Williams, *America*, 32 (see chap. 1, n. 95).

39. Sowell, "Affirmative Action," 21; Sowell, *Preferential Policies*, 145.

40. Williams, *Do the Right*, 8 (see chap. 1, n. 95).

41. This view was in keeping with the model of "symbolic representation" by which the great majority of people had calculated the gains of the civil rights movement. For further discussion of "symbolic representation" and its relevance to the study of contemporary black conservatism, see West, *Race Matters*, 35–49 (see intro., n. 20); Marable, *Beyond*, 188–89 (see intro., n. 17); Charles P. Henry, "Clarence Thomas and the National Black Identity," *Black Scholar* 22, no. 1 (1991): 40–41.

42. The most comprehensive critique of the "reverse racism" position can be found in Stanley Fish, "Reverse Racism, or How the Pot Got to Call the Kettle Black," in *Affirmative Action: Social Justice or Reverse Discrimination?* ed. Francis J. Beckwith and Todd E. Jones (Amherst, Mass.: Prometheus Books, 1997): 142–51. See also John F. Dovidio, Jeffrey A. Mann, and Samuel L. Gaertner, "Resistance to Racism: The Implications of Aversive Racism," in *Affirmative Action in Perspective*, ed. Fletcher A. Blanchard and Faye J. Crosby (New York: Springer-Verlag, 1989), 83–102; James W. Nickel, "Discrimination and Morally Relevant Characteristics," in *The Affirmative Action Debate*, ed. Steven M. Cahn (New York: Routledge, 1995), 3–4; Fair, *Notes*, xvii–xx.

43. For further discussion, see David R. Goldfield, *Black, White, and Southern: Race Relations and Southern Culture 1940 to the Present* (Baton Rouge: Louisiana State University Press, 1990), 211, 274–75; Marable, *Race, Reform*, 174–78.

44. For further discussion, see Nick Thompson, "Confessions of a White Affirmative Action Baby," *Journal of Blacks in Higher Education*, no. 11 (1996): 101. Thompson simply made the point that conservatives in the United States had a tradition of thwarting racial change by "making valid arguments but probably not honest ones." He wrote: "In 1964 these conservative forces argued against the Civil Rights Act on the grounds that it might lead to a racial backlash—or a 'police state' as Barry Goldwater said. In 1968 they validly argued against the Open Housing Act. In 1980 the Reagan administration argued, in the Bob Jones University case, in favor of tax-exempt status for discriminatory schools on the

grounds (later ridiculed by the Supreme Court) that the IRS was usurping its power by meddling too much in private affairs. . . . The basic point is this: Never did anyone, besides perhaps David Duke, base their arguments on the grounds that people of color were gaining too much power; however, every time a bill came up that would increase the power of people of color, the same people opposed it on other grounds."

45. For a discussion, see John K. Wilson, "The Myth of Reverse Discrimination in Higher Education," *Journal of Blacks in Higher Education*, no. 10 (1995–96): 89–90.

46. See, for example, Williams, *More Liberty*, 44–46 (see chap. 1, n. 95); Parker and Brownfeld, "Returning," 3–22 (see chap. 1, n. 184); Wortham, *Other Side*, 21–23.

47. Steele, *Content of Our Character*, 111–25 (see chap. 1, n. 111); Williams, "Question of Fairness," 72. James L. Robinson, *Racism or Attitude?: The Ongoing Struggle for Black Liberation and Self-Esteem* (New York: Plenum Press, 1995), 65–86; Conti and Stetson, *Challenging*, 65–67.

48. Glenn Loury, "How to Mend Affirmative Action," *Public Interest* 127 (1997): 41–43.

49. Steele, *Content of Our Character*, 1–20 (see chap. 1, n. 111); Wortham, *Other Side*, 160.

50. Thomas Sowell had been making this case since the 1970s. See, for example, the following by Sowell: "A Black Conservative Dissents," *New York Times Magazine*, August 8, 1976, 15; *Affirmative Action Reconsidered: Was It Necessary in Academia?* (Washington, D.C.: American Enterprise Institute, 1975), 17; "How Affirmative Action Hurts Blacks," *Forbes* 160, no. 7 (1997): 64. See also Steven L. Carter, *Reflections of an Affirmative Action Baby* (New York: Basic Books, 1991), 47–69.

51. Steele, *Content of Our Character*, 119.

52. Ibid., 90.

53. Ibid., 112–13.

54. Sowell, quoted in Russell Nieli, ed., *Racial Preference and Racial Justice: The New Affirmative Action Controversy* (Washington, D.C.: Ethics and Public Policy Center, 1991), 416.

55. Sowell, quoted in Gennady Stolyarov, "Three Ethical Arguments Against Affirmative Action: A Call to Abolish an Unjust and Racist Practice," *Society*, June 1, 2007, http://www.associatedcontent.com/article/264310/three_ethical_arguments_against_affirmative.html?page=2.

56. Carter, *Reflections*.

57. Ibid., 11–27.

58. Ibid., 12.

59. Ibid., 102.

60. McWhorter, *Losing the Race*, xi (see chap. 1, n. 158).

61. Ibid., 232–34.

62. Glenn Loury, "Economic Discrimination: Getting to the Core of the Problem," *Harvard Journal of African American Public Policy* 1 (1992): 91–110, quoted in "Professor Glenn C. Loury Berates the Abolitionist Crusade Against Racial Preferences," *Journal of Blacks in Higher Education*, no. 23 (1999): 41–42.

63. Glenn Loury, "Incentive Effects of Affirmative Action," *Annals of the American Academy of Political and Social Science* 23 (1992): 21.

64. McWhorter, *Losing the Race*, 82–89.

65. Ibid., 179–83.

66. Ibid., 232–33.

67. Ibid., 233.

68. Ibid., 229.

69. Quoted in Manning Marable, *Speaking Truth to Power: Essays on Race, Resistance, and Radicalism* (Boulder, Colo.: Westview Press, 1996), 66–67.

70. Ibid., 67.

71. McWhirter, *End of Affirmative Action*, 132–33.

72. Stephen Thernstrom and Abigail Thernstrom, quoted in Leo Reisberg, "A Professor's Controversial Analysis of Why Black Students are 'Losing the Race,'" *The Chronicle of Higher Education* 46, no. 49 (2000): A51.

73. See also, for example, Madeline E. Heilman, Caryn J. Block, and Jonathan A. Lucas, "Presumed Incompetent: Stigmatization and Affirmative Action Efforts," *Journal of Applied Psychology* 77 (1992): 538–47; Charles Murray, "Affirmative Racism: How Preferential Treatment Works Against Blacks," *New Republic*, December 31, 1984, 18–23; Warren Brookes, "The Side Effects of Quotas," *Washington Times*, August 10, 1990, 20; J. Lawlor, "Study: Affirmative-Action Hirers' Abilities Doubted," *USA Today*, August 31, 1990, 3.

74. Kilson, "Anatomy," 8–10 (see intro., n. 58); Martin Kilson, "Realism about the Black Experience: A Reply to Shelby Steele," *Dissent* 42 (1990): 520.

75. Reed, "Steele Trap," 274 (see chap. 1, n. 61).

76. Stephen Steinberg, *Turning Back: The Retreat from Racial Justice in American Thought and Policy* (Boston: Beacon Press, 1995): 168–71.

77. For example, in 1981, Nell Irvin Painter—now a black female professor of history at Princeton University—wrote to the *New York Times*: "I never questioned the justice of my position. I should have a job, a good one. I had worked hard as a graduate student and had written a decent dissertation. I knew foreign languages, had travelled widely and had taught and published. I thought I had been hired because I was a promising young historian. . . . I didn't think my teaching at a first-rate university required an extraordinary explanation." Nell Irvin Painter, "Hers; Whites Say I Must Be on Easy Street," *New York Times*, December 10, 1981. See also Henry Louis Gates, Jr., "Affirmative Reaction: A Conversation with Cornel West on Talent, Tradition, and the Crisis of the Black Male," *Transition* 68 (1995): 175–76; Page, *Showing My Color*, 215–18 (see chap. 1, n. 133).

78. See, for example, Martin Kilson, "Affirmative Action," *Dissent* 37 (1995): 469–70; Marable, *Beyond*, 85–90; Kelley, *Yo'*, 95–96 (see intro., n. 13); Fair, *Notes*, 177–82.

79. See, for example, Gates, "Affirmative Reaction," 175.

80. Jennifer L. Hochschild, "Affirmative Action and the Rumor of Black Inferiority," *Journal of Blacks in Higher Education*, no. 8 (1995): 64.

81. For further discussion, see Faye J. Crosby and Sharon D. Herzberger, "The Effectiveness of Affirmative Action," in *Affirmative Action: The Pros and Cons of Policy and Practice*, ed. Richard F. Tomasson, Faye J. Crosby, and Sharon D. Herzberger (Lanham, Md.: Rowman and Littlefield Publishers, 2001): 60–62; Marylee C. Taylor, "Impact of Affirmative Action on Beneficiary Groups: Evidence from the 1990 General Social Survey," *Basic and Applied Social Psychology* 15 (1994): 143–78; Barbara R. Bergmann, *In Defense of Affirmative Action* (New York: Basic Books, 1996), 131–48.

82. Gates, "Affirmative Reaction," 175.

83. For further discussion, see Zillar R. Eisenstein, *The Color of Gender: Reimagining Democracy* (Berkeley: University of California Press, 1994), 60–61, 67–68; Ran-

dolph, "Black Neoconservatives," 155–56 (see chap. 1, n. 87). Julianne Malveaux, "Why Are the Black Conservatives All Men?" *Ms.*, March–April 1991, 60–61.

84. See the great lengths to which they (and their supporters) go to promote their self-help exploits. Williams, *Do the Right*, xi–xii; Goode, "Conscience," 36–39 (see chap. 1, n. 173); Kauffman, "Interview" (see chap. 1, n. 6).

85. For further discussion of the seemingly untenable nature of this black conservative position, see Crosby and Herzberger, "Effectiveness," 64; Brent Staples, "The Presumption of Stupidity," *New York Times*, March 5, 1995, 14; Russell J. Summers, "The Influence of Affirmative Action on Perceptions of a Beneficiary's Qualifications," *Journal of Applied Social Psychology* 21, no. 15 (1991): 1265–276.

86. Stanley Fish, "The Nifty Nine Arguments against Affirmative Action in Higher Education," *Journal of Blacks in Higher Education*, no. 27 (2000): 81.

87. For further discussion, see Hochschild, "Affirmative Action," 65.

88. William G. Bowen and Derek Bok, *The Shape of the River: Long Term Consequences of Considering Race in College and University Admissions* (Princeton, N.J.: Princeton University Press, 1998).

89. Ibid., 268.

90. William M. Banks, *Black Intellectuals: Race and Responsibility in American Life* (New York: W. W. Norton, 1998), 181.

91. Foner, quoted in "What about the Charge That Affirmative Action Reinforces a Sense of Group Inferiority?" *Journal of Blacks in Higher Education*, no. 20 (1997–98): 21.

92. For a discussion, see, for example, "The Black Student Meets the Meritocracy: Entrenched Affirmative Action for Whites," *Journal of Blacks in Higher Education*, no. 40 (2003): 25–27.

93. Quoted in Banks, *Black Intellectuals*, 181.

94. Kilson, "Anatomy," 10–12; West, *Race Matters*, 93–99.

95. See, for example, Bergmann, *In Defense*, 32–61. Chapter 4 will provide a more in-depth discussion of the evidence of employment discrimination in American life.

96. See, for instance, Parker and Brownfeld, "Returning," 3; Ward Connerly, "The Sweet Music of Equal Treatment," in *Affirmative Action: Social Justice or Reverse Discrimination?* ed. Francis J. Beckwith and Todd E. Jones (Amherst, Mass.: Prometheus Books, 1997), 68; Williams, *Do the Right*, 24.

97. West, *Race Matters*, 78, 96–97.

98. Ibid., 78–79. For similar critiques, see Marable, *Speaking Truth to Power*, 67; Randall Kennedy, "Persuasion and Distrust," in *Racial Preference*, ed. Russell Nieli (Washington, D.C.: Ethics and Public Policy Center, 1990), 51; Toler, "Black Conservatives," 1–30 (see intro., n. 58), 20; Kilson, "Anatomy," 10–13.

99. West, *Race Matters*, 79; Fish, "Reverse Racism," 150–51.

100. Sowell, *Civil Rights*, 49–56, 133–34. For further discussion, see also Sowell, *Economics and Politics*, 131–32, 199–200; Sowell, *Preferential Policies*, 140–41; Thomas Sowell, "Racism Under New Management is Still Racism," *Human Events* 52, no. 44 (1996): 19.

101. Theodore L. Cross and Robert Bruce Slater, "Only the Onset of Affirmative Action Explains the Explosive Growth in Black Enrollments in Higher Education," *Journal of Blacks in Higher Education*, no. 23 (1999): 110–15.

102. Steele, quoted in "A Collection of Views of Black Conservatives on Affirmative Action," *Journal of Blacks in Higher Education*, no. 20 (1998): 9–10.

103. Thernstrom and Thernstrom, *America in Black and White*, 538.

104. Stephen Steinberg, "Nathan Glazer and the Assassination of Affirmative

Action," *New Politics* 9, no. 3 (2003), http://www.wpunj.edu/newpol/issue35/Steinberg35.htm.

105. Steinberg, *Turning Back*, 182.

106. Ibid., 182.

107. Ibid., 181–83. See also Steinberg, "Nathan Glazer."

108. Steinberg, *Turning Back*, 167. For more detail, see Edward Franklin Frazier, *Black Bourgeoisie: The Rise of a New Middle Class in the United States* (New York: Free Press, 1957), 129–95.

109. For a discussion of the impact of affirmative action on black employment mobility, see Jonathan S. Leonard, *The Effectiveness of Equal Employment Law and Affirmative Action Regulation* (Berkeley: University of California Press, 1985); Jonathan S. Leonard, "The Impact of Affirmative Action on Employment," *Journal of Labor Economics* 2 (1984): 439–63; Jonathan S. Leonard, "What Was Affirmative Action?" *The American Economic Review* 76, no. 2 (1986): 359–63; Jonathan S. Leonard, "The Impact of Affirmative Action Regulation and Equal Employment Law on Black Employment," *Journal of Economic Perspectives* 4 (1990): 47–63; Gerald D. Jaynes and Robin M. Williams, ed., *A Common Destiny: Blacks and American Society* (Washington, D.C.: National Academy Press, 1989), 269–329; Sharon M. Collins, "The Making of the Black Middle Class," *Social Problems* 30 (1983): 369–81; Garland Pinkston, Jr., *Affirmative Action to Open the Doors of Job Opportunity* (Washington, D.C.: Citizens' Commission on Civil Rights, 1984), 121–47; John F. Zipp, "Government Employment and Black-White Earnings Inequality 1980–1990," *Social Problems* 41 (1994): 363–82.

110. Cross and Slater, "Only the Onset," 110–15.

111. Ibid., 110.

112. "Thomas Carlyle and Affirmative Action," *Journal of Blacks in Higher Education*, no. 24 (1999): 5.

113. Conti and Stetson, *Challenging*, 64.

114. See, for example, Sowell, *Economics and Politics*, 200–201; Sowell, *Civil Rights*, 134; Clarence Thomas, "Abandon the Rules: They Cause Injustice," *USA Today*, September 5, 1985; Williams, "Tragic Vision," 412 (see chap. 1, n. 103).

115. Sowell, "Affirmative Action," 21.

116. Ibid.

117. See, for example, Clarence Thomas, "Affirmative Action Goals and Timetables: Too Tough? Not Tough Enough!" *Yale Law & Policy Review* 5 (1987): 403.

118. Sowell, "Affirmative Action," 21–41.

119. Robert Woodson, "Affirmative Action is No Civil Right," *Harvard Journal of Law and Public Policy* 19, no. 3 (1996): 773–79.

120. For decades, according to Woodson, civil right leaders had been "using affirmative action to pad their pockets and then pull out their civil-rights credit card and plead race when they get caught." Robert Woodson, television appearance on "Tony Brown's Journal," first aired July 13, 1990. Quoted in Conti and Stetson, *Challenging*, 182.

121. See Woodson, "Affirmative Action," 773–79.

122. Robert Woodson, "Capitol Hill Hearing Testimony," in *An Overview of Affirmative Action: Hearing before the Subcommittee on the Constitution, Federalism, and Property Rights of the Committee on the Judiciary*, ed. Hank Brown (Washington, D.C.: Diane Publishing, 1995), 49.

123. See, for example, Jaynes and Williams, *Common Destiny*, 269–329; Pinkston, *Affirmative Action*, 121–47; Leonard, *Effectiveness of Equal Employment Law*; Leonard, "What Was Affirmative Action?" 359–63; Leonard, "Impact of Affirmative

Action on Employment," 439–63; Leonard, "Impact of Affirmative Action Regulation," 47–63; Collins, "Making of the Black Middle Class," 369–81; Zipp, "Government Employment," 363–82. Sowell and company never addressed these studies in their books.

124. For evidence of this, see Conti and Stetson, *Challenging*, 50.

125. The book's thesis was stated simply in the opening sentence: "Race relations in America have undergone fundamental changes in recent years, so much so that now the life chances of individual blacks have more to do with their economic class position than with their day-to-day encounters with whites." Wilson, *Declining Significance of Race*, 1 (see intro., n. 27).

126. Ibid., 110.

127. William J. Wilson, *The Truly Disadvantaged: The Inner City, the Underclass and Public Policy* (Chicago: University of Chicago Press, 1987).

128. Ibid., 110–20. For further discussion, see Michael Lind, *The Next American Nation: The New Nationalism and the Fourth American Revolution* (New York: Free Press, 1995), 175–79.

129. Wilson, *Truly Disadvantaged*, 120–24.

130. William J. Wilson, "Race Neutral Programs and the Democratic Coalition," *American Prospect* 1 (1990): 81.

131. Loury, *One By One*, 109–10 (see chap. 1, n. 70).

132. Ibid., 110. See also Glenn Loury, "How to Mend Affirmative Action," *Public Interest* 127 (1997): 42–43.

133. Loury, *One By One*, 19–24, 41–42, 110.

134. West, *Race Matters*, 95.

135. Loury, "How to Mend," 43.

136. See, for example, Manning Marable, *Black Liberation in Conservative America* (Boston: South End Press, 1997), 263–64. That the impetus for racism is not narrowly economic in focus was given dramatic exposure in a 1991 broadcast of the ABC program *Prime Time Live*. In a revealing twenty-minute segment, journalists followed two young men of equal education, cultural sophistication, and economic status around St. Louis, Missouri, in search of employment, housing, a new car, and services at community stores. The two differed only in one respect: one was black and the other, white. But that, it turned out, was the critical difference. Job vacancies that had been filled when the black applicant inquired were miraculously available when the white applicant arrived fifteen minutes later. The rental accommodation that was available for lease to the white applicant was not available only minutes later to the black applicant. The white applicant was given better terms on his car loan and immediately obtained service at shops and supermarkets. The black man did not. After viewing the program, philosopher Stanley Fish concluded that "Racism is a cultural fact, and although its effects may to some extent be diminished by socioeconomic variables, those effects will still be sufficiently great to warrant the nation's attention and thus the continuation of affirmative action policies." Fish, "Reverse Racism," 144.

137. Orlando Patterson, "Affirmative Action: The Sequel," *New York Times*, June 22, 2003. For further discussion, see also Kenneth S. Tollett, "Racism and Race-Conscious Remedies," *American Prospect* 5 (1991), 192. Tollet wrote: "I take umbrage at Wilson's repeated criticism of affirmative action for benefiting primarily the middle class or those who need help least and not helping the underclass. . . . It is as if one were to criticize penicillin for not curing or anticipating and preventing AIDS or cancer."

138. Marable, *Beyond*, 89.

139. Ibid., 88–95.

140. Indeed in 1969 the black liberal Bayard Rustin had opposed Nixon's Philadelphia Plan on the assumption that it would "split" labor unions and the civil rights movement. In reality, this meant that racist lily-white unions that were the target of the plan would have continued to discriminate against black workers. For a discussion, see Stephen Steinberg, "Occupational Apartheid," in *Race and Ethnicity in the United States: Issues and Debates*, ed. Stephen Steinberg (Malden, Mass.: Blackwell Publishers, 2000), 69–70.

141. For further discussion, see Herbert Hill, "Myth-Making as Labor History: Herbert Gutman and the United Mine Workers of America," *Politics, Culture and Society* 2 (1988): 132–95; Steven Shulman, "Racism and the Making of the American Working Class," *Politics, Culture and Society* 2 (1988): 365.

142. For a discussion, see Steinberg, *Turning Back*, 180.

143. Ibid., 147–48.

144. Ibid., 166–68, 195–96.

145. William L. Taylor, "Brown, Equal Protection, and the Isolation of the Poor," *Yale Law Journal* 95 (1986): 1714.

146. Ibid., 1714. For further details about the Philadelphia Plan, see Arthur A. Fletcher, "Whatever Happened to the Philadelphia Plan?" *Business and Society Review/ Innovation* 5 (1973): 24–28.

147. Steinberg, *Turning Back*, 148.

148. Kilson, "Affirmative Action," 469.

149. Ibid., 469.

150. For further discussion, see Marcus Alexis, "The Effect of Admission Procedures on Minority Enrollment in Graduate and Professional Schools," in *Working Papers: Bakke, Weber and Affirmative Action*, ed. Rockefeller Foundation (New York: Rockefeller Foundation, 1979), 52–71.

Indeed, according to the former Secretary of Education Lamar Alexander, "ninety-eight percent of race-specific scholarships do not involve constitutional problems." In other words, in university admissions, 98 percent of race-specific scholarships were also to the economically disadvantaged. Fish, "Reverse Racism," 133.

151. See, for example, Thomas Sowell, "Choosing a College," *Jewish World Review*, April 21, 1999, http://www.jewishworldreview.com/cols/sowell.html. Williams, *More Liberty*, 127–29; Steele, *Content of Our Character*, 138–39; John McWhorter, "Who Should Get Into College?" *City Journal*, spring 2003, http://www.city-journal.org/html/13_2_who_should_get.html.

152. Sowell, quoted in "Professor Thomas Sowell Holds to the Discredited Myth That Blacks Admitted to Harvard Under Affirmative Action Might Be Better Off at a Less Selective School," *Journal of Blacks in Higher Education*, no. 40 (2003): 21.

153. "Perpetuating the Falsehood That Affirmative Action Students Will Have a Lower Dropout Rate If They Attend Less Selective Colleges," *Journal of Blacks in Higher Education*, no. 36 (2002): 50.

154. Walter Williams, "Black Students as Meal Tickets," *Jewish World Review*, February 9, 2000, http://www.jewishworldreview.com/cols/williams020900.asp.

155. Ibid., 50.

156. Williams, *More Liberty*, 129.

157. Steele, quoted in "The Myth that Affirmative Action Causes High Student Dropout Rates," *Journal of Blacks in Higher Education*, no. 17 (1997): 63.

158. McWhorter, "Who Should Get."

159. Sowell, *Black Education*, 129–53 (see chap. 1, n. 38).

160. Thernstrom and Thernstrom, *America in Black and White*, 396.

161. See, for example, Theodore L. Cross, "The Myth That Preferential College Admissions Create High Black Student Dropout Rates," *Journal of Blacks in Higher Education*, no. 1 (1993): 71; "The Thernstrom Fallacy: Why Affirmative Action Is Not Responsible for High Dropout Rates of African American College Students," *Journal of Blacks in Higher Education*, no. 20 (1998): 90.

162. "Professor Thomas Sowell Holds," 21.

163. Williams, "Black Students."

164. See, for example, "Professor Thomas Sowell Holds," 21; "Perpetuating the Falsehood," 50.

165. "Professor Thomas Sowell Holds," 21.

166. "Myth that Affirmative Action," 63.

167. Walter Williams, "Virginia State University Tyranny," *Jewish World Review*, May 2, 2001, http://www.jewishworldreview.com/cols/williams050201.asp.

168. See, for example, Glenn Loury, "America's Moral Dilemma: Will It Be Color Blindness or Racial Equality?" *Journal of Blacks in Higher Education*, no. 27 (2000): 90.

169. Loury, *One By One*, 114.

170. "Glenn Loury on the Undercutting of Black Incentives to Go to College," *Journal of Blacks in Higher Education*, no. 16 (1997): 34–35.

171. Loury, "America's Moral Dilemma," 90–94.

172. Ibid.

173. Ibid., 90.

174. Loury, *One By One*, 109.

175. Ibid.; Loury, "America's Moral Dilemma," 90–94.

176. Stephen Steinberg, "Two Cheers for Glenn Loury—Or Maybe Just One," *New Politics* 9, no. 1 (2002), http://www.wpunj.edu/newpol/issue33/steinb33.htm.

177. Loury, "Beyond Civil Rights," 22–25 (see chap. 1, n. 66).

178. Loury, "America's Moral Dilemma," 90.

179. There will be a discussion of role-modeling—its merits and flaws—in Chapter 3 of this book.

180. For a discussion of Woodson's support for role-modeling, see Clarence Page, "Toward a New Black Agenda," *Chicago Tribune*, April 17, 1985. For a discussion of Steele's support for role-modeling, see Banner-Haley, *Fruits of Integration*, 79.

181. Banner-Haley, *Fruits of Integration*, 75; Williams, "We Can Be Proud," 53–55 (see chap. 1, n. 103); Walter Williams, "The Sad Passing of a Black Tradition," *Lincoln Review* 8, no. 3 (1989): 47–48.

182. Enacted in 1996, Proposition 209 banned race-based admissions at California's public universities. For further discussion, see "Has Proposition 209 Discouraged Black Students from Seeking Places in Private Universities in California?" *Journal of Blacks in Higher Education*, no. 26 (1999–2000): 42–43; B. Drummond Ayres, Jr., "Conservatives Forge New Strategy to Challenge Affirmative Action," *New York Times*, February 16, 1995.

183. See Connerly's justification of this decision in a letter he wrote to King's son in 1997. http://www.acri.org/news/mlkiii.html.

184. Kelley, *Yo'*, 90; Dillard, *Guess*, 52 (see intro., n. 30).

185. Alan L. Keyes, *Master of the Dream: The Strength and Betrayal of Black America* (New York: William Morrow, 1995); Ken Hamblin, *Pick a Better Country: An*

Unassuming Colored Guy Speaks His Mind About America (New York: Simon and Schuster, 1996); Gary Franks, *Searching for the Promised Land: An African American's Optimistic Odyssey* (New York: Regan Books, 1996).

186. Ward Connerly, *Creating Equal: My Fight Against Race Preferences* (San Francisco: Encounter Books, 2000). See also Connerly, "Sweet Music," 64–69; Ward Connerly, "Don't Box Me In: An End to Racial Checkoffs," *National Review,* April 16, 2001, 24–26; American Civil Rights Institute, "Connerly Commemorates Anniversary of 'I Have a Dream,'" news release, September 11, 1998; Ward Connerly, "My Fight Against Race Preferences: A Quest Towards Creating Equal," *Chronicle of Higher Education* 46, no. 27 (2000): 27–30.

187. On more than one occasion, these personal circumstances provoked charges of a conflict of interest.

188. For more information on the CCRI, see http://www.publicaffairsweb.com/ccri/.

189. For further discussion, see "The California Black Regent Who is Leading the Charge Against Affirmative Action," *Journal of Blacks in Higher Education,* no. 10 (1995): 30–31; Dungee, "Two Faces of Clarence Thomas,"140 (see intro., n. 84); Randolph, "Black Neoconservatives," 154; Reed, "Descent of Black Conservatism," 18–20 (see intro., n. 83). When the story confirming Connerly's status as an affirmative action beneficiary first appeared in the *San Francisco Examiner,* he denied it. When it reappeared soon after in the *Los Angeles Times,* Connerly claimed that he "regretted" registering and participating in the "repugnant race-based program." Quoted in C. Ingram and E. Woo, "Affirmative Action FOE Widens Attack," *Los Angeles Times,* May 10, 1995, A3. Significantly, however, Connerly did not return the money to the state of California.

190. Connerly, quoted in Barry Bearak, "Questions of Race Run Deep for Foe of Preferences," *New York Times,* July 27, 1997.

191. For further discussion, see Robert Michael Franklin, *Liberating Visions: Human Fulfillment and Social Justice in African American Thought* (Minneapolis: Fortress Press, 1990); David Howard-Pitney, *The Afro American Jeremiad: Appeals for Justice in America* (Philadelphia: Temple University Press, 1990).

192. Martin Luther King, Jr., *Where Do We Go from Here: Chaos or Community?* (New York: Harper and Row, 1967), 30–69.

193. Dillard, *Guess,* 49. See also Sheridan, "New Accommodationists," 167–68 (see intro., n. 58).

194. Dillard, *Guess,* 48–55; Indeed, by the end of his life, King's faith in the "American Dream" had diminished significantly. See, for example, his remarks in a 1967 speech: "Yes, I am personally the victim of deferred dreams, of blasted hopes." Quoted in James H. Cone, *Martin and Malcolm and America: A Dream or a Nightmare* (New York: Orbis Books, 1991), 213. For further discussion of King's political evolution, see Stewart Burns, "From the Mountaintop: The Changing Political Vision of Martin Luther King Jr.," *History Teacher* 27, no. 1 (1993): 7–18; Harry A. Reed, "History and Memory, Reflections on Dreams and Silences," *Journal of Negro History* 84, no. 2 (1999): 150–66; William M. King, "The Reemerging Revolutionary Consciousness of The Reverend Dr. Martin Luther King Jr.," *Journal of Negro History* 71 (1986): 1–22.

195. Dillard, *Guess,* 50–52.

196. Martin Luther King, Jr., "Negroes Are Not Moving Too Fast," *Saturday Evening Post,* November 7, 1964.

197. Martin Luther King, Jr., *Why We Can't Wait* (New York: Harper and Row, 1964), 134.

198. King, *Where Do We Go*, 187.

199. Ibid., 186.

200. Ibid., 187.

201. Ibid., 183–93.

202. Mary Frances Berry, "Vindicating Martin Luther King, Jr.: The Road to a Color-Blind Society," *Journal of Negro History* 81 (1996): 143.

203. For further discussion of King's practical support for black institutions, despite his philosophical emphasis on color-blindness, see Kenneth B. Nunn, "Rights Held Hostage: Race, Ideology, and the Peremptory Challenge," *Harvard Civil Rights-Civil Liberties Law Review* 63 (1993): 71–72; Harold Cruse, *Plural But Equal: A Critical Study of Blacks and Minorities in America's Plural Society* (New York: William Morrow, 1987), 238–41, 256–57; Marable, *Speaking Truth to Power*, 65–66.

Chapter 3. Partisans of the Poor?

1. For further discussion of these trends within black America, see Manning Marable and Leith Mullings, "The Divided Mind of Black America: Race, Ideology and Politics," *Race and Class* 36, no. 1 (1994): 62–66; Marable, *Black Liberation*, 24–26 (see chap. 2, n. 138); "Setting the Record Straight on the State of Black Inequality in the United States," *Journal of Blacks in Higher Education*, no. 21 (1998): 46–47; Mark Newman, *The Civil Rights Movement* (Edinburgh: Edinburgh University Press, 2004), 155–57.

2. Cone, *Martin and Malcolm*, 89 (see chap. 2, n. 196).

3. Michael Harrington, *The Other America: Poverty in the United States* (New York: Macmillan, 1962).

4. See, for example, Robert Charles Smith, *Racism in the Post Civil Rights Era: Now You See It, Now You Don't* (New York: State University of New York Press, 1995), 107–8; Myron Magnet, *The Dream and the Nightmare: The Sixties Legacy to the Underclass* (New York: William Morrow, 1993), 117; David Stoesz and Howard Jacob Karger, *Reconstructing the American Welfare State* (Lanham, Md.: Rowman and Littlefield Publishers, 1992), 47; B. Jones, "From the Sixties to the Eighties: The Economic Status of Black Americans," in *Readings in American Political Issues*, ed. Franklin D. Jones and Michael O. Adams (Dubuque, Iowa: Kendall-Hunt, 1987), 371; Robert H. Haveman, "The War on Poverty and the Poor and Non-poor," *Political Science Quarterly* 102, no. 1 (1987): 65; Byron G. Lander, "Group Theory and Individuals: The Origin of Poverty as a Political Issue in 1964," *Western Political Quarterly* 24, no. 3 (1971): 514–26.

5. Kenneth B. Clark, *Dark Ghetto: Dilemmas of Social Power* (New York: Harper and Row, 1965); Elliot Liebow, *Tally's Corner: A Study of Negro Streetcorner Men* (Boston: Little, Brown and Company, 1967); Ulf Hannerz, *Soulside: Studies in Ghetto Culture and Community* (New York: Columbia University Press, 1969); Lee Rainwater, *Behind Ghetto Walls: Black Families in a Federal Slum* (Chicago: Aldine Publishing, 1970). See also Lee Rainwater, "Crucible of Identity: The Negro Lower-Class Family," *Daedalus* 95 (1966): 166–216.

6. Noting that one-quarter of black marriages dissolved, that one-quarter of black babies were illegitimate, and that one-quarter of black families were headed by females, Moynihan talked of a "tangle of pathology" within the black community. Daniel P. Moynihan, *The Negro Family: The Case for National Action* (Washington, D.C.: Department of Labor, Office of Policy Planning and Research, 1965).

The report, the effects of the controversy it generated, and many of the key documents related to it were subsequently compiled in Lee Rainwater and William L. Yancey, *The Moynihan Report and the Politics of Controversy* (Cambridge, Mass.: MIT Press, 1967).

7. Moynihan, *Negro Family*, 30.

8. Government actions, Moynihan wrote, must "have the effect . . . of enhancing the stability and resources of the Negro American family." Quoted in Jennifer L. Hochschild, "When Books on Race Don't Help Us Know the Truth," *Journal of Blacks in Higher Education*, no. 12 (1996): 70.

9. See, for example, the comments of James Farmer of the Congress of Racial Equality: "As if living in the sewer, learning in the streets and working in the pantry weren't enough of a burden for millions of American Negroes, I now learn that we've caught matriarchy and the tangle of pathology. . . . By laying the primary blame for present-day inequalities on the pathological condition of the Negro family and community, [the Moynihan Report] has provided a massive academic cop-out for the white conscience." He added: "We are sick unto death of being analyzed, mesmerized, bought, sold, and slobbered over, while the same evils that are the ingredients of our oppression go unattended." Quoted in Rainwater and Yancey, *Moynihan Report*, 409–10.

10. For a discussion, see Kevin L. Yuill, "The 1966 White House Conference on Civil Rights," *Historical Journal* 41, no. 1 (1998): 259–82.

11. Ibid.

12. This emerging conservative consensus directly contradicted the findings of the Johnson-appointed Kerner Commission charged with investigating the causes of the riots. The commission's 1968 publication, popularly known as the Kerner Report, explicitly rejected the view that the riots had stemmed from senseless violence on the part of dysfunctional ghetto youth. Rather, it concluded that "white racism is essentially responsible for the explosive mixture which has been accumulating in our cities since the end of World War II." National Advisory Commission, *Report of the National Advisory Commission on Civil Disorders* (Washington, D.C.: U.S. Government Printing Office, 1968), 10.

13. Banfield's most famous work was *The Unheavenly City* (Boston: Little, Brown, 1970).

14. Ibid., 125.

15. The similarities between *The Unheavenly City* and the writings of Edward Ross, a white supremacist from the early twentieth century, are striking. Ross argued that European people were "future oriented"—emphasizing reason and the ability to defer gratification—while blacks "live from hand to mouth taking no thought of tomorrow." Edward A. Ross, "The Cause of Race Superiority," *Annals of the American Academy of Political and Social Science* 18 (1901): 67–89.

16. For a detailed discussion of the various government initiatives, see Robert C. Liberman, *Shifting the Color Line: Race and the American Welfare State* (Cambridge, Mass.: Harvard University Press, 1998); Jill Quadagno, *The Color of Welfare: How Racism Undermined the War on Poverty* (New York: Oxford University Press, 1994); Sar A. Levitan, "The Community Action Program: A Strategy to Fight Poverty," *Annals of the American Academy of Political and Social Science* 385 (1969): 63–75.

17. For a discussion of AFDC specifically, see Kenneth J. Neubeck, "The Demise of AFDC as a Legacy of White Racial Backlash," in *Welfare Racism: Playing the Race Card Against America's Poor*, ed. Kenneth J. Neubeck and Noel Cazenave (New York: Routledge, 2001), 115–44.

18. In 1978 Dorothy Newman wrote that "the public perception has been that idle black welfare recipients lived on Easy Street, despite the fact that in the only terms that count—money—welfare took only a little over 10 percent of the black households . . . out of poverty, but two times as many of the whites." Dorothy Newman, *Protest, Politics and Prosperity: Black Americans and White Institutions 1940–1975* (New York: Pantheon Books, 1978), 255.

19. For a discussion, see Porter, "Affirming," 50–74 (see chap. 2, n. 24).

20. "The American Underclass," *Time*, August 29, 1977.

21. In the largest American cities—New York, Chicago, Los Angeles, Philadelphia, Detroit, Houston, Baltimore, Dallas, Cleveland, and Indianapolis—the number of blacks living in extreme poverty areas doubled between 1970 and 1980. Loïc J. D.Wacquant and William J. Wilson, "The Cost of Racial and Class Exclusion in the Inner City," *Annals of the American Academy of Social and Political Science* 501 (1989): 8–25. In its annual study, *The State of Black America, 1978*, the Urban League charged that the situation facing blacks had actually grown worse since the racial disorders of the 1960s. Bernard E. Anderson, *The State of Black America, 1978* (New York: National Urban League, 1978).

22. "American Underclass," 14–15.

23. Gunnar Myrdal, *Challenge to Affluence* (New York: Harper and Brothers, 1962), 53.

24. See, for example, Richard McGahey, "Poverty's Voguish Stigma," *New York Times*, March 12, 1982; Andrew Hacker, "The Lower Depths," *New York Review of Books*, August 12, 1982, 15–40; William Raspberry, "Will the Underclass Be Abandoned?" *Washington Post*, May 14, 1985; Mortimar B. Zuckerman, "The Black Underclass," *U.S. News and World Report*, April 19, 1986, 78; Nicholas Lehmann, "The Origins of the Underclass," *Atlantic*, June 1986, 31–61; Myron Magnet, "America's Underclass: What to Do?" *Fortune*, May 11, 1987, 130–50; P. Hammil, "America's Black Underclass: Can It Be Saved?" *Reader's Digest*, June 1988, 105–10; Richard Stengel, "The Underclass: Breaking the Cycle," *Time*, October 10, 1988, 41–42.

25. George Gilder, *Wealth and Poverty* (New York: Basic Books, 1981); Lawrence M. Mead, *Beyond Entitlement: The Social Obligations of Citizenship* (New York: Free Press, 1986).

26. "Charles Murray: White America's Deadly Seducer," *Journal of Blacks in Higher Education*, no. 6 (1994–1995): 72.

27. Charles Murray, *Losing Ground: American Social Policy, 1950–1980* (New York: Basic Books, 1984).

28. For a discussion, see Robert Greenstein, "Losing Faith in Losing Ground," *New Republic*, March 25, 1985, 12–17.

29. Bernadette P. Chachere, "The Economics of Thomas Sowell: A Critique of *Markets and Minorities*," *Review of Black Political Economy* 12, no. 2 (1983): 169. Banfield was in fact a great admirer of Sowell's work. On the dust jacket of *The Economics and Politics of Race* (front inside flap), Banfield wrote: "In this new book Sowell gives us the facts and analytic tools with which to understand ethnic and racial experiences in *all* countries. No scholar thinks or writes more lucidly than he. No one has shown his skill at solving the ethnic and racial equivalents of Rubik's Cube."

30. Thomas Sowell, "Crippled by Their Culture," *Wall Street Journal Online*, April 26, 2005, http://www.opinionjournal.com/editorial/feature.html?id=110006608.

31. Thomas Sowell, ed., *Essays and Data on American Ethnic Groups* (Washington,

D.C.: Urban Institute, 1978), 258; Sowell, *Markets*, 8 (see chap. 1, n. 50); Sowell, *Economics and Politics*, 107 (see chap. 1, n. 38); Sowell, *Civil Rights*, 77 (see chap. 1, n. 38).

32. See, for example, Sowell, *Essays and Data*, 258.

33. Sowell, *Ethnic America*, 187 (see chap. 1, n. 44).

34. Ibid., 218.

35. Reynolds Farley and Walter Allen, *The Color Line and the Quality of Life in America* (New York: Oxford University Press, 1989), 362–407; Stephen Steinberg, *The Ethnic Myth: Race, Ethnicity, and Class in America* (Boston: Beacon Press, 1989), 267–80; Suzanne Model, "Caribbean Immigrants: A Black Success Story?" *International Migration Review* 25, no. 2 (1991): 248–76; Suzanne Model, "West Indian Prosperity: Fact or Fiction?" *Social Problems* 42, no. 4 (1995): 535–53; See also Mathijs Kalmijn, "The Socioeconomic Assimilation of Caribbean American Blacks," *Social Forces* 74, no. 3 (1996): 911–30.

36. In the 1960s many had even come to regard these practices as "acts of resistance," as calculated strategies to reduce surplus extraction on the plantation. This was why the whip was considered "indispensable" wherever the institution existed. For further discussion, see Orlando Patterson, *Slavery and Social Death: A Comparative Study* (Cambridge, Mass.: Harvard University Press, 1982), 3.

37. See, for example, Orlando Patterson, *The Sociology of Slavery: An Analysis of the Origins, Development and Structure of the Negro Slave Society in Jamaica* (London: MacGibbon and Kee, 1967), 216–21; Barry W. Higman, *Slave Populations of the British Caribbean 1807–1834* (Baltimore: Johns Hopkins University Press, 1984), 251–55; Eric Williams, *Capitalism and Slavery* (London: Andre Deutsch, 1964), 121; Michael Craton, *Testing the Chains: Resistance to Slavery in the British West Indies* (Ithaca, N.Y.: Cornell University Press, 1982), 174; Joseph P. Reidy, *From Slavery to Agrarian Capitalism in the Cotton Plantation South: Central Georgia 1800–1880* (Chapel Hill: University of North Carolina Press, 1992); Ira Berlin and Philip D. Morgan, eds., *The Slaves' Economy: Independent Production by Slaves in the Americas* (London: Frank Cass, 1991).

38. See, for example, William Alexander Darity and Rhonda M. Williams, "Peddlers Forever? Culture, Competition, and Discrimination," *American Economic Review* 75, no. 3 (1985): 256–61.

39. See, for example, Steinberg, *Ethnic Myth*, 267–80; Watts, "Review of Thomas Sowell," 471–85 (see chap. 1, n. 45).

40. William J. Wilson, "Class Cleavages and Ethnic Pluralism," *Contemporary Sociology* 11, no. 4 (1982): 372. See also Adam Kuper, *Culture: The Anthropologists' Account* (Cambridge, Mass.: Harvard University Press, 1999), x–xi, 245–47.

41. Ian McKay, "Historians, Anthropology, and the Concept of Culture," *Labor/Le Travailleur* 8/9 (1981/82): 228–29.

42. Focusing on New York in the 1920s and 1930s, James Weldon Johnson accounted for the disproportionately large number of black professionals of West Indian ancestry by suggesting that Caribbean immigrants, in contrast to African Americans, had "something of a genius for business." James Weldon Johnson, *Black Manhattan* (New York: Alfred A. Knopf, 1930), 153. Three decades on, George Schuyler, Nathan Glazer, and Daniel Moynihan were expressing their admiration for the resourcefulness and resilience of the West Indians too. In spite of "race," they were said to possess the fundamental cultural ingredients for success: a capacity for thrift, sobriety, hard work, and deferred gratification. "The Reminiscences of George Schuyler" (New York: Oral History Office, Butler Library, Columbia University, 1960), 73; Nathan Glazer and Daniel P. Moynihan,

Beyond the Melting Pot: The Negroes, Puerto Ricans, Jews, Italians, and Irish of New York City (Cambridge, Mass.: MIT Press, 1963), 35. See also Roi Ottley and William Weatherby, eds., *The Negro in New York: An Informal Social History* (New York: Oceana Publications, 1967), 192.

43. Farley and Allen, *Color Line*, 396.

44. Ibid., 403. By 1980 African American family incomes stood at 70 percent of the national average, compared with 62 percent in 1969.

45. Ira Reid, *The Negro Immigrant: His Background, Characteristics and Social Adjustment 1899–1937* (New York: Columbia University Press, 1939), 121.

46. Stanley Lieberson, *A Piece of the Pie: Black and White Immigrants Since 1980* (Berkeley: University of California Press, 1980).

47. See, for example, Watts, "Review of Thomas Sowell," 479–80.

48. Ibid., 479. Steinberg, *Ethnic Myth*, 267–80; Model, "West Indian," 538. Kalmijn, "Socioeconomic Assimilation," 914.

49. These people were distinctive in two critical respects: their socioeconomic and educational credentials set them apart not only from most West Indians they "left behind" but also from most African Americans they encountered in their new home. Before emigrating to the United States, a high proportion had held professional, white-collar jobs in the Caribbean. Model, "West Indian," 538.

50. For a discussion, see Peter R. Shergold, "Relative Skill and Income Levels of Native and Foreign Born Workers: A Reexamination," *Explorations in Economic History* 13, no. 4 (1976): 459.

51. See, for example, Walter Williams, "The Legacy of Slavery Hustle," *Capitalism Magazine*, July 16, 2001, http://www.capmag.com/article.asp?ID=968.

52. Herbert Gutman, *The Black Family in Slavery and Freedom 1750–1925* (New York: Pantheon Books, 1976).

53. Williams, "Legacy of Slavery."

54. Ibid. See also Walter Williams, "The Welfare Debate," *Society* 33, no. 5 (1996): 13–14.

55. Sowell, *Race and Culture*, 220 (see chap. 1, n. 38).

56. Ibid., 220.

57. Quoted in Peter B. Edelman, "The War on Poverty and Subsequent Federal Programs: What Worked, What Didn't Work, and Why? Lessons for Future Programs," *Clearinghouse Review Journal of Poverty Law and Policy* 40 (2006): 7.

58. Ronald Reagan, "Governor of California Inaugural Address," January 4, 1971, http://californiagovernors.ca.gov/h/documents/inaugural_33b.html.

59. For an assessment of Reagan's approach to the welfare state, see, for example, Raymond J. Struyk, "Administering Social Welfare: The Reagan Record," *Journal of Policy Analysis and Management* 4, no. 4 (1985): 481–500; Sheldon Danziger, "Budget Cuts as Welfare Reform," *The American Economic Review* 73, no. 2 (1983): 65–70; John O'Connor, "U.S. Social Welfare Policy: The Reagan Record and Legacy," *Journal of Social Policy* 27 (1998): 37–61.

60. For a discussion of these earlier attitudes, see Marvin E. Gettleman, "Charity and Social Classes in the United States 1974–1900," *American Journal of Economics and Sociology* 22, no. 2 (1963): 313–29.

61. Michael Lind, *Up from Conservatism: Why the Right Is Wrong for America* (New York: Free Press, 1996), 192–93.

62. Sowell, "Politics and Opportunity," 7 (see intro., n. 7).

63. See, for example, Williams, *All It Takes*, 111–12 (see chap. 1, n. 95). Steele, "New Black," 18–19 (see chap. 1, n. 119); J. A. Parker, "Is the NAACP Now Irrelevant?" *Lincoln Review* 4, no. 1 (1983): 3–7; J. A. Parker, "Charges of New Rac-

ism Are a Smokescreen for the Problems Black Leaders Refuse to Face," *Lincoln Review* 7, no. 3 (1987): 1–8.

64. See, for example, Thomas Sowell, "War on Poverty Revisited," *Capitalism Magazine*, August 17, 2004, http://www.capmag.com/articlePrint.asp?ID=3864.

65. Walter Williams, "Religion Helps Underclass Overcome Many Problems," *Human Events* 53, no. 2 (1997): 9.

66. For a detailed discussion, see Glenn Loury and James Q. Wilson, eds., *Families, Schools and Delinquency Prevention* (New York: Springer-Verlag, 1987).

67. Walter Williams, "Sex, Families, Race, Poverty, Welfare," *American Enterprise* 6 (1995): 33.

68. See, for example, Loury, *One By One*, 138 (see chap. 1, n. 70).

69. See, for example, Williams, *All It Takes*, 111–12. Williams wrote: "But while charity might be man's greatest virtue, it is no cure for poverty. . . . People actually choose welfare as a permanent way of life because it is their right."

70. See, for example, Parker, quoted in Hill et al., "Black America," 30 (see intro., n. 31); Thomas, quoted in Hill et al., "Black America," 32; Thomas Sowell, "Preserving a Vision: Part III," *Jewish World Review*, May 31, 2006, http://jewishworldreview.com/cols/sowell060106.asp; Williams, *All It Takes*, 108.

71. Williams, *Do the Right*, 13 (see chap. 1, n. 95).

72. Parker, quoted in Hill et al., "Black America," 32.

73. "Welfare," according to Thomas, was "detrimental to people because it sucked out of them any motivation, any ambition." He suggested politicians "cut it off and force people to work and learn and pull themselves up by their bootstraps." "You can't tinker with it," Thomas insisted of welfare. "We've been tinkering with it for twenty years. We've just got to shut it down." Quoted in Thomas, *Clarence Thomas*, 208–9 (see chap. 1, n. 21). For Wortham's views on the ineffectiveness of government generally and welfare more specifically, see Wortham, "Victimhood," 15 (see chap. 1, n. 189).

74. For further discussion, see James P. Smith and Finis R. Welsch, *Closing the Gap: Forty Years of Economic Progress for Blacks* (Santa Monica, Calif.: Rand Corporation, 1986), 19.

75. "Thomas Sowell on Meet the Press," special edition 1, *Manhattan Report*, no. 8 (1981): 12.

76. Indeed, political scientist Mack Jones wrote: "It was state intervention in response to societal tension precipitated by militant struggle which led to the constellation of court decisions, statutes, and executive orders which broke the back of the caste system." Jones, "Political Thought," 35 (see intro., n. 25).

77. Reagan's comments before the NAACP 72nd Annual Convention, Denver, Colorado, June 29, 1981. Quoted from http://www.reagan.utexas.edu/archives/speeches/1981/62981a.htm.

78. Ibid.

79. Walter E. Williams, "Response to Five Policy Proposals," in *The Fairmont Papers: Black Alternatives Conference*, ed. Institute for Contemporary Studies (San Francisco: Institute for Contemporary Studies, 1980), 105.

80. See John Petrie's collection of Thomas Sowell quotations at: http://jpetrie.myweb.uga.edu/sowell.html.

81. Jones, "Political Thought," 23–49.

82. Franklin, quoted in Gettleman, "Charity and Social Classes," 324.

83. Woodson, quoted in Conti and Stetson, *Challenging*, 165 (see intro., n. 22).

84. In 1986, for example, Loury wrote: "It is important to understand that I am

not arguing here against the ancient and still valid notion that there is a public responsibility in a decent society to contribute to the alleviation of poverty, black or otherwise. In the areas of education, employment training, and provision of minimal subsistence to the impoverished, the government must be involved." Loury, "Prescription for Black Progress," 437 (see chap. 1, n. 76). Woodson, as we know, strongly supported the "mediating structures" approach pioneered by Peter Berger and Richard Neuhaus. "Wherever possible," Berger and Neuhaus wrote in *To Empower a People*, "public policy should utilize mediating structures for the realization of social purposes." Berger and Neuhaus, *Empower People*, 6–7 (see chap. 1, n. 145).

85. Loury, "Linking Public and Private Efforts," 19 (see chap. 1, n. 72).

86. Indeed, in the same 1987 article Woodson wrote: "Another significant problem with the traditional approach to poverty is that it tends to reward failure. If you are poor and truant from school, there is a program for you. If you are poor and alcoholic, there is a program for you. If you are poor and pregnant, there is yet another. But if you are merely in the low income category, if you obey your parents, if you are struggling to achieve in school, if you refrain from sexual activity, there is no program for you. You just don't qualify." Robert Woodson, "Poverty: Why Politics Can't Cure It," *Imprimis* 17, no. 7 (1988), http://www.hillsdale.edu/news/imprimis/archive/issue.asp?year=1988&month=07. See also Woodson, "Empowering," 54 (see chap. 1, n. 146).

87. Woodson, *On the Road*, 23 (see chap. 1, n. 145); Woodson, "Poverty: Why Politics Can't Cure It."

88. Loury wrote that mandatory work requirements showed "respect for the recipients, by according them the expectation that they are capable of meeting commonly held norms about how people should conduct their lives." Loury, "Two Paths," 20–21 (see chap. 1, n. 70).

89. Thomas Sowell, *Compassion versus Guilt and Other Essays* (New York: William Morrow, 1987), 43–44.

90. In his book *Pick a Better Country*, the black conservative radio host Ken Hamblin described poor "dysfunctional" blacks as "black trash." On the blurb, Sowell endorsed this sentiment and the book generally, writing: "Hamblin has [an] irreverent attitude toward the politically correct dogmas of the day and a gift for the right word or image that captures how outrageous the liberal malarkey is." Hamblin, *Pick a Better Country* (see chap. 2, n. 187).

91. Thomas Sowell, "Random Thoughts," *Capitalism Magazine*, September 22, 2005, http://www.capmag.com/article.asp?ID=4413.

92. Williams, *Do the Right*, 27–29.

93. Years later journalists Mayer and Abramson found that Thomas's remarks were false because his sister was not on welfare at the time of the conference. Having received none of the educational advantages that he had taken for granted, Thomas's sister, Emma Mae Martin, had assumed primary care of their mother and was working two part-time jobs to get off welfare. Mayer and Abramson, *Strange Justice*, 74–75 (see intro., n. 38). The black feminist Julianne Malveaux was incensed, writing: "For providing that kind of support in her family, Emma Mae Martin earned her brother's public scorn." Quoted in Marable, *Beyond*, 96 (see intro., n. 17).

94. See, for example, the remarks of J. A. Parker in J. Parker, *Freeing Black Americans from the Liberal Plantation* (pamphlet), Washington, D.C., 1994. Parker wrote: "As President of the Lincoln Institute, I invite you to help us continue our work of building support for conservative principles in the black community

and thereby free more black Americans from the liberal plantation." For further discussion of this black conservative rhetorical strategy, see Smith, "Individual Ethos," 128 (see intro., n. 62).

95. For a discussion, see Neubeck, "Demise of AFDC," 115–44.

96. See, for example, Robert B. Hill, *Economic Policies and Black Progress: Myths and Realities* (Washington, D.C.: National Urban League, 1981), 60; Peter Gottschalk, "AFDC Participation Across Generations," *American Economic Review* 80, no. 2 (1990): 367–71.

97. Frances Piven and Richard A. Cloward, "The Contemporary Relief Debate," in *The Mean Season: The Attack on the Welfare State*, ed. Fred Block, Richard A. Cloward, Barbara Ehrenreich, and Frances Piven (New York: Pantheon Books, 1987), 64–65.

98. Teresa L. Amott, "Black Women and AFDC: Making Entitlement Out of Necessity," in *Women, the State, and Welfare*, ed. Linda Gordon (Madison: University of Wisconsin Press, 1990), 281.

99. Katherine McFate, "Blacks and Welfare: Sorting Out the Facts," in *Readings in American Political Issues*, ed. Franklin D. Jones and Michael O. Adams (Dubuque, Ia.: Kendall-Hunt, 1987), 427. Significantly, McFate wrote, "between 1972 and 1980, while the number of children in black female-headed households was increasing by 20 percent, the number of black children supported by AFDC was falling by 5 percent. The women who were purportedly having children to 'get on welfare' were neither applying for nor receiving AFDC support."

100. Wilson, *Truly Disadvantaged*, (see chap. 2, n. 129).

101. Ibid., 135–36.

102. See, for example, Bernard R. Boxill, "Wilson on the Truly Disadvantaged," *Ethics* 101, no. 3 (1991): 579–92; Bernard C. Watson, "Review: The Truly Disadvantaged," *Journal of Negro Education* 57, no. 2 (1988): 222–24.; Mali Pohlmann, "Review: The Truly Disadvantaged," *Journal of Politics* 51, no. 1 (1989): 239–41.

103. For a more detailed discussion of these developments, see Barry Blueston and Bennett Harrison, *The Deindustrialization of America: Plant Closings, Community Abandonment, and the Dismantling of Basic Industry* (New York: Basic Books, 1982), 25–48.

104. West, *Race Matters*, 87 (see intro., n. 20).

105. For further discussion, see William J. Wilson, *When Work Disappears: The World of the New Urban Poor* (New York: Vintage Books, 1996); Jennifer L. Hochschild, *Facing Up to the American Dream: Race, Class, and the Soul of the Nation* (Princeton, N.J.: Princeton University Press, 1995).

106. West, *Race Matters*, 86.

107. Ibid.

108. Ibid.

109. Ibid., 85–88. West wrote: "On the practical and political level, the only feasible alternative to the welfare state is to create more jobs for poor people—something the private sector is simply uninterested in doing, for it is not in its economic interests to do so. Thus, the market rationality of the private sector relegates poor people to subsistence levels of living and/or unemployment. In contemporary American politics, to attack the welfare state without linking this attack to a credible jobs program (one that is more than likely supported by the public sector) is to reduce the already limited options of black poor people" (86–87).

110. Loury, "God and the Ghetto," A14 (see chap. 1, n. 75).

111. Ibid.

112. William Ryan, *Blaming the Victim* (New York: Pantheon Books, 1971), xiii.

113. See, for example, Kelley, *Yo'*, 15–19 (see intro., n. 13); Adolph Reed, *Class Notes: Posing as Politics and Other Thoughts on the American Scene* (New York: New Press, 2001), 93–100. For a more detailed discussion of race's continuing significance in American life, see Douglass S. Massey and Nancy A. Denton, *American Apartheid: Segregation and the Making of the Underclass* (Cambridge, Mass.: Harvard University Press, 1993).

114. Kelley, *Yo'*, 18.

115. Reed, *Class Notes*, 95.

116. Ibid.

117. Ibid., 98–99; Kelley, *Yo'*, 19.

118. Kelley, *Yo'*, 19.

119. Ibid. Reed, *Class Notes*, 98–100.

120. Reed, *Class Notes*, 98.

121. Ibid., 99.

122. Kelley, *Yo'*, 3. The "dozens," as defined by Kelley, refers to "a kind of game or performance" in which young black men talk, with humor, about each other's mothers.

123. Fred Barnes, "The Minority Minority," *New Republic*, September 30, 1991, 20.

124. For evidence of this black 1990s self-help discourse, see Don Aucoin and Peter S. Canellos, "A Community Takes Responsibility: Black Manifesto Urges a New Social Contract," *Boston Globe*, May 8, 1992; F. Robinson, "Self-Help Can Chip Away at Mountain of Despair," *Atlanta Journal-Constitution*, July 26, 1990; R. Morganfield, "Nation of Islam Spreads Self-Help Message," *Houston Chronicle*, September 11, 1994; Jerry M. Guess, "NAACP Stays True to Self-Help Principle," *Wall Street Journal*, May 14, 1992.

125. For a detailed discussion of the March, see Manning Marable, "Black Fundamentalism: Louis Farrakhan and the Politics of Conservative Black Nationalism," *Dissent* 45, no. 2 (1998): 69–76.

126. Adolph Reed, "Black Politics Gone Haywire," *Progressive*, December 1, 1995.

127. See, for example, Woodson, *On the Road*, 23.

128. Loury, "Prescription for Black Progress," 437.

129. Walter Williams, "The Poor Are Getting Richer," *Human Events* 55, no. 31 (1999): 13.

130. Anne Wortham, "Individualism: For Whites Only?" *Reason*, February 1979, 31.

131. Loury, *One By One*, 73.

132. Woodson, quoted in Conti and Stetson, *Challenging*, 157.

133. Loury, *One By One*, 36.

134. Williams, *More Liberty*, 49–50 (see chap. 1, n. 95).

135. See, for example, ibid., 48–50. But arguably the most detailed black conservative discussion of black self-help in American history is to be found in Robert Woodson's 1987 book, *On the Road to Economic Freedom*.

136. Thomas, quoted in Kauffman, "Interview" (see chap. 1, n. 6).

137. Sowell, *Economics and Politics*, 183–206; Sowell, *Race and Culture*, 146.

138. Hazlett and Klausner, "Reason Interview," 49 (see intro., n. 31).

139. Thomas Sowell, "Blacks and Self-Help," *Washington Times*, August 21, 1991.

140. John Hope Franklin, "Booker T. Washington, Revisited," *New York Times*, August 1, 1991.

141. Ann Withorn, "Helping Ourselves: The Limits and Potential of Self-Help," *Social Policy* 11, no. 3 (1980): 21.

142. U.S. Bureau of the Census, *Statistical Abstract of the United States 1993* (Washington, D.C.: U.S. Government Printing Office, 1993), 469.

143. T. Sowell, quoted in William F. Buckley, ed., *On the Firing Line* (New York: Random House, 1989), 321. See, for example, Sowell, "Culture—Not Discrimination," 74 (see chap. 1, n. 41).

144. Kelley, *Yo'*, 78–102. For a broader discussion of the disinvestment under Reagan, see Frank Levy, *Dollars and Dreams: The Changing American Income Distribution* (New York: W. W. Norton, 1988); Martin Carnoy, *Faded Dreams: The Economics and Politics of Race in America* (Cambridge: Cambridge University Press, 1994), 150–71.

145. Bernard H. Ross and Myron A. Levine, *Urban Politics: Power in Metropolitan America* (Ithaca, N.Y.: F. E. Peacock Publishers, 2001), 12.

146. Marable, *Race, Reform*, 183 (see intro. n. 14).

147. John Herbers, "Poverty Rate, 7.4%, Termed Highest Since '67," *New York Times*, July 26, 1982.

148. McGhee, quoted in S. Rule, "Black Middle Class Slipping, Study by Urban League Says," *New York Times*, August 4, 1982.

149. Monte Piliawsky, "From Black Agenda to National Policy: A Few Proposals," *Southern Changes* 4 (1982): 12–13.

150. Steele, *Content of Our Character*, 9 (see chap. 1, n. 111).

151. Conti and Stetson, *Challenging*, 105–6.

152. Parker, quoted in Hill et al., "Black America," 37.

153. Thomas, quoted in ibid.

154. See, for example, Williams, *All It Takes*, 27–29; Walter Williams, "The Minimum Wage and Davis-Bacon Act: Comment," *Journal of Labor Research* 3, no. 4 (1982): 408–10; Walter Williams, "Minimum Wage Devastates Young and Unskilled," *Human Events* 52, no. 21 (1996): 9; Walter Williams, "Minimum Wage, Maximum Folly," *Human Events* 62, no. 15 (2006): 11; Thomas Sowell, "Gambling with Jobs," *National Minority Politics* 6, no. 1 (1994): 19.

155. Clarence Thomas, quoted in Hill et al., "Black America," 37.

156. Thomas Boston, *Race, Class and Conservatism* (London: Unwin Hyman, 1988).

157. See, for example, Jonathan S. Leonard, "The Interaction of Residential Segregation and Employment Discrimination," *Journal of Urban Economics*, no. 21 (1987): 323–46; John E. Farley, "Disproportionate Black and Hispanic Unemployment in US Metropolitan Areas: The Roles of Racial Inequality, Segregation and Discrimination in Male Joblessness," *American Journal of Economics and Sociology* 46, no. 2 (1987): 129–50; Keith R. Ihanfeldt and David L. Sjoquist, "The Impact of Job Centralization on the Economic Welfare of Central City Blacks," *Journal of Urban Economics*, no. 26 (1989): 110–30; Mark Alan Hughes and Jannice Fanning Madden, "Residential Segregation and the Economic Status of Black Workers: New Evidence for an Old Debate," *Journal of Urban Economics*, no. 29 (1991): 110–30.

158. Watts, "Case of a Black Conservative," 310 (see intro., n. 33).

159. Margery Turner, Michael Fix, and Raymond Struyk, *Opportunities Denied, Opportunities Diminished: Discrimination in Hiring* (Washington, D.C.: Urban Institute, 1991).

160. Ibid., 1.

161. Ibid.

162. Joleen Kirschenman and Kathryn Neckerman, "We'd Love to Hire Them But . . . The Meaning of Race for Employers," in *The Urban Underclass*, ed. Christopher Jencks and Paul E. Peterson (Washington, D.C.: Brookings Institution, 1992), 203–12.

163. Ibid., 210.

164. Robert Woodson, "The Poor and Conservatives versus The Poverty Industry," *The Heritage Foundation*, October 1, 1987, http://www.heritage.org/Research/Religion/HL128.cfm.

165. R. Greenstein et al., *Still Far from the Dream: Recent Developments in Black Income, Employment and Poverty* (Washington, D.C.: Center on Budget and Policy Priorities, 1988).

166. Elijah Anderson, "The Social Context of Youth Employment Programs," in *Youth Employment and Training Programs: The YEDPA Years*, ed. Charles L. Betsey, Robinson G. Hollister, and Mary R. Papageorgiou (Washington, D.C.: National Academy Press, 1985), 348–66.

167. Steinberg, *Turning Back*, 179–80 (see chap. 2, n. 78).

168. Clay Smith Jr., "A Black Lawyer's Response to the Fairmont Papers," *Howard Law Journal* 26, no. 1 (1983): 219–20.

169. Ibid., 219.

170. Ibid., 218–20.

171. Ibid., 219–20.

172. Dorothy Height, "Family and Community: Self-Help—A Black Tradition," *The Nation* 249, no. 4 (1989): 136.

173. See, for example, Banner-Haley, *Fruits of Integration*, 53–80 (see chap. 2, n. 3).

174. Loury, *One By One*, 22.

175. Woodson advocated the establishment of "Junior Achievement"–type clubs to "teach entrepreneurial values like thrift, hard work and showing up on time." Moreover, he argued, "entrepreneurial values have application beyond just business; and I think that steps should be taken to spread them among low-income people." See Hill et al., "Black America," 40. Woodson further stressed the importance of "Mom-and-Pop" stores because "certain values are communicated to the children so that they can go on to college." Robert Woodson, "Is the Black Community a Casualty of the War on Poverty?" *Heritage Lectures*, no. 45 (1990): 6.

176. Glenn Loury, "Internally Directed Action for Black Community Development: The Next Frontier of the Movement," *Review of Black Political Economy* 13, no. 1 (1984): 38. Loury's lament indicated support for this notion of elite responsibility for poor blacks. He wrote: "Having achieved professional success, they [middle-class blacks] appear not to recognize that their own accomplishments are rooted in the kind of personal qualities that enable one best to take advantage of the opportunities existing in American society. As a result, the opportunity for their lives to stand as examples for the lower class of the community goes relatively unexploited" (38).

177. Page, "Toward a New Black Agenda" (see chap. 2, n. 182).

178. For further discussion, see, for example, Gordon Lafer, "Minority Unemployment, Labor Market Segmentation, and the Failure of Job-Training Policy in New York City," *Urban Affairs Quarterly* 28, no. 2 (1992): 206–35.

179. Martin Kilson, "Anatomy," 7 (see intro., n. 58). For further discussion, see Jerry G. Watts, *Heroism and the Black Intellectual: Ralph Ellison, Politics and Afro-American Intellectual Life* (Chapel Hill: University of North Carolina Press, 1994), 21–23; Banks, *Black*, 231–41 (see chap. 2, n. 92); Marable, *Beyond*, 167–73.

180. So, too, was their emphasis on the few instances in which blacks had climbed to the top, as if social mobility was available to all blacks, irrespective of circumstances.

181. Kofi Buenor Hadjor, *Another America: The Politics of Race and Blame* (Boston: South End, 1995), quoted in Robin Kelley, "The Crisis: Is Self-Help the Capitalism of Fools?" *Village Voice*, March 5, 1996, 8.

Chapter 4. Visions of School Reform

Note to epigraphs: Marable, *Black Liberation*, 90 (see chap. 2, n. 138).
Williams, *More Liberty*, 118 (see chap. 1, n. 95). For similar sentiments, see Walter Williams, "Miserable Schools, Not Lott, Real Enemy of Urban Blacks," *Human Events* 59, no. 1 (2003): 10.

1. For further discussion, see, for example, Jonathan Kozol, "Still Separate, Still Unequal: America's Educational Apartheid," *Harper's Magazine*, September 1, 2005, 41–54; Gary Orfield and Susan E. Eaton, *Dismantling Desegregation: The Quiet Reversal of Brown v. Board of Education* (New York: New Press, 1996); Maureen T. Hallinan, "Sociological Perspectives on Black-White Inequalities in American Schooling," extra issue: Current of Thought: Sociology of Education at the Dawn of the Twenty-first Century, *Sociology of Education* 74 (2001): 51.

2. Walter Williams, "Public Education for Blacks Is a Disgraceful Disaster," *Human Events* 60, no. 15 (2004): 25.

3. Juan Williams, *Enough: The Phony Leaders, Dead-End Movements, and Culture of Failure That Are Undermining Black America—and What We Can Do About It* (New York: Random House, 2006), 95.

4. Marable, *Black Liberation*, 90.

5. For an overview of the history of black education in America, see Ronald E. Butchart, "Outthinking and Outflanking the Owners of the World: A Historiography of the African American Struggle for Education," *History of Education Quarterly* 28, no. 3 (1988): 333–66.

6. For a concise overview, see Henry A. Giroux, "Thunder on the Right: Education and the Ideology of The Quick Fix," *Curriculum Inquiry* 5, no. 1 (1985): 57–62.

7. The literature on *Brown* is, of course, extensive. Any list is invidious, but the following sources provide useful overviews of both the judgment's foundations and implications. For books, see Richard Kluger, *Simple Justice, The History of Brown v. Board of Education and Black America's Struggle for Equality* (New York: Vintage, 1975); J. Harvie Wilkinson III, *From Brown to Bakke: The Supreme Court and School Integration: 1954–1978* (New York: Oxford University Press, 1979); John R. Howard, *The Shifting Wind: The Supreme Court and Civil Rights from Reconstruction to Brown* (New York: State University of New York Press, 1999); Jack Greenberg, *Crusaders in the Courts: How a Dedicated Band of Lawyers Fought for the Civil Rights Revolution* (New York: Basic Books, 1994). For articles, see Michael J. Klarman, "How *Brown* Changed Race Relations: The Backlash Thesis," *Journal of American History* 81 (1994): 81–118; Raymond Wolters, "From *Brown* to *Green* and Back: The Changing Meaning of Desegregation," *Journal of Southern History* 70, no. 2 (2004): 317–26; M. Tushnet and K. Levin, "What Really Happened in *Brown v. Board of Education*," *Columbia Law Review* 9 (1991): 1867–930; J. Morgan Kousser, "Separate, but *Not* Equal: The Supreme Court's First Decision on Racial Discrimi-

nation in Schools," *Journal of Southern History* 46 (1980): 17–44; Marian Wright Edelman, "Twenty Years after Brown: Where Are We Now?" *New York University Education Quarterly* 5, no. 4 (1974): 2–10.

8. Marable, *Beyond*, 18–19 (see intro., n. 17).

9. The great scholar and activist W. E. B. Du Bois argued that, for African Americans, education had a special, critical purpose: to find the means to end oppression. Butchart, "Outthinking," 333. For further discussion of DuBois's thinking on this issue and for broader perceptions about the historical value of education in the black community, see Derrick P. Alridge, "Guiding Philosophical Principles for a DuBoisian-Based African American Educational Model," *Journal of Negro Education* 68, no. 2 (1999): 182–99; Vincent P. Franklin, "Introductory Essay: Changing Historical Perspectives on Afro-American Life and Education," in *New Perspectives on Black Educational History*, ed. Vincent P. Franklin and James D. Anderson (Boston: G. K. Hall, 1978), 1–18; Mwalimu Shujaa,"Education and Schooling: You Can Have One Without the Other," in *Too Much Schooling Too Little Education: A Paradox of Black Life in White Societies*, ed. Mwalimu Shujaa (Trenton, N.J.: Africa World Press, 1993), 13–36.

10. "NAACP Sets Advanced Goals," *New York Times*, May 18, 1954, as quoted in Gerald N. Rosenberg, *The Hollow Hope: Can Courts Bring About Social Change?* (Chicago: University of Chicago Press, 1991), 43.

11. Johnson remarked: "If segregation is unconstitutional in educational institutions, it is no less so unconstitutional in other aspects of our national life." James T. Patterson, *Brown v. Board of Education: A Civil Rights Milestone and Its Troubled Legacy* (New York: Oxford University Press, 2001), 71.

12. New York *Amsterdam News*, May 22, 1954, quoted in Clive Webb, "A Continuity of Conservatism: The Limitations of *Brown v. Board of Education*," *Journal of Southern History* 70, no. 2 (2004): 327.

13. Quoted in David J. Garrow, "Why Brown Still Matters," *Nation* 278, no. 17 (2004): 45.

14. For a detailed overview of white Southern "backlash" against *Brown*, see Numan V. Bartley, *The Rise of Massive Resistance: Race and Politics in the South During the 1950s* (Baton Rouge: Louisiana State University Press, 1999); Neil R. McMillen, *The Citizens' Council: Organized Resistance to the Second Reconstruction, 1954–1964* (Urbana: University of Illinois Press, 1971); Klarman, "How Brown," 81–118.

15. For a comprehensive overview of the slow pace of change in the decade after *Brown*, see Charles T. Clotfelter, *After Brown: The Rise and Retreat of School Desegregation* (Princeton, N.J.: Princeton University Press, 2004). See also "A Mixed Verdict on Brown," *Wilson Quarterly* 28, no. 3 (2004): 96; Webb, "Continuity of Conservatism," 327–28; Newman, *Civil Rights Movement*, 94 (see chap. 3, n. 1).

16. Thernstrom and Thernstrom, *America in Black and White*, 351, 358–59 (see chap. 2, n. 5).

17. For a discussion of the shift from desegregation to integration in civil rights circles and subsequently, amongst the Justices of the Supreme Court, see Wolters, "From Brown," 317–26.

18. Sowell, *Black Education*, 248 (see chap. 1, n. 38).

19. Ibid., 251–63.

20. Edward Banfield, quoted on the back-cover blurb of *Black Education*.

21. Thaddeus Spratlen, "Book Review: Black Education—Myths and Tragedies," *Journal of Black Studies* 3, no. 4 (1973): 511.

22. Sowell, *Personal*, 282 (see chap. 1, n. 43).

23. Reagan, quoted in Larry Cuban, "A Nation at Risk?" in *School: The Story of American Public Education*, ed. Sarah Mondale and Sarah Patton (Boston: Beacon Press, 2001), 184.

24. Ibid., 186.

25. Reagan, quoted in Gerald Holton, "An Insider's View of a Nation at Risk and Why It Still Matters," *Chronicle of Higher Education* 49, no. 33 (2003): B13.

26. Thomas Sowell, *Education: Assumptions Versus History* (Stanford, Calif.: Hoover Institution Press, 1986), 104–5. For similar sentiments, see Williams, *All It Takes*, 113–27 (see chap. 1, n. 95).

27. Williams, *All It Takes*, 114; Sowell, *Pink and Brown*, 106–8 (see chap. 2, n. 38). See, more recently, Thomas Sowell, "School Perfomances," *Jewish World Review*, September 24, 2003, http://www.jewishworldreview.com/cols/sowell092403. asp.

28. Williams, *All It Takes*, 117.

29. For statistical information about blacks' support for government intervention in education, see Howard Schuman, Charlotte Steen, and Lawrence Bobo, *Racial Attitudes in America: Trends and Interpretations* (Cambridge: Free Press, 1985), 144–45. In the case of busing, however, black support was often "qualified," the policy being seen by many as a "last resort." "I'm in favor of busing to achieve integration," said one black mother in Philadelphia. "Obviously, you can't achieve it any other way. The schools work on a neighborhood system, and the neighborhoods are segregated. Separate but equal doesn't work [because] the white politicians don't care about black schools." Quoted in Wilkinson, *From Brown to Bakke*, 232. For further discussion of such black "support," see Lee Sigelman and Susan Welch, *Black Americans' Views of Racial Inequality: The Dream Deferred* (New York: Cambridge University Press, 1991), 121.

30. For a concise discussion, see McKee J. McClendon, "Racism, Rational Choice, and White Opposition to Racial Change: A Case Study of Busing," *Public Opinion Quarterly* 49, no. 2 (1985): 214–33. See also Thomas B. Edsall and Mary D. Edsall, *Chain Reaction: The Impact of Race, Rights and Taxes on American Politics* (New York: W. W. Norton, 1991).

31. For further discussion, see Frederick Ohles, Shirley M. Ohles, and John G. Ramsy, *Biographical Dictionary of Modern American Educators* (Westport, Conn.: Greenwood Press, 1997), 23; Michael Arnone, Eric Hoover, Jeffrey Selingo, and Welch Suggs, "Ronald Reagan Remembered," *Chronicle of Higher Education* 50, no. 41 (2004): A24–A25; John McLaughlin, "Reagan's Social Mission," *National Review* 34, no. 17 (1982): 1070; Jaynes and Williams, *Common Destiny*, 346 (see chap. 2, n. 111).

32. National Commission on Excellence in Education, *A Nation at Risk: The Imperative of Educational Reform* (Washington, D.C.: U.S. Government Printing Office, 1983), 5.

33. Ibid.

34. Ibid., 27.

35. See, for example, Lawrence C. Stedman and Marshall S. Smith, "Recent Reform Proposals," *Contemporary Education Review* 2 (1983): 85–104; Charles Vert Willie and Sarah Susannah Willie, "Black, White and Brown: The Transformation of Public Education in America," *Teachers College Record* 107, no. 3 (2005): 489–90; David C. Berliner and Bruce J. Biddle, *The Manufactured Crisis* (Reading, Mass.: Addison-Wesley, 1995).

36. For a discussion, see John E. Chubb, "Ignoring the Market: A Nation at Risk Virtually Overlooked School Choice," *Education Next*, spring 2003, 329–61.

37. Reagan, quoted in Wilbur Edel, *The Reagan Presidency: An Actor's Finest Performance* (New York: Hippocrene Books, 2000), 132.

38. See, for example, James S. Coleman and Thomas Hoffer, "Achievement and Segregation in Secondary Schools: A Further Look at Public and Private School Differences," *Sociology of Education* 55 (1982): 162–82; James S. Coleman and Thomas Hoffer, *Public and Private High Schools: The Impact of Communities* (New York: Basic Books, 1987).

39. L. Gordon Crovitz, "On Brown v. Board of Education, Call Him Thurgood Thomas," *Wall Street Journal*, July 31, 1991, A11.

40. Thomas, "Civil Rights as a Principle," 392–93 (see chap. 1, n. 4).

41. Ibid.

42. Clark's research was cited in a footnote in the *Brown* opinion.

43. Clark's position on educational segregation is set out clearly in Kenneth B. Clark, *Prejudice and Your Child* (Middletown, Conn.: Wesleyan University Press, 1963); Kenneth B. Clark, "Racial Progress and Retreat: A Personal Memoir," in *Race in America: The Struggle for Equality*, ed. Herbert Hill and James E. Jones (Madison: University of Wisconsin Press, 1993), 3–18.

44. Max Deutscher and Isidor Chein, "The Psychological Effects of Enforced Segregation: A Survey of Social Science Opinion," *Journal of Psychology* 26 (1948): 259.

45. Thomas, quoted in David J. Garrow, "On Race, It's Thomas v. an Old Ideal," *New York Times*, July 2, 1995, 4.

46. Thomas Sowell, "Blacks and Education: Half a Century after Brown, Part 2," *Capitalism Magazine In Defense of Individual Rights*, May 13, 2004, http://www.CapMag.com/article.asp?ID=3679. See also Walter Williams, "School Integration Is Not Necessary to Create Black Academic Excellence," *Human Events* 52, no. 23 (1996): 9.

47. Sowell, quoted in McWhorter, *Authentically*, 193 (see chap 1., n. 154).

48. To this end, Sowell wrote: "I happen to have been one of those black children who went to a segregated school in the South. The fact that there were no white kids in our school was something that no one I knew ever expressed any concern over or even noticed. There were no white kids in our neighborhood or anywhere we went. Why would we be struck by the fact that there were no white kids in our schools—much less be so preoccupied with that fact as to interfere with our learning the three R's?" Thomas Sowell, "We Are Still Paying the Price for the Faulty Reasoning in Brown," *History News Network*, May 13, 2004, http://hnn.us/roundup/entries/5160.html.

49. Thomas, quoted in Garrow, "On Race," 4.

50. Thomas, quoted in Scott Jaschik, "Justice Thomas Stresses the Role of Predominantly Black Colleges," *The Chronicle of Higher Education* 41, no. 41 (1995): A22. Years earlier, remembering his days at St. Pius X High School in Savannah, Georgia, Thomas wrote, "We did have a bad physical plant; we did have constant problems with paying the bills, and so forth, and we did have poor books. [But] we also had an excellent education." Clarence Thomas, "Response to Thomas Sowell's 'False Assumptions about Black Education,'" *The Fairmont Papers: Black Alternatives Conference, December 1980*, ed. Institute for Contemporary Studies (San Francisco: Institute for Contemporary Studies, 1981), 81. "Despite their origins in the shameful history of state-enforced segregation," Thomas argued, all-black schools "can be both a source of pride to blacks who have attended them and a source of hope to black families who want the benefits of learning for their children.'" See James Traub, "Ghetto Blasters: The Case for All-Black Schools," *New Republic*, April 15, 1991, 21.

51. Thomas, quoted in Williams, "Question of Fairness," 72–79 (chap. 1, n. 4).

52. Ibid.

53. McWhorter, *Authentically*, 193.

54. Reed, *Class Notes*, 15 (see chap. 3, n. 113).

55. For a discussion, see Patterson, *Brown v. Board Education*, 1–20; Thernstrom and Thernstrom, *America in Black and White*, 84–85; Henry M. Levin, "Education and Earnings of Blacks and the *Brown* Decision," in *Have We Overcome? Race Relations since Brown*, ed. Michael V. Namorato (Jackson: University Press of Mississippi, 1979), 81–84.

56. Even the conservative legal scholar Robert Bork appeared to understand this point. In his book *The Tempting of America*, Bork wrote: "By 1954, when *Brown* came up for decision, it had been apparent for some time that segregation rarely, if ever, produced equality. Quite aside from any question of psychology, the physical facilities provided for blacks were not as good as those provided for whites. That had been demonstrated in a long series of cases. . . . The Court's realistic choice, therefore, was either to abandon the quest for equality by allowing segregation or to forbid segregation in order to achieve equality. There was no third choice. Either choice would violate one aspect of the original understanding but there was no possibility of avoiding that. Since equality and segregation were mutually inconsistent . . . both could not be honored. When that is seen, it is obvious that the Court must choose equality and prohibit state-imposed segregation. The purpose that brought the fourteenth amendment into being was equality before the law, and equality, not separation, was written into the law." Robert Bork, *The Tempting of America: The Political Seduction of the Law* (New York: Free Press, 1990), 82. For further discussion, see Charles J. Ogletree, *All Deliberate Speed: Reflections on the First Half Century of Brown v. Board of Education* (New York: W. W. Norton, 2004); Levin, "Education and Earnings," 85.

57. Significantly, this is also how Thurgood Marshall explained the NAACP's emphasis on Clark's social-science research in *Brown*. Asked by the journalist Juan Williams whether it had been a mistake to insist on racial integration instead of improvement in the quality of schools for black children, Marshall (upon retirement) responded that the seating of black children next to white children in school had never been the point. It had been necessary, he said, "only because all-white school boards were generously financing schools for white children while leaving black students in overcrowded, decrepit buildings with hand-me-down books and underpaid teachers." Marshall had "wanted black children to have the right to attend white schools as a point of leverage over the biased spending patterns of the segregationists who ran schools—both in the 17 states where racially separate schools were required by law and in other states where they were a matter of culture." "If black children had the right to be in schools with white children," he reasoned, "then school board officials would have no choice but to equalize spending to protect the interests of their white children." Juan Williams, "Don't Mourn Brown v. Board of Education," *New York Times*, June 29, 2007.

58. For a discussion, see Roy Brooks, *Integration or Separation?: A Strategy for Racial Equality* (Cambridge, Mass.: Harvard University Press, 1996).

59. For a comprehensive discussion of the black nationalist tradition in African American history, see Dean E. Robinson, *Black Nationalism in American Politics and Thought* (New York: Cambridge University Press, 2001); Essien Udosen Essien Udom, *Black Nationalism: The Search for an Identity* (New York: Dell Publishing, 1964).

60. Thomas, quoted in Williams, "Question of Fairness," 73. For further discussion, see Williams, "Was Malcolm X a Republican," 190–95, 269.

61. Harold Cruse, *Plural But Equal: A Critical Study of Blacks and Minorities and America's Plural Society* (New York: William Morrow, 1987), quoted in Garrow, "On Race," 4.

62. Alex M. Johnson, "Bid Whist, Tonk and *United States v. Fordice*: Why Integrationism Fails African Americans Again," *California Law Review* 81 (1993): 1401.

63. Bell, quoted in Garrow, "Why *Brown* Still Matters," 46.

64. For an overview of the policy of busing, see, for example, Thomas J. Cottle, *Busing* (Boston: Beacon Press, 1977); Bernard Schwartz, *Swann's Way: The School Busing Case and the Supreme Court* (New York: Oxford University Press, 1986); James Bolner and Robert Shanley, *Busing: The Political and Judicial Process* (New York: Praeger Publishers, 1974).

65. For a discussion, see Nathanial R. Jones, 'The Judicial Betrayal of Blacks—Again: The Supreme Court's Destruction of the Hopes Raised by Brown v. Board of Education," *Fordham Urban Law Journal* 32, no. 1 (2004): 117–29; Wilkinson, *From Brown to Bakke*, 193–215.

66. See, for example, Ronald P. Formisano, *Boston Against Busing: Race, Class and Ethnicity in the 1960s and 1970s* (Chapel Hill: University of North Carolina Press, 1991).

67. Sowell, *Civil Rights*, 69 (see chap. 1, n. 38).

68. Ibid., 68.

69. Ibid., 71.

70. Ibid.

71. Wortham, *Other Side*, xii (see chap. 1, n. 89).

72. Ibid., 194.

73. Woodson, quoted in Conti and Stetson, *Challenging*, 160 (see intro., n. 22).

74. Woodson, "New Politics in Action," 47.

75. Clarence Thomas, "Being Educated Black," in *The Fairmont Papers: The Black Alternatives' Conference, 1980*, ed. Institute for Contemporary Studies (San Francisco: Institute for Contemporary Studies, 1981), 82.

76. Thomas, "Civil Rights as a Principle," 393.

77. Glenn Loury, "Integration Is Yesterday's Struggle," *New Crisis*, December/January 1998, 22.

78. Ibid.

79. Ibid.

80. Smith, "Black Lawyer's," 212 (see chap. 3, n. 168).

81. Percy Sutton, "A Skeptic Persuaded?" in *The Fairmont Papers*, 153.

82. Formisano, *Boston Against Busing*, 192.

83. Thomas Paine (with an introduction by Eric Foner), *The Rights of Man* (New York: Penguin Press, 1984), 245.

84. Milton Friedman, "The Role of Government in Education," in *Economics and the Public Interest*, ed. Robert A. Solo (New Brunswick, N.J.: Rutgers University Press, 1955), 123–44.

85. See, for example, James S. Coleman, *Equality of Educational Opportunity* (Washington, D.C.: U.S. Government Printing Office, 1966); Sowell, *Black Education*, 242–50.

86. Robin D. Barnes, "Black America and School Choice," *Yale Law Journal* 6, no. 8 (1997): 2379; Michael W. Apple and Thomas Pedroi, "Conservative Alliance Building and African American Support for Vouchers: The End of *Brown's*

Promise or a New Beginning?" *Teacher's College Record* 107, no. 9 (2005): 2068–105; Davison M. Douglas, "The End of Busing?" *Michigan Law Review* 95, no. 6 (1997): 1716–18.

87. "School Vouchers: An Educational Conundrum for Black America," *Journal of Blacks in Higher Education*, no. 35 (2002): 79–80. Frank Margonis and Laurence Parker, "Choice: The Route to Community Control?" *Theory into Practice* 38, no. 4 (1999): 203–8; Douglas, "End of Busing," 1717–18.

88. See, for example, Sowell, *Black Education*, 242–50; Sowell, *Pink and Brown*, 108; Walter Williams, "Competition of Monopoly," *Jewish World Review*, June 13, 2007, http://jewishworldreview.com/cols/williams061307.php3; Williams, *All It Takes*.

89. Wortham quoted in Center for Economic Education, *The Case for Educational Vouchers* (Chattanooga, Tenn.: Center for Economic Education, 1986), 3–4.

90. Thomas Sowell, *Inside American Education: The Decline, the Deception, the Dogmas* (New York: Free Press, 1993). For these words, see the book's back-cover blurb. See also Sowell, quoted in Sylvester P. Theisen, "A Broad Indictment," *College Teaching* 41, no. 3 (1993): 118.

91. Sowell, *Education*, 105.

92. Woodson, quoted in H. Spencer, "Education: The Battle Is On for the Minds of Black Children," *Destiny*, March/April 1991, 33.

93. Loury argued: "the condition of poor blacks could be materially advanced if the choices of parents with regard to the nature of education for their children could be expanded. Many of these parents would seek out alternative educational options for their children if they could get some financial assistance . . . vouchers would enable parents to avail themselves of private education for their children, should they be willing to make the necessary attendant sacrifices. This option and its exercise by some parents would create pressures on the public institutions and the unions that represent their employees which well might lead to an improved educational environment for all poor students." "Race and Affirmative Action: An Interview with Glenn Loury," 1985, http://www.users.bigpond.com/smartboard/rights/chap17.htm. For Woodson's position, see Woodson, *On the Road*, 99 (see chap. 1, n. 145).

94. Conti and Stetson, *Challenging*, 178.

95. Parker, quoted in Hill et al., "Black America," 39 (see intro., n. 31).

96. Woodson, *On the Road*, 99.

97. Woodson, "Poverty: Why Politics Can't Cure It," 3 (see chap. 3, n. 86).

98. Woodson, "Is the Black Community," 7 (see chap. 3, n. 175).

99. Woodson, "Poverty: Why Politics Can't Cure It," 3.

100. Woodson, "Is the Black Community," 9.

101. Thomas Sowell, *Patterns of Black Excellence* (Washington, D.C.: Georgetown University, Ethics and Public Policy Center, 1977). See also Sowell, *Pink and Brown*, 106–8.

102. Williams, *All It Takes*, 113–14.

103. Jim Waring, "Educational Vouchers: The Case for Public Choice Reconsidered," *Public Budgeting and Finance* 16 (1996): 66.

104. James E. Ryan, "Brown, School Choice, and the Suburban Veto," *Virginia Law Review* 90, no. 6 (2004): 1636.

105. Ibid., 1635–37. For further discussion, see Barnes, "Black America," 2382; David A. Bositis, "The Politics of School Choice: African Americans and Vouchers," in *Educational Freedom in Urban America: Brown v. Board after Half a Century,*

ed. David Salisbury and Casey Lartigue Jr. (Washington, D.C.: Cato Institute, 2001), 179–80.

106. Ryan, "Brown, School," 1636–37.

107. Ibid.

108. Sowell, *Pink and Brown*, 106.

109. See, for example, Charles Glenn, "The Significance of Choice for Public Education," *Equity and Choice* 3 (1985): 5–10; Fred M. Hechinger, "About Education: The Right to Choose a School—A Pillar of Democracy or an Invitation to Election?" *New York Times*, March 29, 1989, 15; Myron Liberman, *Privatization and Educational Choice* (New York: St. Martin's Press, 1989); Joe Nathan, "Before Adopting School Choice: Review What Works and What Fails," *American School Board Journal* 176, no. 7 (1989): 28–30.

110. Leon F. Beauchman, "Beware the Voucherman," *Oakland Post*, November 1, 2000. See also Marie Rohde, "Minority Test Scores at Catholic Schools Mirror Lag in City," *Milwaukee Journal*, August 1, 1991, 1. Rohde noted that the Milwaukee Catholic school system once provided a breakdown of their average scores by race. The black-white achievement gap was as large as that among the city public school students, even though the black Catholic school students most likely were more advantaged than the black public school students.

111. Donald R. Moore and Suzanne Davenport, "Cheated Again: School Choice and Students at Risk," *School Administrator* 46, no. 7 (1989): 12–15. Moore's and Davenport's study focused on the impact of school choice programs in Boston, Chicago, Philadelphia, and New York.

112. See, for example, Donald R. Moore and Suzanne Davenport, "High School Choice and Students at Risk," *National Center on Effective Schools Newsletter*, fall 1988, 2–4; William Snider, "The Call for Choice: Competition in the Educational Marketplace—A Special Report," *Education Week*, May 18, 1988, 1–24.

113. See, for example, Judith Pearson, "Myths of Choice: The Governor's New Clothes," *Phi Delta Kappa* 70 (1989): 821–23; William Snider, "In Nation's First Enrollment State, the Action Begins," *Education Week*, March 15, 1989, 18–19.

114. For a detailed discussion, see Kevin B. Smith and Kenneth J. Meier, *The Case Against School Choice: Politics, Markets and Fools* (New York: M. E. Sharpe, 1995).

115. Sowell, *Pink and Brown*, 106.

116. For further discussion, see Gary B. Nash, "The Great Multicultural Debate," in *Race and Ethnicity in the United States: Issues and Debates*, ed. Stephen Steinberg (Malden, Mass.: Blackwell Publishers, 2000), 277–93.

117. Marable, *Beyond*, 118.

118. For a discussion, see Diane Ravitch, "Multiculturalism: E Pluribus Plures," *American Scholar* 59 (1990): 339.

119. Dinesh D'Souza, *Illiberal Education: The Politics of Race and Sex on Campus* (New York: Free Press, 1991).

120. Sowell, quoted in Theisen, "Broad Indictment," 118.

121. Quoted in Peter Schrag, "Class Warfare," *Nation*, May 10, 1993, 639.

122. Walter Williams, "Celebrating Multiculturalism and Diversity," *World Net Daily*, January 1, 2003, http://www.worldnetdaily.com/news/article. asp?ARTICLE_ID=30278.

123. For a detailed discussion of Afrocentrism, see, for example, Clarence E. Walker, *We Can't Go Home Again: An Argument About Afrocentrism* (Oxford: Oxford University Press, 2001); Stephen Howe, *Afrocentrism: Mythical Pasts and Imagined*

Homes (London: Verso, 1999); Mary Lefkowitz, *Not Out of Africa: How Afrocentrism Became an Excuse to Teach Myth as History* (New York: Basic Books, 1997).

124. Molefi Kete Asante, *Afrocentricity* (Trenton, N.J.: African World Press, 1988), 5, 29.

125. Sowell, *Inside American Education*, 99.

126. Steele, quoted in Suzanne Fields, "Afrocentric Curriculum Cheats Kinds," *Insight on the News*, October 11, 1993, http://findarticles.com/p/articles/mi_m1571/is_n41_v9/ai_14657313.

127. Woodson, quoted in Conti and Stetson, *Challenging*, 168.

128. Anne Wortham, "Errors of the Afrocentrists," *Political Notes*, no. 104 (1995): 4.

129. Ibid.

130. Ibid.

131. Appiah, quoted in Stanley Crouch, "The Afrocentric Hustle," no. 10 (1995–96): 79. The most impressive and comprehensive critique of Afrocentrism (along these lines) is offered by Clarence Walker, Professor of History at the University of California (Davis). Walker, *We Can't Go Home Again*.

132. King wrote in his last work, *Where Do We Go from Here?*: "It is not a sign of weakness, but a sign of high maturity, to rise to the level of self criticism." Quoted in Loury, *One By One*, 194.

133. West, *Race Matters*, 76 (see intro., n. 20).

134. Marable, *Beyond*, 121.

135. Glenn Loury, "Pride and Prejudice," *New Republic*, May 19, 1997, 25.

136. Ibid.

137. Ibid.

138. Sowell, *Inside American Education*, 72–73.

139. Stephen Thernstrom and Abigail Thernstrom, *No Excuses: Closing the Racial Gap in Learning* (New York: Simon and Schuster, 2003), 1.

140. Salisbury and Lartigue, eds., *Educational Freedom*, 14.

<endfile>

Index

Abramson, Jill, 14
affirmative action: achievements of, 57–58, 71, 85; black resistance to, 56, 60; constitutionalism-based arguments against, 61; definition of, 55–56; economic arguments against, 61–63, 66–67, 79–80; evolution of (as legislation), 55–58; failures of, 75–77, 80–81; in higher education, 81, 84–85; historical arguments for, 73–74, 79; ideology of, 58; individualism-based arguments against, 61–63, 65, 69, 72–73, 75–76, 81–82, 90; institutional racism and, 57, 92, 117–18, 120, 178n8; in the labor market, 76–81; Martin Luther King's use in attacking, 86–89; morality-based arguments against, 76–77; Nixon's policies on, 57; philosophy of, 58; pragmatism-based arguments against, 73, 78; psychological arguments against, 64–72; social capital theory and, 34–35; white resistance to, 55, 58–59, 62–64, 68. *See also* Jim Crow (laws); poverty (black); racism; *specific scholars and policies*
African Americans. *See* blacks
Afrocentrism (educational movement), 149–53
Aid to Families with Dependent Children (AFDC), 94, 107
Alexander, Lamar, 186n150
Alien Nation (Brimelow), 149
Allan, Walter, 98
America in Black and White (Thernstrom and Thernstrom), 73
American Enterprise Institute, 4, 18, 45, 167n68

"American Nightmare." *See* poverty
Amherst College, 31
Amsterdam News (publication), 127
Anderson, Elijah, 119
Anderson, Myers, 114
Appiah, K. Anthony, 151
Asante, Molefi, 150
Association of Black Sociologists, 159n28
Atlas Shrugged (Rand), 27
Auletta, Ken, 95
Authentically Black (McWhorter), 46
authenticity (racial), 25, 32, 37, 52, 60, 106. *See also* black conservatives; *specific black scholars*

Baker, Houston, 11
Bakke, Allan, 178n20
Baldwin, James, 41
Banfield, Edward, 94–96, 110, 191n29
Banks, William, 71
Barnes, Fred, 4
Beauchman, Leon, 147
Bell, Derrick, 60, 137
The Bell Curve (Murray and Herrnstein), 18
Bennett, William, 36, 167n68
Berger, Peter, 43–44
Beyond Entitlement (Mead), 95
"Black Alternatives' Conference." *See* Fairmont Conference
Black Bourgeoisie (Frazier), 74
black conservatives: connections to black nationalism, 137–38; defenses against "blaming the victim" charges, 42, 112; emergence as political force, 3–4, 16; failures to engage counterarguments, 63, 68, 83–84, 109, 111–12, 145–47; on failures of *Brown*, 133, 138; influences

Acknowledgments

No person is an island. Our debts to others stretch far back into the mists of time. And so it is not surprising that I have accumulated numerous debts at the University of Western Australia (UWA) and the University of Newcastle, where I have been, respectively, a student and academic over the past thirteen years. Both institutions have been extraordinarily generous to me in so many ways, but especially helpful toward the completion of this book was the support I received from the 2007 UWA Whitfeld Fellowship and, later, from a 2008 Newcastle Staff Research Grant. I would also like to acknowledge the professionalism of the University of Pennsylvania Press because no young historian could aspire to work with a more supportive publishing team.

My main debts, however, are to the people around me. At the University of Western Australia, where I studied between 1996 and 2007, I would like to thank Ernie Jones, Philippa Maddern, Sarah Brown, Robyn Owens, Tim Pitman, and especially Richard Bosworth and Rob Stuart, for their friendship and guidance over the years. At the University of Newcastle, where I am currently employed, my colleagues Philip Dwyer, Roger Markwick, Wayne Reynolds, Hilary Carey, Jane Bellemore, Victoria Haskins, James Bennett, Terry Ryan, and Terry Lovat deserve special mention for welcoming me so warmly to my new academic home and for making university life what it ought to be: a collegial experience.

I am similarly indebted to three academics with whom I have not been institutionally affiliated but who nevertheless took time off from their busy work schedules to read this manuscript and offer constructive feedback. Chris Dixon at the University of Queensland, Raymond A. Mohl at the University of Alabama (at Birmingham), and Shane White at the University of Sydney all provided the right admixture of criticism and encouragement of this project, and it is much the better for it. Shane's input, however, went beyond the offering of interpretational advice; in truth, it was he who put the project on the road to publication by introducing author and Press. Needless to say, I am very grateful to him.

In writing a book, one inevitably confronts personal crises and seeks the counsel of friends. I would like to acknowledge my very best friends—Jeremy Martens, Simon Thackrah, and Dave Edelman—for the interest they showed in my research from the beginning and for the encouragement they gave me along the way. No five people have offered me greater encouragement than my parents, Vicki Vanden Driesen and David Ondaatje; my step-parents, Jan Vanden Driesen and Grace Ondaatje; and my girlfriend Shannon Thompson. No words can adequately convey how important their love and support was to the eventual completion of *Black Conservative Intellectuals in Modern America*. I am a lucky boy indeed to have such fine people in my corner and in my life.

This acknowledgments page would be glaringly incomplete, however, without recognition of Tony Barker. For twelve years now, Tony has been a teacher and mentor to me. He has taught and thought in ways that I aspire to match and from which I have tried to learn. He has given me generosity, both intellectual and emotional. He, more than anyone else, made my university student experience a source of great joy and pleasure. Always encouraging, supportive and available for discussion, Tony's advice at every stage of this project was arguably what made its completion possible. He read the manuscript numerous times (including a final proofreading), offering helpful ideas and suggestions. All mistakes are, nonetheless, my own.

Finally, I would like to dedicate *Black Conservative Intellectuals in Modern America*—my first book—to three towering figures in my life, all of whom passed away, unexpectedly and tragically, during the final stages of writing. To "Aunty" (Nerissa de Niese), "Pa" (Vivian Blazé), and especially "Nanna" (Charmaine Blazé): Your contributions to the subtlety, range, and happiness of my life are infinite. I am who I am because of you.